STRIKE THE HAMMER

THE BLACK FREEDOM STRUGGLE IN ROCHESTER, NEW YORK, 1940–1970

Laura Warren Hill

CORNELL UNIVERSITY PRESS

Ithaca and London

First published 2021 by Cornell University Press

Library of Congress Cataloging-in-Publication Data

Names: Hill, Laura Warren, author.
Title: Strike the hammer : the Black freedom struggle in
    Rochester, New York, 1940–1970 / Laura Warren Hill.
Description: Ithaca [New York] : Cornell University Press,
    2021. | Includes bibliographical references and index.
Identifiers: LCCN 2020030994 (print) | LCCN 2020030995
    (ebook) | ISBN 9781501754258 (hardcover) |
    ISBN 9781501756047 (paperback) |
    ISBN 9781501754418 (pdf) | ISBN 9781501754425 (epub)
Subjects: LCSH: African Americans—Civil rights—
    New York (State)—Rochester—History—20th century. |
    Civil rights movements—New York (State)—
    Rochester—History—20th century. | Black power—
    Economic aspects—New York (State)—Rochester. |
    Black power—New York (State)—Rochester—
    History—20th century. | Rochester (N.Y.)—
    Race relations—History—20th century. |
    Rochester (N.Y.)—Race relations—Economic aspects.
Classification: LCC F129.R79 N44 2021 (print) |
    LCC F129.R79 (ebook) | DDC 305.8009747/89—dc23
LC record available at https://lccn.loc.gov/2020030994
LC ebook record available at https://lccn.loc.gov
    /2020030995

This book is dedicated to the men and women of Rochester's Black Freedom Struggle, and in memory of Dr. Marcus Alexis, Loma Allen, David Finks, Clarence Ingram, John Mitchell, Constance Mitchell, Horace Becker, and Reuben Davis, who kindly shared their stories with me.

CONTENTS

Introduction

Striking the Hammer while the Iron Is Hot

> Power concedes nothing without a demand. It never
> did and it never will. Find out just what a people will
> submit to, and you have found out the exact amount
> of injustice and wrong which will be imposed upon
> them; and these will continue till they are resisted with
> either words or blows, or with both. The limits of
> tyrants are prescribed by the endurance of those
> whom they oppress.
>
> —Frederick Douglass, West India Emancipation
> speech, 1857

This book is a story of transformations wrought by an event that happened on July 24, 1964, in Rochester, New York. On that day, the city's Black community erupted in rebellion, the suppression of which required calling up the National Guard. Barely a week earlier, another uprising had taken place in the fabled Black mecca of Harlem. The rebellions in both places, Rochester and Harlem, shared a common spark: police brutality and misconduct, which would also be true of subsequent urban uprisings in that era. The events on opposite sides of New York State happened at a crucial moment in the modern African American experience. To some, the timing seemed incongruous. At the beginning of the same month as the back-to-back uprisings in Harlem and Rochester, July 1964, the first major legislative achievement of the civil rights movement, the Civil Rights Act of 1964, had come into effect. The twin rebellions in New York State in 1964 were a foretaste of what was to come as the Southern-based civil rights movement, fresh from its legislative victories (the Civil Rights Act would be followed by the equally consequential Voting Rights Act of 1965) gave way to a different kind of Black political mobilization centered largely, although not exclusively, in the urban North. The civil rights movement had dismantled Jim Crow as a system of legalized racism, with consequences that were more immediately evident in the South than in the North. The new Black political mobilization, building on the energy arising from the rebellions and fashioning theories of

1

a Black political economy, sought to address the structures of socioeconomic marginalization and impoverishment that survived the legal dismantling of Jim Crow, North as well as South. From this standpoint, the perceived incongruity of explosive rebellions in Black communities, hard on the heels of legislative victories advancing Black rights, was more apparent than real.

Rochester emerged as an important laboratory, and national model, in the transition from the old to the new. This too seemed incongruous. Yet belying stereotypes casting it as a nondescript municipality on the northern edge of the Lower 48, perched on one side of Lake Ontario and with Canada on the other side, Rochester became a key center of the new Black political mobilization. It was indeed an improbable achievement. To begin, Rochester was not a major urban center. In 1960, it ranked just thirty-eight among the nation's cities by population, behind Long Beach, California, and Birmingham, Alabama.[1] Nor did Rochester have a Black majority, or anything close to it. The city's Black population, while growing, stood at just 7.4 percent of the total in 1960. Again, Rochester did not conform to preconceptions of where and why Black uprisings occurred, any more than it seemed emblematic of the Black Freedom Struggle in the twentieth century. For these reasons and more, the events in Rochester have been variously mischaracterized, when they have not been ignored altogether. Even so, Rochester rose to the forefront. Where it led, other urban centers would follow.

As a result of the rising in Rochester, a newly energized African American community used the public outpouring of discontent to launch one of the most innovative, and largely uncharted, campaigns for Black freedom in the twentieth century. In so doing, Black Rochester became a national leader in the quest for the new Black political economy in the Black Power moment. Rochester ministers and community activists spearheaded two developing tendencies within Black Power. The first, Black theology, was closely related to the second, Black economic development.[2] That the two—Black theology and Black economic development—emerged in Rochester is not surprising, given the city's deep history of multipronged and closely related social movements, including abolition (as personified by Frederick Douglass), women's rights (as personified by Susan B. Anthony and Harriet Tubman), and the Social Gospel (as personified by Walter Rauschenbusch).[3] Furthermore, Rochester was home to a radical socialist tendency most often associated with Emma Goldman. If Black Rochester was "hot" in 1964, it was in part because it was heir to a long local history of striking back against the twin pillars of inequality and injustice, in the context of the larger national and global struggle for Black freedom.

A new generation of scholars has begun to examine the transition from civil rights to Black Power organizing in other northern cities, enriching the Freedom North literature.[4] Rochester has much to contribute to this discourse, illustrating as it does the various options that uprisings potentially made possible. Rochester demonstrates that the southern success of sit-ins, protests, and boycotts failed to convince many that those tactics were replicable in the North and the West. Rebellion, it seemed, was just as effective, more so even, than the forms of agitation and resistance that had proven efficacious in the South. In this way, this book builds on more recent research, which compellingly demonstrates that nonviolent protest was insufficient for securing Black freedom at midcentury and beyond.[5]

The case of Rochester is instructive, however, not simply for what it can tell us about violence, nonviolence, and police brutality at the very moment that notions of "law and order" were being introduced nationally.[6] This book shows how Black activists in Rochester used the uprising and the fear of Black violence to make increased demands on the city and to launch new kinds of movements. To pursue economic development in their communities, participants in the Rochester movement privileged Black capitalism. This book places the reemergence of Black capitalism firmly within the Black Power tradition, in a way that few movement historians have done.[7]

The Rochester movement explored the economic possibilities of Black capitalism as a movement tactic and contested its meaning and value in the age of Black Power.[8] Traditionally, Black freedom activists, particularly from the civil rights era, have been understood largely in their role as consumers rather than as producers.[9] This book takes seriously the producer impulse that emerged with Black capitalism. At the time, many proponents of Black capitalism advanced an individualistic, rather than a collectivist, agenda. Consequently, many in the movement dismissed Black capitalism as antithetical to its larger goals. As a strain within the Black Power movement, Black capitalism continues to be dismissed as a reactionary venture devised by a Republican president, Richard Nixon, to blunt the Black Power movement.[10] Yet many in Rochester saw the promise of collective empowerment, dignity and equality *within* capitalism, challenging notions of what it meant to be "radical" or to seek radical change or liberation, and harkening back to a longer Black nationalist impulse.

This book recovers the populist stories of both corporate responsibility and the revived pursuit of Black capitalism that sprung up in the era of Black Power.[11] At its core, Rochester's foray into Black Power was decidedly economic. Leaders and followers—traditional and militant alike—sought to improve the economic conditions of African Americans, most notably among the poor. In so doing, they pioneered strategies and forms of protest that came to be modeled across the nation, challenging perceptions that Black capitalism was antithetical to the freedom movement. Thus, one finds in Rochester both a contest to define Black capitalism and myriad efforts to bring it to fruition. As a result, Black activists pushed locally headquartered corporations (Kodak and Xerox) into adopting novel forms of social responsibility. Rochester was not just at the forefront of these efforts, but a pioneer in this new moment.

The trajectory of Rochester, with its emphasis on economic strategies, demonstrates that Black Power movements are not reducible to violent forms of protest. The case of Rochester also challenges assumptions about actors, about periodization, and about strategies in the transition from civil rights to Black Power. If the economic underpinnings of Black Power have been given short shrift in the history of the Black Power movement, so too has the role of Christian ministers. Whereas Christian values have long been associated with the movement for civil rights, Black Power has more often been treated as a movement devoid of sanctity, irreverent even. Given the historical trend to paint Black Power as a violent foil to the nonviolent civil rights movement, the role of Christian ministers and Christian organizations in the quest for Black Power and Black capitalism has remained understudied.[12] Here too, Rochester has plenty to tell. In the wake of the uprising, ministers—Black and white—who preached the Social Gospel in the tradition of Walter Rauschenbusch and demanded economic and social accountability from all facets of the community, drove the Black Power movement. Those same Christian ministers, including many who kept counsel with Malcolm X, took Rochester to task for its poor race record. This was a fighting ministry, devoid of the turn-the-other-cheek gentility so often attributed to civil rights. What is more, the Rochester movement garnered the support and contribution of national church bodies, including the National Council of Churches, the United Presbyterian Church in the USA, and the national Church of Christ. All told, Rochester paints a picture of strange bedfellows and unexpected turns in the quest for Black freedom. And yet these alliances and turns are only "strange" if we continue to ignore the movements that took place in cities such as Rochester.

This book is a study of the long civil rights and Black Power movements in a northern city, where the Black community quite literally struck for equality, self-determination, and economic advancement while the iron was still hot from the 1964 urban rebellion. This work first traces the growth and development of the Black community between 1940 and 1964, paying special attention to the role migrant communities play in shaping movement tactics and how leadership must adapt to such communities to remain effective.

This book then charts the engagement by a small group of dedicated activists, known locally as the "Young Turks," who sought to replace a prewar Black leadership that they viewed as complacent and more accommodating to the white power structure than in improving the lives of African Americans. The Young Turks hoped to engage the Black masses using the traditional civil rights strategies of voter registration and protest. But before a movement with stable organizations and recognized leadership could coalesce, the rebellion erupted in the summer of 1964. This book argues that the uprising quickly became Rochester's twentieth-century watershed moment. The rising served as a fundamental precondition for the transformation of the Black freedom movement in that city, birthing a new set of leaders and leadership styles more attentive to the energy of the Black migrants.

This community study then follows the various segments of postrebellion Rochester as they struggled to organize in response to the crisis, charting the efforts and accomplishments as well as the conflicts and confrontations that emerged within the Black community and with the city's power structure. By 1970, a newly organized Black movement, led largely by Black ministers and driven overwhelmingly by Black women, had provided several concrete outlets for Black hopes and aspirations in Rochester. It had simultaneously reshaped notions of corporate responsibility nationally and had contributed mightily to a newly emerging campaign for Black capitalism.

Each chapter tells the story of a crucial moment in the formation or development of Black Rochester in the latter half of the twentieth century. Chapter 1 charts the emergence of a sizable Black population in the city. This Black renaissance began not in the city center but in the fields and orchards surrounding the city, an agricultural belt responsible for growing a significant portion of the nation's food supply. As World War II sapped the nation's labor supply, local white agricultural workers abandoned the fields for better-paying factory jobs in Rochester, Buffalo, and Syracuse, creating a labor shortage in the fields. Consequently, farmers turned to places like Sanford, Florida, and to the "East Coast Migrant Stream," which brought Black agricultural migrants, along with their culture and customs, from the depths of Florida, through the Carolinas and Virginia, and then into New York State. Over time, many of the agricultural migrants would leave the stream, opting instead to put down roots in the North, with Rochester becoming a popular destination.

The new influx of Black migrants created a demographic shift, the likes of which Rochester had never seen before. At the start of the century, the city's Black population consisted of 601 people, less than half of 1 percent of the total. While a slow trickle continued until 1940, the real boom began in that year. Between 1940 and 1970, the Black population increased from roughly 3,000 to nearly 50,000.[13] The city leaders refused to acknowledge the strain this massive demographic shift put on the Third and Seventh Wards, where Rochester's Black population was concentrated. African Americans, new and old, agricultural and otherwise, were relegated to living in these two city wards—long designated migrant neighborhoods—that simply were not equipped to house so many people. Redlining and restrictive covenants kept them from settling anywhere else. It was this unprecedented influx that gave rise to the group of Black activists known as the Young Turks, who helped to elect a Black woman, Constance Mitchell, as ward supervisor. Mitchell's election marked a significant change in Rochester politics. The coordination it required signaled a new dedication to civil rights organizing and protest in the city. It also overturned a previous generation of Black leadership.

The Young Turks and others also moved to address the police brutality and harassment that increasingly accompanied life in the two city wards. Chapter 2 documents several brutal clashes between African Americans and the police. These incidents engendered a loose coalition of Black organizations and a number of sympathetic white ministers. While police clashes occurred throughout most cities in the postwar era, the Rochester cases garnered significant attention for several reasons. In one case, the US Justice Department interceded. In another case, famed Nation of Islam leader Malcolm X also joined the protest efforts. This chapter argues that police brutality became a salient issue for a broad cross section of the Black community, which included ministers who cultivated and promoted a unified response. For Black Rochester, unity included diverse elements of the community. The local National Association for the Advancement of Colored People (NAACP) worked closely with Malcolm X and local Nation of Islam leaders to organize a unity rally, much to the chagrin of the NAACP's national office, which chastised the Rochester branch for consorting with reputed Black separatists. Here, the events in Rochester challenge popular perceptions, which suggest irreconcilable differences between organizations such as the NAACP and the Nation of Islam. While the two organizations may have highlighted their differences nationally, the Rochester branches often cooperated on issues of mutual interest and concern. In particular, the Rochester affiliates of the NAACP and the Nation of Islam joined forces to oppose police repression locally. Chapter 2 argues further that Rochester's Christian ministers sought relevancy as the Black freedom movement in that city began to take shape.

Despite their success in rallying the Black community around the issue of police brutality, neither the ministers nor the Young Turks built a sustained movement. Chapter 3 traces the eruption of the Black community in response to police brutality. On July 24, 1964, one of the era's very first "race riots" occurred in Rochester. As police were called to a street dance to remove an intoxicated young man, many bystanders, who had had enough of aggressive police tactics, struck back. What began as a response to police brutality ended as an indictment of the economic conditions in Rochester's ghettoes. This chapter argues that the three-day rebellion, which ended with the calling up of the National Guard, became a watershed moment in the city of Rochester. The moral economy of the uprising is also noteworthy. With an impressive degree of precision, those in rebellion—men and women, youth and senior citizens—attacked the police and private property with vengeance, but exempted community institutions and stores with a reputation for fairness. When all was said and done, nearly nine hundred people had been arrested, three hundred and fifty had sustained injuries, including the chief of police, and millions of dollars of property had been damaged.

In the wake of Rochester's rebellion, an organizing frenzy began. A group of white ministers, who had previously aided Black Rochesterians in their struggle to create a police review board, now expanded their commitment to the struggle for racial justice. Acting through the local council of churches, they joined forces with Rochester's Black ministers to found and fund an organizational structure capable of building a Black movement. Chapter 4 tells this story. It traces an abortive engagement with the Southern Christian Leadership Conference and a more successful one with Chicago's Saul Alinsky and his Industrial Areas Foundation. Within a year of the uprising, three new groups were competing for the hearts and minds of Black Rochester. The FIGHT organization was decidedly militant and aggressive, trumpeting its claim to be the true representative of the Black poor. FIGHT consolidated 135 member organizations into an undeniably powerful body. At the same time, the city's power structure formed Action for a Better Community (ABC) to serve as a clearinghouse for President Johnson's War on Poverty funds. Not surprisingly, the two entities, FIGHT and ABC, found themselves at odds as they plotted a course for Black economic development. Still a third organization, the Urban League, set up shop in Rochester for the first time, after city officials had rejected it for decades. This chapter argues that in order for FIGHT to attract and retain the loyalty of the masses, it adopted what scholar Angela Dillard has called an "oppositional identity."[14] In so doing, FIGHT alienated much of the Black middle class and its white allies; however, it garnered tremendous concessions from corporate Rochester along the way.

If FIGHT mourned the loss of its middle class allies, it hardly skipped a beat. Chapter 5 shows how FIGHT targeted the Eastman Kodak Company. By its second annual convention in 1966, FIGHT decided to press the film conglomerate to hire and train the hard-core unemployed.[15] Begun as a local struggle, this crusade jumped to the national scene in 1967, making major waves in the business world. Kodak had successfully avoided any type of labor negotiations for more than eighty years, a fact that made business executives envious nationally. When FIGHT came calling, the corporate leaders simply handled the organization as they had always done in Rochester: Kodak representatives explained their own programs and suggested that FIGHT get in line. Not to be deterred, FIGHT continued to pressure Kodak locally, engaging the media and even drawing national Black Power leader Stokely Carmichael to join its efforts. As Kodak refused to budge, FIGHT employed a newly emerging proxy strategy, persuading Kodak shareholders to apply pressure on the company. Publications such as the *Wall Street Journal* and the *New York Times* warned corporations that times were changing and that they should beware of Black Power organizations such as FIGHT. Under intense scrutiny, Kodak ultimately signed a working agreement with FIGHT. This chapter argues that FIGHT's campaign against Kodak—complete with new strategies and the ability to capture national media coverage—significantly rewrote the rules of corporate responsibility in the era of Black Power.

Shaken by the FIGHT-Kodak struggle, Rochester corporations endeavored to develop Black business opportunities in the city. In the process, they implemented new and competing forms of Black capitalism that attracted attention from far and near. Chapter 6 documents the various plans to encourage Black entrepreneurship. Here, Kodak, wary of further negative publicity, spearheaded the creation of the Rochester Business Opportunities Council (RBOC). A collaboration between the locally headquartered corporations, several universities, and private citizens alike, RBOC provided funds, training, and technical assistance to Black individuals seeking to start or expand a business. This form of Black capitalism represented what Thomas Sugrue calls "a romance with small, family-run businesses and a celebration of the independent entrepreneur."[16] But there were others in Rochester who envisioned a different form of Black capitalism, a more collective capitalism wherein the Black community would operate businesses for the common good. In this alternative vision of Black capitalism, profits would be reinvested in daycare centers, affordable housing, and shopping centers. Because FIGHT was in the vanguard of cooperative Black capitalism, the organization attracted an unusual partner. The Xerox Corporation, which also supported RBOC, spearheaded independent industrial opportunities in conjunction with FIGHT. Eventually, Xerox and FIGHT unveiled FIGHTON, a Community Development Corporation intended to provide training, jobs, managerial experience, and profits to the Black community. The two paths to Black entrepreneurship—the individual and the cooperative—were strikingly different in their philosophies and attracted a range of supporters. Chapter 6 argues that this local struggle to provide economic opportunities in Black neighborhoods contributed significantly to the contest to define Black capitalism nationally.

Altogether, this book traces some thirty years of engagement and organizing in Black Rochester. No facet of life shaped Rochester in this period more than the emergence of a sizable Black population able to organize and command the attention of city hall and of the major corporations. By the end of the period, a telling diffusion of power had occurred. No longer could the corporations alone chart the city's course. No longer could the "haves" unilaterally prescribe a cure for the "have-nots."

Chapter 1

Black Rochester at Midcentury
Agricultural Migration, Population, and Politics

At midcentury, Rochester was in flux. Demo-
graphically, politically, and spatially, Rochester faced rapid changes, which
had only accelerated with the onset of World War II. The most dramatic
change was racial. Demographic forces, long underway in northern and western cities throughout the United States, explained in part the movement of a
sizable number of African Americans into the city of Rochester, swelling two
of the city's wards. At the same time, white flight or the rapid exodus of white
people from the inner city exacerbated the racial shift. Neighborhoods that
once consisted of Germans, Italians, Polish, and various other white ethnic
groups increasingly became Black neighborhoods, as the whites moved to the
outer reaches of Rochester and its suburbs.

Institutions that had long catered to white immigrants—settlement houses
and churches—either regrouped to serve the newcomers in this moment, as
the settlement houses attempted, or moved to the suburbs with their congregants, as did several churches. Storekeepers, who once lived above their businesses and among their customers, maintained their shops but increasingly
moved their families out of those neighborhoods and away from the communities they served. By 1950, Rochester's total population began a slow decline
that would continue for several decades. The city's Black population, however,
entered a period of rapid increase. For many, the changes represented more
than just a demographic shift. One settlement house, for example, saw the

influx of African Americans as qualitatively different from what had happened in previous generations: "Now the entire character of the neighborhood had changed until it seemed imperative that the Settlement should be primarily a character building agency."[1]

While consistent with national changes in migration patterns, which relocated unprecedented numbers of southerners to the North and West, the Rochester sojourn does not fully reflect the typical Great Migration story. These were not rural migrants heading to urban locales in search of factory work. Instead, they were agricultural migrants who first resided seasonally in nearby farming communities, all the while accumulating extensive knowledge of the greater metropolitan area, prior to permanent relocation. The steady increase of partially acculturated migrants helped foster generational challenges to longtime Black leadership in the city, which ultimately spurred a new wave of organizing.

Another set of migrants, smaller in number but with more formal education, moved into the city alongside the agricultural migrants. These Black newcomers, the Young Turks, as they came to be known, were inspired by changes taking place in the South as a result of the civil rights movement, and they hoped to apply similar strategies to the North. The Young Turks quickly swelled the local branch of the National Association for the Advancement of Colored People (NAACP), and they promoted new forms of organization and agitation.

When accounts of the Rochester uprising circulated nationally in 1964, any mention of Black agency, community formation, organization, or leadership were truncated or omitted in favor of narratives about Black disorder and pathology. Told that way, Black Rochester appeared disorganized, chaotic, lacking in leadership, and unable to identify and name its oppression. Nothing was further from the truth.

The East Coast Migrant Stream

During the 1950s, war veteran Robert F. Williams migrated to Rochester, lured there by the promise of factory work at the Eastman Kodak Company. He spent several weeks pounding the pavement in search of work, to no avail. He would later testify to the limited industrial opportunities in Rochester for Black men: "I walked that place inch by inch, and there was no job to be had." Without money to return home, Williams went to the nearby orchards and fields to secure work picking beans, cherries, and apples. Unlike many migrants to Rochester (and other northern cities), Williams stayed only long enough to earn money to return south, in his case, to his native North Carolina.[2] Once there, he went on to become the famed activist and author of *Negroes with Guns*.

Williams's story reflects the larger trajectory and the impact of the Great Migration on the urban landscape.[3] Black migrants were drawn away from the South to industrial opportunities frequently during times of war, when labor shortages were exacerbated by restrictions on immigration.[4] This Black migration changed the complexion of the nation's largest cities, including New York, Los Angeles, Chicago, Detroit, and Pittsburgh. "In the 1900s," James Gregory offers, "only 8 percent of the nation's total Black population" lived outside the South. By 1970, more than 10.6 million African Americans lived outside the South, 47 percent of the nation's total.[5] Gregory further notes that while this changed the face of the nation's major cities, the migrants "were also going to regions that previously had known little racial diversity."[6] Though sensitive to minor differences in sex, familial circumstance, and time and route of departure, the migration narrative remains largely the same whenever it is told. Large numbers of Black southerners left behind the segregation and violence of the Jim Crow South in search of industrial job opportunities—or in the case of women, domestic service positions—in the North, thus improving their economic stability.

Rochester was not exempt from these forces. An economic boom placed Rochester in a much better position economically than other upstate New York cities. The Eastman Kodak Corporation, headquartered in Rochester, continued to dominate the film and camera industry and served as Rochester's leading industrial employer. The city also benefited greatly from the expansion of the Haloid Company, which became Xerox, as it capitalized on new xerography patents. While Kodak and Xerox commanded international attention, other manufacturing industries also fueled this local boom. For many reasons, however, Rochester's labor shortage did not translate into industrial opportunities for Black migrants.

Rochester did provide opportunities for agricultural migrants. A less studied and less understood facet of the Great Migration is the trickle-down effect industrial expansion had on rural and agricultural areas in the North. Take for example the more than 40,000 African Americans who moved to Rochester between 1950 and 1970, which more than tripled the Black population (see table 1). As the story of Robert Williams demonstrates, their presence was *not* the result of an open industrial labor market grateful for their presence. Rochester's corporate world relied on a highly skilled and technically trained workforce. Kodak and Xerox required laborers to have at least a high school diploma whether the job in question required this level of education or not.[7] They also preferred to fill industrial openings with local, white agricultural laborers eager

Table 1.1   Rochester's Black Population, 1930–1970

YEAR	TOTAL ROCHESTER POPULATION	BLACK POPULATION	BLACK POPULATION (%)	BLACK POPULATION INCREASE PER DECADE (%)	BLACK POPULATION INCREASE OVER 1930 (%)
1930	328,132	2,679	0.8	—	—
1940	324,975	3,262	1.0	21.8	21.8
1950	332,488	7,590	2.3	132.7	183.3
1960	318,611	23,586	7.4	210.8	780.4
1970	296,233	49,647	16.8	110.5	1,753.2

Sources: Adolph Dupree, "Rochester Roots/Routes, Part III," About . . . Time, August 1984, 24; Ruth Forsyth, The Rochester Area Selected Demographic and Social Characteristics (Rochester, NY: Monroe Community College, 1984); Campbell Gibson, "Population of the 100 Largest Cities and Other Urban Places in the United States, 1790–1990," Population Division Working Paper No. 27, Population Division, US Bureau of the Census, June 1998; and Norman Coombs, "History of African-Americans in Rochester, NY," unpublished paper, http://people.rit.edu/nrcgsh/arts/rochester.htm, April 23, 2012, Wayback Machine.

to abandon the grueling work and long hours in the fields in exchange for stable, year-round work that promised better wages and benefits.[8] The absence of white laborers, of course, created substantial openings for field hands to maintain and harvest crops throughout the summer and fall. At the same time, increasing mechanization in the southern agricultural landscape had left many Black agricultural workers jobless.[9]

The East Coast Migrant Stream fashioned a solution for both the short-staffed farms and the underemployed or unemployed Black southerners. This stream of migrants originated in Florida, ultimately depositing workers throughout thirty-six rural counties in New York State; the bulk were concentrated in western New York, including the area around Rochester.[10] It was common for farm owners in the area to instruct a trusted employee to return to his (women were rarely, if ever crew leaders) hometown to recruit twenty-five to eighty more people to work the season. In this way, migrants were frequently acquainted through familial or communal networks with one another prior to leaving the South. Once a migrant had an agreeable experience on a particular farm, he or she often traveled to the same farm yearly, sometimes as an individual working with a crew, other times as a member of an independent family unit. While it was not a lucrative undertaking, families could make enough to support themselves if they worked through the myriad crops. One migrant remembered that in upstate New York, "you could start in June and work right straight through until November because you had tomatoes, you had beans, you had cherries, you had apples, your pears, your prunes, you know, all of those things would keep you busy all the way through."[11] While those were central agricultural crops in New York, migrants also planted, tended, and harvested strawberries, potatoes, cabbage, celery, and onions.

Unlike most migrants whose travel was restricted by the rail system, agricultural migrants were not limited by the tracks; rather, they came in migrant trucks, owned cars, or traveled North with friends or family who owned vehicles. The car afforded greater flexibility in traveling and returning, and it became the source of fond family memories. Ruby Ford, born in 1956 in Haines City, Florida, recalled coming "with my father and mother, sisters and brothers; there was ten of us then. We all came up in one car."[12] Emmarilus McCants Jenkins, born to migrant parents in North Rose, New York, remembered preparing to return to Florida for the first time as a married woman; pregnant with her first son, she went into labor the night before they were to leave the camp. The family car allowed them to stay until both mother and son were able to travel safely.[13]

This flexibility in movement also facilitated economic flexibility. Families could determine when and where to stop along the stream. Pandora Tinsley Cole, born in 1940, traveled the circuit for twenty-five years before permanently settling in upstate New York. She traveled with her mother as a child, first to Hendersonville, North Carolina, then to Dover, Delaware, where they picked beans, and then on to Wayne County (next to Monroe County, where Rochester is located), where she picked cherries and apples in the orchards. Like many migrants who remained in the stream, Cole eventually "started working in [the] canning plant where [she] worked on machines, canning beans and beets, and applesauce."[14] The fields and orchards yielded such a large quantity of produce that canning factories for companies such as Mott's, headquartered at the time in Rochester, were often built on site.[15]

Some families moved directly from Florida to New York each year, avoiding working along the way. Migrant crews, particularly those comprised of families, found it undesirable to set up camp at more than two farms throughout the season.[16] Montrose Cole, born in 1969, worked the migrant stream alongside her father, who taught her to pick apples. She recalled coming to Wayne County from Haines City, Florida: "I've been coming up here on the seasons all my life. . . . It usually takes us a day and a half to come; we leave in the morning, and should get up that next night—late that next night. . . . We always go to this truck stop in Pennsylvania, which is nice."[17]

The yearly rituals that families developed, remembered so fondly by some migrants, demonstrate both familial order and communal organization. They further suggest that families were attuned to their own economic and educational needs, and the various obstacles that could prevent progress in either

of these areas. While many migrants continued to work the stream by returning to Florida each winter, a growing number of migrants "settled out" in the
Rochester area. These settled-out migrants, or "stagrants," sought better opportunities by choosing to remain year-round, significantly altering the racial
demography of upstate New York by 1960. Agricultural work was often the
only option available to many laborers. While some recalled the rhythms and
routines of migrant life fondly, structural forces made it a difficult way to make
a living. Working the fields of upstate New York satisfied wanderlust, offered
a respite from southern heat and violence, and provided marginally better pay.
However, federal legislation and corrupt farm owners tipped the scales against
the migrant workers.

The unpredictable conditions in which migrant families lived and worked,
combined with abysmal housing, exacerbated negative perceptions of agricultural migrant work, including by migrants themselves. As one former migrant
stated, "This isn't a man's work. This is just too dirty. I'd like to see people doing
other work, not like this."[18] Other migrants saw honest work made unpredictable and therefore unprofitable. Another reported, "This traveling stuff is not
good. You can't predict the weather, you can't predict what's going to happen,
you can't predict the good days or the bad days, so nine times out of ten you
end up with some kind of complication and no work. You do pretty good for a
week and then have no work at all so it just doesn't add up to anything."[19]

These difficulties prompted migrants to look for alternatives whenever possible. Ivory Simmons, a migrant born in Vero Beach, Florida, in 1929 came to
New York State in the 1950s to work in the camps. He left the migrant stream
as quickly as possible, highlighting the decision many migrants made. "There
are a lot of disadvantages in being a migrant," he offered. "I guess that's why
I decided to not be a transient. I started to stay because I wanted to put some
roots somewhere, and if I was going to be in this part of the world then I might
as well stay here permanently instead of coming back and forth."[20] Wayne
County resident Charles Jackson recalled, "I had to leave Florida because I
owed my children a better future. I needed more money. The farms up north
did pay more than the southern farms. With my educational limitations, it
would have been hard to find work even in a factory."[21]

While Simmons and Jackson viewed leaving the migrant stream in personal and familial terms, structural forces made migrant agricultural work
precarious, transferring the risk of doing business to the employees rather
than the employer. Two decades earlier, in the 1930s, the acquiescence of
the southern ruling class to Roosevelt's New Deal programs required that both
farmworkers and domestics, who were disproportionately Black, be excluded
from many initiatives, including social security, which provided benefits if an

employee was injured or became disabled. Likewise, federal legislation that guaranteed overtime and unemployment benefits excluded farmworkers.[22] Individual states compounded these federal structural inequalities, requiring permanent residency in order to qualify for services such as Medicaid and food stamps. If a state did not exclude farmworkers from their programs in theory, migrants were often prohibited in practice. On one Wayne County farm, for example, 124 individuals qualified for food stamps after being without work for an extended period of time. The farm where they worked, however, was only approved to house eighty-six migrant laborers that season.[23] To protect himself from reprisal for overcrowding, the owner simply removed thirty-eight individuals from the list provided to the food stamp caseworker. Frequent migration also frequently hindered recertification for aid after a family had crossed state lines, given the extensive paperwork and documentation required.[24] Practices such as these prompted many to consider alternate arrangements.

Agricultural migrant workers did not make the decision to remain in the North lightly or without forethought. The decision was made only after gaining familiarity with the area and weighing the benefits and drawbacks of northern living. Migrants who worked the fields in western New York often traveled to Rochester on Saturdays to purchase supplies unavailable in the rural towns, to hear jazz and blues in a city club, or to get their hair cut or styled. This contact with the urban center convinced many agricultural workers that leaving the migrant stream and settling permanently in Rochester would improve their lot. As increased numbers made this decision, they eventually sent for wives, children, and extended family members. At certain moments, the decision seemed universal.

Though never an agricultural farmworker himself, Eugene Barrington provides an interesting case study of the group migration process. Barrington arrived in Rochester from his native Sanford, Florida, the single largest source of Black migrants to Rochester.[25] As a child, Barrington was deeply affected by stories of Rochester. He recalled that his friends eagerly awaited the return of the migrant children every winter so they could hear new stories about Rochester. The cultural currency migrant children accumulated with travel to the Rochester area came to be called "the Rochester Mystique." Such was the migrant flow that Edward Blacksheare, the principal of the Black Croombs Academy in Sanford, claimed that by 1969, roughly thirty years after the relationship between the two cities began, thirty to forty of 150 high school graduates would leave for Rochester each year.[26] Barrington himself was a case in point. After completing high school in Florida, he attended Syracuse University, where he completed his doctorate in social science in 1976.

Barrington was so taken with the power of the Rochester Mystique that he titled his dissertation "New Beginnings: The Story of Five Black Entrepreneurs Who Migrated from Sanford, Florida to Rochester, New York." The text highlighted the importance of the migrant stream in his upbringing and in the development of his worldview but also in the group experience of Sanfordians. He argued persuasively that large numbers of African Americans made the conscious and informed decision to depart Sanford permanently because they perceived better opportunities in Rochester.[27] In the course of his research, Barrington explored migrants' perceptions of their decisions to relocate permanently to Rochester. One reply is instructive: "Couldn't git ahea'. . . . Who wanna work on somebody else's farm for nothing anyway? Most of us wuz working for nothing. I knowed the place [referring to Rochester]. The farms wuz close by. We'd come into the city to have a good time. A lotta people started moving here from Sanford and around. Jobz was plentiful. I thought I could make a good start here."[28] Another recalled, "Money was the main reason. You could git a little security up here witout a whole lotta education. It was better than home." Still another offered, "I wanted to git off that farm. Ain't never liked that damn farm. It got hot. You didn't make no money. Had to leave that shit. Got out when I could."[29]

While most hoped to improve their own prospects, many believed their children would make use of educational opportunities to better their life chances. Thus, the migrant stream did not drop dislocated Black families prone to social pathology on upstate New York. Individuals and families who had resided in the area for many years believed they could work to support and improve their familial situations by making the situation permanent.

Migrants turned stagrants, Sanford-born and otherwise, believed their fortunes would improve in Rochester, but they were largely disappointed. Many found unscrupulous landlords waiting to profit from their arrival. Constance Mitchell and her husband, John, homeowners in Rochester's Third Ward, realized something was very wrong when twenty mailboxes appeared on a single dwelling across the street from their home. They recalled, "Slumlords had taken great big old mansions and cut them all up. And made what they called, 'efficiency apartments' which was just a refrigerator and a two burner little stove and a room."[30] Landlords then rented these efficiency apartments to entire extended families and charged twice the rent one would expect to pay elsewhere in Rochester. The city was expansive enough to accommodate the 780 percent increase in Black residents; however, real estate agents and landlords refused to show Black tenants and potential homeowners housing options outside the two city wards where ethnic immigrants and African Americans had traditionally resided (see figure 1.1). Between 1940 and 1960, these practices created a housing crisis of astronomical proportions. The increased strain on housing also taxed community services: uncollected garbage increased; wear and tear on housing, parks, and streets increased; and tensions ran high.

For many African American residents, the abominable housing situation was a defining feature of their lives. Buddy Granston moved to Rochester in 1947 as an eight-year-old child. He recalled more than sixty years later, "When I got here I lived in what they called 'the bottom' over in the Joseph Avenue,

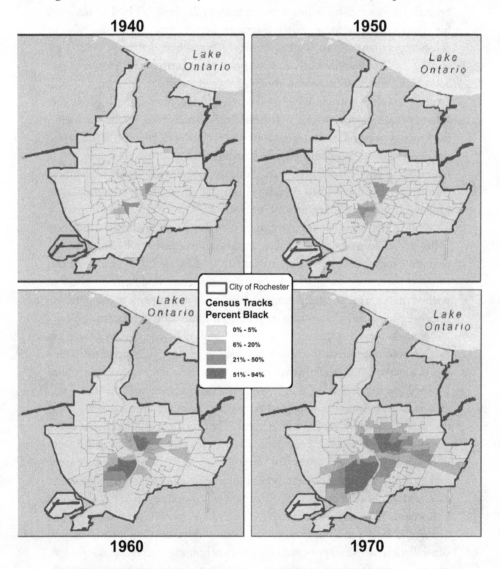

FIGURE 1.1.   Black Population Percentage by Census Tract for the City of Rochester, NY, 1940–1970. Created by Binghamton University's GIS Core Facility.

Ormond Street area. . . . The housing was horrendous and it was rough; it really was rough. And we called that the bottom and we didn't feel bad about it because when you're at the bottom you have nowhere to go but up."[31] Daryl Porter, who grew up in these overcrowded neighborhoods, remembered the conditions similarly but highlighted the sense of community among the residents. He recalled that when a family's gas and electric were shut off for nonpayment, the community came to their aid. A walk through any of these neighborhoods would have revealed extension cords strung from one apartment to the next through windows and over fire escapes.[32] Communal aid aside, such housing conditions created health problems for many residents. Trent Jackson, an Olympic athlete who grew up in Rochester, remembered, "It was a time when your mother and father would wake up in the middle of the night and come to your room to check on you because of rats."[33] Indeed, his younger sister was hospitalized because of a rat bite.

While it was the agricultural migrants who most often ended up in these "efficiency" apartments, the influx of migrants and the practice of redlining reduced available housing for African Americans of all socioeconomic levels. When Earl Caldwell, a young Black reporter recruited by the *Rochester Democrat and Chronicle*, arrived in 1963, he expected to move into a promised "apartment in a luxury building" near the press offices. Once in Rochester, no one at the press seemed to recall this promise. Instead, Caldwell was asked to participate in an investigative news story. The paper had received numerous complaints from "Black activists" regarding housing discrimination. In fact, the NAACP's Walter Cooper, a research chemist at Eastman Kodak, had answered advertisements for sixty-nine apartments and was refused by each.[34] Claims such as Cooper's had been difficult for the newspaper to investigate prior to Caldwell's arrival. With Caldwell on board, the paper could send both Caldwell and a white reporter, Bill Vogler, to answer advertisements posted in the paper. Caldwell recalls the experience:

After we had visited about five or six apartments, Vogler asked me, "Are you sure you're actually going into these places?" He did not understand. I would just reach the door and promptly be told, "The apartment has already been rented." Right after I was told that no apartment was available, Vogler would visit the same place and be invited inside. He'd get a whole spiel on how great the apartment was, why he'd like it and what the neighborhood had to offer. My experience was so different that at times it would be downright embarrassing. We visited apartment after apartment. It was always the same: no to me, yes to him. I just kept making notes of everything that happened.[35]

Caldwell described his experiences in a front-page story. He was later offered an apartment, which he accepted, but what most surprised him was the response of those Black activists. "The day after the story was published," he explained, "Blacks began showing up in the newsroom 'to meet Earl Caldwell.' Some people called these visitors troublemakers. They called themselves activists, which meant they were in the forefront of stoking, shaping and channeling the anger they said was growing in Rochester's two Black communities."[36]

This defining feature of Black life in Rochester—the burgeoning housing crisis—was not the only one the stagrants found in their new city. While the city leaders relied on real estate agents to corral the newcomers, Rochester's Black leaders produced a strong web of institutions, churches, and social networks throughout the years. For generations, these folks had worked tirelessly to take care of each other and to push bit by bit for Black opportunity, justice, and equality.

Black Leadership in the Flower City

Local journals, organizations, and histories pay annual tribute to the Black community's long experience in Rochester. These tales proudly begin with Frederick Douglass's adoption of Rochester as the place he "shall always feel more at home . . . than anywhere else in the country."[37] They continue with the elaborate tracing of Harriet Tubman's great nieces and nephews, who resided in the Rochester area, and then catalog myriad examples of ordinary African American leaders who made a contribution locally, and in some cases, nationally.[38] Here, even the casual observer is struck by a strong sense of racial purpose and pride. The oral tradition and the written word chronicle both the strivings and accomplishments of Black Rochester despite the pervasive racism and segregation. To cope, Black leaders turned inward to build strong, stable Black institutions ranging from churches to athletic clubs. When African Americans faced exclusion from a Rochester institution, as they frequently did, they often built their own, as in the cases of the Elks Lodge and the Masonic Temple. If building their own institution was impractical or improbable, as in the case of an African American equivalent to the University of Rochester's School of Medicine and Dentistry, Black leaders would quietly and gently agitate for admission, as Dr. Charles Lunsford and Dr. Van Levy did for decades. In short, Black Rochester proudly looked to itself and to its leadership to solve its problems and to meet its ongoing needs.[39]

Throughout the twentieth century, the leadership styles present in Black Rochester reflected the times. As the times changed, so too did the leaders and their styles. In the first half of the century, Black luminaries adopted a conservative path, turning inward to lift as they climbed. Turning inward did not necessarily mean disengagement from the white community, however. On the contrary, it often meant adopting an accommodationist stance with white leaders. The aforementioned Dr. Lunsford, for example, came to Rochester from Macon, Georgia, in the early part of the twentieth century. A veteran of both Howard University Medical School and the Freeman's Hospital in Washington, DC, Lunsford brought with him to Rochester a deep appreciation for Black institutions. As Rochester's first licensed African American physician, he established a joint practice with dentist Dr. Van Levy, also an African American. Over the years, the two built a thriving practice in Rochester, serving both Black and white clients. Lunsford and Van Levy made house calls, provided free services to the poor, and developed a reputation as community leaders. Lunsford served as long-time NAACP president, while Van Levy helped to form Rochester's Negro Business League, becoming its first secretary.

While the pair made a considerable impression on Rochester, they too faced institutional segregation and racism. In 1922, Van Levy applied to the University of Rochester's School of Medicine and Dentistry to study specialized surgery, but the school's dean refused to consider his application on account of his race. Rather than take to the streets, picketing or protesting at the medical school, which both Van Levy and Lunsford felt would be vulgar, the pair arranged several meetings with George Eastman, founder of the Eastman Kodak Company and, more importantly, the University of Rochester's most generous benefactor.[40] The two doctors privately took Eastman to task for his racial hypocrisy, believing he held the key to desegregating the medical school. They demanded to know why "he was willing to give money to Tuskegee, Hampton and Meharry and then would not employ the graduates of those institutions in his factory."[41] In one meeting with Eastman, Lunsford and Van Levy also threatened to raise the stakes. Van Levy recalled, "I told him I thought it would be interesting news for the New York papers to get hold of and finally things began to happen."[42] Slowly, throughout the following two decades, the University of Rochester's School of Medicine and Dentistry began to admit Black students, and Eastman Kodak, for its part, hired a handful of Black scientists. While the initial numbers were negligible, the doctors' accomplishments proved important.[43] Their targeting of Eastman for his racist hiring practices is instructive: where George Eastman led, Rochester would follow. It was a lesson well learned by the Black community.

While in that instance Lunsford and Van Levy did not go to the press, they did make good on their threat of a public hearing. Between 1922 and 1939, Lunsford organized a citizens committee comprised of both Black and white members to bring clergy and professionals into formal dialogue in order that they might increase brotherly love while initiating gradual change in Rochester. In 1939, New York State provided them a public venue to air their grievances. Black Harlem had risen up in rebellion in 1935, a first for that neighborhood. In response, state officials had formed the New York Temporary Commission on the Urban Colored Population and charged the new committee with visiting various cities across the state to hold public meetings. Lunsford ensured that Rochester would be included.

At the hearing in Rochester, Lunsford demonstrated his perfectly honed diplomatic skill. The citizens committee did not attack Rochester's corporations or its government in any systemic form. Rather, its members accused Rochester teachers of diverting Black students from pursuing higher education and encouraging them to join the labor market instead. When so accused, the superintendent of schools claimed he had no knowledge of this practice. Rather than further embarrass the superintendent in front of the statewide committee or damage his own relationship with city leaders, Lunsford created an opportunity to save face, offering that the superintendent likely did not know of this practice. He cautioned the superintendent, however, that he knew about it now and reminded him that his teachers were under his command.[44] Shortly thereafter, a token handful of Black teachers were hired in the public school system. These were important strides in a city that was just beginning to witness increased numbers of African Americans, drawn to the city primarily to improve educational opportunities for their families.

Lunsford agitated in Rochester, but he did so in accordance with the status quo. He located the source of power and arranged a meeting. He quietly but firmly put forth the needs of the community as he envisioned them. Despite his long track record of uplifting the race, Lunsford would disapprove of the direction of the modern civil rights movement at midcentury. He became one of the first to speak out against the organization over which he once presided. It seems he opposed the burgeoning militancy of the NAACP.[45]

Like Lunsford before him, Father Quintin Primo, who would later become Bishop Primo in Chicago, came to Rochester to serve. In 1947, during Lunsford's term as NAACP president, Primo was called to convert Rochester's Black Episcopal mission church to a parish church. Once settled in Rochester, Primo immersed himself in the religious, social, and political fabric of the community. As a Black minister heading a Black church in a white diocese, Primo quickly learned that much of his time would be spent navigating Rochester's racial politics. One of a handful of Black churches at the time, St. Simon's, under Primo's care, emerged as a formidable community institution and Primo as a central community leader. In fact, within a few short years, he capitalized on his standing in both white and Black communities to succeed Lunsford as president of Rochester's integrated NAACP. As in Lunsford's time, the NAACP was a clearinghouse for all things African American. There were many white members; by some counts, the organization was majority white. When the city leadership wanted Black representation on a committee or for an issue, they generally turned to the president of the NAACP. For these reasons, the president was typically someone agreeable to the white community and accepted by the Black community.

Father Primo's popularity as a community leader was no accident. He self-consciously sought avenues to connect with community members and to nurture their civic and religious involvement. When Constance Mitchell first relocated to Rochester in 1950, she encountered Primo one afternoon at an intersection near his church. Primo immediately recognized that Mitchell was new in town. Identifying her as such, he engaged her in conversation, inquiring after her opinion of the city. She informed him, rather tartly, that she did not care for the city at all. Years later, Mitchell fondly recalled that it was a fortuitous meeting with Primo, who had only been in Rochester for three years himself. Interpreting her distaste for the city as loneliness, Father Primo saw an opportunity to mediate Mitchell's isolation and to enlist a new foot soldier in his church and community projects. Primo invited Mitchell to work with the Baden Street Settlement, then in a transition to serve the burgeoning African American population, as a chaperone at their youth dances. Mitchell consented to serve, which eventually led to her involvement in the Delta RESSICs (Recreational, Educational, Social, Special Interest and Civic), a group organized at Baden Street, which taught literacy classes, organized clothing drives, arranged childcare and offered various forms of tutoring in the migrant camps on the farms surrounding Rochester.[46]

Father Primo took great pride in this ability to engage his community in unique and unexpected ways and to make coalitions with civic groups. Just as he engaged Constance Mitchell on the street corner, he sought ways to ingratiate himself with a new congregation skeptical of his worldliness. At the church guild's annual community card party, Primo proved to be quite the pinochle player, causing "the word [to] spread like wildfire in the community. 'The new priest at St. Simon's plays cards.'"[47] Primo's willingness to play cards, an activity that some in the church considered a sin, garnered respect from the larger community. Primo pitched his card playing as symbolic of the worldly work he was doing to integrate white neighborhoods, to improve professional opportunities for African Americans, and to provide access for them to professional training and postsecondary education. Organizations such as the Masonic lodge took note of this community engagement, applauded his efforts, and then joined him to build community cooperation. These alliances undoubtedly assisted Primo in his 1959 bid for the presidency of the Rochester NAACP, then the second-largest NAACP local in New York State.

Though Primo believed himself a popular president, he soon created a host of problems for himself in his role as a race broker. Primo, it seems, relied heavily on a group of relatively new members to prepare him for public events. These newcomers were like-minded: young professionals who had been politicized by the winds of racial change blowing in the South. One newspaperman dubbed these new arrivals, Constance Mitchell and Walter Cooper among them, the Young Turks, a name that stuck. From identifying relevant community issues to writing speeches, the young men and women served as NAACP committee heads and performed much of the organization's legwork. In return, they expected Father Primo, as one of Rochester's "powerful actors who served as an intermediar[y] between the races" to represent their best interests and mediate their concerns with white leaders.[48] Community activist Glenn Claytor, a new face in Rochester, recalled that someone like Primo was not "an uncommon figure in many American cities in the early '50s, where a small number of people sort of interfaced between the authorities—whether it be the banks or the police or whomever."[49] In Rochester, Primo, like Dr. Lunsford before him, "was the person you went to for just about anything that involved a non-white dealing with the power structure. These individuals sometimes were accepted by the power structure as spokesmen, and of course, that was an accommodation. And it was better than no accommodation."[50] In his role as NAACP president with an educated and aggressive new membership, Primo walked a precarious path.

Unfortunately, Primo misjudged the changing needs and desires of his constituency as they entered the 1960s. He was not prepared to engage in large-scale confrontations with the white power structure, as his changing Black constituents would increasingly demand. Instead, Primo approached racism one issue at a time. The reverend earned his stripes primarily for work on housing desegregation, facilitating the purchase of homes in white neighborhoods for African American families with the means to do so. Importantly, Primo did not challenge the structural forces that reinforced redlining. Instead, he sought individual opportunities for middle class Black families. Primo recalled that during his presidency, white NAACP members, or white intermediaries, would purchase a home and hold it for sixty to ninety days before transferring the deed to the rightful Black owners. In this way, Black families were able to integrate white neighborhoods that resisted their presence. In fact, Father Primo himself faced great difficulty purchasing his own home in a white suburb when

he arrived in Rochester. Perhaps it was politically expedient, but Primo cred-
ited the white members of the NAACP for their steadfast efforts.[51]

The new group of Black activists, the Young Turks, challenged both Primo
and the traditional ways of negotiating power in Rochester. Rather than
dismantle housing segregation one house at a time or serve as a supportive
NAACP auxiliary for southern struggles, they hoped to address the growing
concerns in their own city. The Young Turks further believed that many of
the old methods were outdated and ineffective. They refused to negotiate mod-
est or incremental change behind the scenes with white power brokers, as
both Lunsford and Primo had done. Instead, they believed the time was ripe
for structural, large-scale initiatives that would bring better opportunity to
more people, most importantly the Black migrants then entering the city. They
used their positions as committee heads to advance their agendas.

In 1962, Dr. Walter Cooper, a research scientist at Kodak, head of the local
NAACP education committee, and one of Primo's speechwriters, began to col-
lect statistics on de facto segregation in Rochester's city schools, segregation
that depended upon housing discrimination.[52] His efforts greatly reflected his
interests. Cooper came from a large, low-income family in a Pennsylvania steel
town. Education, highly valued among his family, provided an escape route
for poor young people seeking opportunities. After meeting with Paul Zuber,
head of New York State's NAACP Housing Committee, Cooper moved from
fact finding to initiating a desegregation lawsuit against the city of Rochester.
Zuber had just won the famous New Rochelle case, wherein a federal judge
established legal precedent by ordering a northern community to desegregate
its schools. Energized, Zuber encouraged Cooper to continue his work.[53]
Cooper was elated to hear that his evidence collection surpassed New Rochelle's
and that a legal challenge from Rochester would likely be successful given that
New Rochelle's segregation issues paled in comparison. Buoyed by this news,
Cooper took the information to Primo and informed the president-priest that
he would "like to report out these findings to the executive committee of the
NAACP." On Cooper's telling, Primo responded that he did not "want to
embarrass his [white] friends downtown."[54] Primo ultimately blocked a legal
challenge from the NAACP.

This was not an isolated incident between Father Primo and the heads of
the various NAACP committees. At about this same time, Rochester's city
council belatedly accepted federal funds to build Chatham Gardens, a low-to-
moderate-income public housing complex that the city desperately needed.
To oversee the project, the council formed a special committee and asked
Father Primo to represent the Black community. This position put him at odds

with his constituency once again. The council intended to build the new project adjacent to existing public housing rather than spread it evenly throughout the city, across traditionally Black and white neighborhoods. Council members believed this would elicit the least amount of (white) public resistance. One council representative reported that he had personally gone through various communities and discussed the issue with his constituency. He found that "they were in unanimity of opposition" to putting the new project in their neighborhoods.[55]

Primo accepted this reasoning without argument, believing that one should not look a gift horse in the mouth. The city needed more public housing, and Primo was willing to compromise on its location to ensure it was built. Rochester *had* resisted public housing much longer than any other city in New York State, the need was urgent, and he feared the council would refuse to build if challenged on the location.[56] The more militant committee heads of the NAACP, however, were not accustomed to capitulating to councils. Led by Glenn Claytor, brother-in-law to Walter Cooper and the head of the NAACP housing committee, these members refused to let Primo speak on their behalf. They publicly challenged both the legality and the wisdom of concentrating public housing in a single ward. This confrontation between city hall, the traditional Black leadership, and the Young Turks marked a new dawn in Black Rochester.

Ignoring the concerns of his Black constituency on multiple occasions became a fateful decision for Primo and for the local NAACP. Primo quickly learned that despite his community engagement and his challenge to housing segregation, his dedicated foot soldiers were loyal to the cause, not to him. When Father Primo's membership came to believe that their president was more interested in preserving his relationship with white leaders than in large-scale, structural change, the Young Turks in the NAACP largely transferred their energies to an organization more suited to their needs. Though they maintained their NAACP membership, Cooper and Claytor, accompanied by several other young and energetic race men and women promptly formed the Monroe County Non-Partisan Political League, an organization committed to public agitation on race issues. The Rochester branch of the NAACP had one further hurrah left in it—a later challenge to police brutality—but Primo's presidency set in motion a series of events that severely weakened the organization by 1964.

Dr. Lunsford's and Father Primo's leadership and experience in Rochester demonstrate two important facets of Black leadership in Rochester at mid-century. The Black community relied upon Black professionals, particularly those who had inroads to the white community, to navigate opportunities and to resolve issues. Primo's story also demonstrates the fallibility of leaders who did not negotiate the new militancy of civil rights activists. By 1963, Primo had become ineffective as a power broker between the white city government and the Black community. His Black constituents undermined him by protesting committees upon which he sat, and white officials could no longer count on him to represent Black Rochester. As a result, he resigned without protest "after the formation of the Monroe County Non-Partisan League, citing a pressing workload of activity outside of the NAACP."[57] He left Rochester months later, having been transferred by the Episcopal diocese to Chicago.

Throughout their years in Rochester, it is likely that both Lunsford and Primo would have encountered Virginia Wilson and her daughters, Lydia and Mildred, other examples of the city's Black mainstays. As founding members of Rochester's Mt. Olivet Baptist Church, arguably the most respectable of Rochester's Black churches, the Wilsons positioned themselves as a welcoming committee of sorts, helping newcomers get acquainted with the city. Where Lunsford and Primo concerned themselves with brotherhood and promoting positive race relations, the Wilsons concerned themselves primarily with improving the lives of Black people. In many ways, they were a social agency unto themselves. They visited jails, took children to the hospital when the need arose, and in general provided for the weakest elements of the Black community, demonstrating an altogether different type of leadership. Their method allowed them to navigate the changing times and the various social movements with little interruption.

In time, Virginia Wilson passed the torch to her youngest daughter, Mildred Johnson, who gladly took up the family mantle. In her many roles in the community, formal and informal, Johnson consistently advocated for the poor and the dispossessed. One case in particular highlights Johnson's "dedicated reign of 'speaking for the little people and holding the big people in account,'" a practice that earned the attention of New York governor Nelson Rockefeller, who subsequently gave Johnson the moniker "Ambassador of the Inner City."[58] At a time when the justice system did not yet include a public defender's office, Johnson brazenly appointed herself public defender throughout Rochester's city courts. Whenever a young African American appeared before the court, Johnson accompanied the family and frequently served as legal counsel, though she had no formal training in this area. City court judge Reuben Davis recalled,

> Mildred would appear on behalf of some seventeen year old who had gotten in trouble and Mildred was there with his mother wanting to get him out without bail because they had no money. Mildred would ensure that he would make every appearance that was required of him.

And you can bet Mildred would see that he was there. Mildred would be at that kid's house at five o'clock in the morning, take him to her house and wait 'til it's time to go to court and then she'd bring him to court. And she would not hesitate to say, "Your honor can I approach the bench?" She got legal language and law. And you dare not to refuse her, 'cause Mildred was such a strong personality she would tell you off right then, you know. And she didn't just do it in my court, she would do it in every city court, the judges—they all say "Oh, here comes Mildred!"[59]

In 1968, under the aegis of the Black Power organization FIGHT, Johnson would go on to establish the city's first formal public defender's office.

Instruments of Change

By the close of the 1950s, the Young Turks took it upon themselves to set up new organizations to advance their causes, as Mildred Johnson and her family had done. If the NAACP would not represent their interests at city hall, they would begin to petition the city council on their own behalf. Among the grievances was the absence in Rochester of an office of the State Commission Against Discrimination (SCAD), the agency designated to record and investigate housing and employment discrimination complaints in New York State. Despite Governor Harriman's 1958 approval of a Rochester SCAD office, no such branch had yet opened. It appears that "Republican legislative opposition reduced the appropriation [to fund the Rochester office] and stalled the approval."[60] As a result, if a Rochester resident wished to file a discrimination complaint, he or she had to travel to Buffalo (approximately seventy miles away) or Syracuse (approximately ninety miles away) to do so.

The absence of a SCAD office changed the nature of Black organizing in Rochester. It convinced the Young Turks that, given their inability to influence local politicians, they needed to elect their own leaders. Several such organizers, including Walter Cooper and Richard (Dick) Wade, a white professor at the University of Rochester, toyed with running a Black candidate for Third Ward supervisor. Recent migration had tipped the racial balance in the Third Ward, and if registered to vote, African American residents could successfully elect a candidate to represent them in city government. The Democrats, for whom majority control had remained out of reach for several decades, were willing to run a Black candidate if it would gain them another seat. Two major obstacles presented themselves: Who would run for the office? And how could enough voters be registered to ensure a successful election? After several conversations, Cooper and Wade approached the Delta RESSICs. Cooper recalled that the Delta RESSICs "comprised . . . the most forward looking and fundamentally better educated Blacks in the community" and would likely provide a suitable man for the job. Instead, when they talked it over with the Delta RESSICs, "the men said 'Well, you know, I'd face pressure from my employer.'" After much conversation, Cooper, betraying his class position, suggested, "It would be logical if we chose a woman because she would not come under any economic pressures—she was not in the work force." Cooper eventually asked Constance Mitchell to run against the Republican incumbent Lester Peck.[61] Mitchell recalled, "The men were primarily concerned about their jobs, because Rochester was a Republican city and they were really looking for Democrats. And they knew that the men weren't going to jeopardize their jobs. 'Cause there was a lot of intimidation during that time, I mean, I can tell you, you know, a long story about what I went though, just being a Democrat."[62] Mitchell, who was a new mother, agreed that a woman needed to run, and she agreed to the task.

In many ways, Mitchell was an ideal candidate, well placed to address the deteriorating conditions in the Third Ward. Having settled in Rochester in 1950, she had become an integral member of several institutions but was still relatively new to the city. Though not an agricultural migrant (Mitchell had moved to Rochester from New Rochelle with her husband, John), she spent a great deal of time working with the settlement houses and tutoring in the migrant camps. Because she was not entrenched in Black Rochester's old-time politicking, many believed Mitchell could make history as "the highest elected official among Black women in the United States."[63] Mildred Johnson, that straight-shooting, self-appointed public defender, visited Mitchell as soon as she learned of her campaign. Mitchell fondly recalled the women's conversation that day:

[Johnson] came to my house and she said, "I had to come to see you. Now, I have to tell you something: You'll make it." And I said, "Why?" And she said, "Well, for one thing, you're the right color—you're not too Black and you're not too light. Second thing is that I understand you're Catholic, you're not Baptist. 'Cause you see, you get caught up in the churches—if you don't belong to the right church you're going to have some problems, so I'm glad to hear that you're Catholic." She was really hilarious, you know. And so we became like *this* [crosses her fingers], because I always came to her for advice about the community that I didn't know about, you know. And I respected her because Mildred was much older than I was.[64]

The campaign focused on bread-and-butter issues affecting both the migrants and long-time residents alike: garbage pickup, parks and recreation, over-crowded schools, poor housing, and importantly, the creation of a Rochester SCAD office. Despite Johnson's prediction that Mitchell would "make it," the campaign was an uphill battle all the way.

Perhaps the most significant aspect of Mitchell's campaign, however, was not the positions she took on the community's most pressing issues. Instead, race-based enforcement of literacy tests, alive and well in the North, took center stage in Mitchell's bid to become Third Ward supervisor. If Mitchell were to be successful, Rochester's new Black migrants first needed to register to vote. New York State, however, still had literacy laws on its books, requiring that all new voters demonstrate an ability to read and write English.[65] To register to vote in New York, an applicant had to have a high school diploma, a discharge from the military, or take and pass a literacy exam. Many of the migrants could not meet any of these requirements. Mitchell characterized the problem: "Many of my voters, you know, were just one step off the migrant train and had very limited education. Some of them only had first, second, third grade education coming out of Florida, because they were bean pickers."[66] While this may have been the case, many of those migrants arrived in Rochester from communities with long traditions of Black organizing, and they valued education, despite their limited access to it. Mitchell and her supporters spent most of their time in grassroots voter education and registration campaigns, which created new opportunities for community education.

In order to prepare these newcomers for the literacy test, Mitchell and others had to learn how to teach. Through trial and error, Mitchell and her campaign staff ran a voter registration school in her living room. Mitchell always had a pot of food on the stove and her daughter on her hip.[67] Teachers at the "Mitchell school"—Cooper and Wade, Dr. William Knox (a research chemist and fellow NAACP member), Obadiah Williamson (a former migrant himself), Mitchell, and others, found that voter registration introduced them to new possibilities for Black Rochester. As Mitchell explained, "The thing about that was that once a person found out that they had a little bit of knowledge, they'd want more."[68] According to Mitchell, these living room sessions expanded into night classes at a local high school. Mitchell and her husband, John, remembered that anyone who completed the voter registration class received a certificate: "We would give them a little certificate, once they completed. You'd swear they'd went off and got a PhD. . . . Everybody wanted to get educated."[69]

While education took center stage in the campaign, it did not replace the grueling work of canvassing neighborhoods, knocking on doors, asking community organizations to get involved, and alleviating people's fear of voting. While it was unlikely one would be shot or killed while voting, as in certain southern locations, there were very real forms of economic coercion taking place in Rochester. Mitchell's Republican opponent, Lester Peck, was remembered as a rather shady and intimidating figure. Peck owned a pharmacy on Plymouth Avenue in the Third Ward where he had long been the ward supervisor. Over the years, Peck used his position in the Republican Party to secure the sole prescription contract for welfare recipients. His central location and his medication monopoly gave him a great deal of influence over his customers. Like many store owners in the ghetto, he also extended credit to his customers, credit that could be withdrawn at will. Peck and his wife reminded their customers on a regular basis of the relationship between voting for Peck and the extension of credit at their store. Community members report that Peck employed a gimmick on Election Day to "check" his customers by shining a light on their hand. The light would reveal if and how they voted, he informed them. The Mitchells countered by sending their voters to the pharmacy to prove that Peck could not discern their vote.[70]

Despite all their efforts and Mildred Johnson's prediction, Peck defeated Mitchell in 1959. However, the Young Turks found the outcome sufficiently encouraging that they immediately began to organize another run against Peck in 1961. Mitchell's small grassroots campaign consisted of no more than a dozen people, but their impact was impressive. Claytor, one of Mitchell's campaign members and later a New York State election inspector, believed they registered more than a hundred people in those short months. While that number was not glaringly significant, he offers a reminder of the context: "In those days there were probably only a couple thousand registered Blacks in the entire city of Rochester. . . . Mathematically, we had an impact."[71]

By the second run, Mitchell and her supporters had matured politically. They continued their education and registration drives but worked harder to include as many neighborhood people as possible in their efforts. Rather than simply electing Mitchell to serve as their leader, the campaign sought to build clout in the Black community. For her part, Mitchell had improved on the platform and had learned to utilize her personal networks more efficiently. Daryl Porter, a teenager who ran with a local gang, recalled that he got his start in politics volunteering for Mitchell's campaign. As a youth, Porter frequently turned to Mitchell for guidance and frequently to get him out of trouble with the local authorities. Mitchell was like a mother to Porter, whose own parents were deceased. So when she ran for ward supervisor in 1961, Porter and his gang went door to door handing out campaign literature for her. The result was twofold: Porter and company had a constructive project to occupy their time, and their wide dispersal of literature exposed a broader cross section of Black Rochester to Mitchell's campaign goals.[72] Porter would later serve as assistant to the mayor of Rochester.

At the same time, the Monroe County Non-Partisan Political League, which was nonpartisan only in name, undertook a series of town hall meetings to further highlight the Black community's lack of political representation. The group invited each candidate for every open Rochester office to field questions from their constituency. As Claytor recalled,

> We would invite candidates to attend public functions and at first, they tried to dis us, and you know, there was no previous record of this kind of involvement in the Black community, so many [candidates] did not show up. And we made sure that they were punished for that. We would put the old empty chair up there and ask the absent person questions and [we] also point[ed] out to the audience that this was an act of great disrespect and indicated that they don't care about you, so maybe you shouldn't care about them in terms of coming to vote. After a while, they did start coming. Candidates were still wary, but the belief that coming to the event was better than not [grew].[73]

Throughout the course of Mitchell's second campaign, more than a dozen such meetings were held, some attracting more than 300 people. On Election Day in 1961, these same Rochesterians, a majority of them Black, went to the polls and pulled the lever for Constance Mitchell. She had finally become "the highest elected official among Black women in the United States."[74]

By this point, a group of young, energetic Black activists had emerged in Rochester. The city's old Black leaders and organizations either conformed and joined the newcomers or were ingloriously swept aside as Black Rochester remade itself. The new leadership utilized both the national momentum of civil rights organizing and the potential of the massive Black in-migration to confront the racial ills in the city's policies and politics. By implementing grassroots education and organizing, they put in place new forms of protest and put the city on notice that Black Rochester would no longer be accommodated in the ways of old. If the city did not immediately respond to this message, it was only a matter of time before it would.

CHAPTER 2

Uniting for Survival

Police Brutality, Organizational Conflict, and Unity in the Black Freedom Struggle

On February 17, 1963, Mildred Johnson addressed a mostly Black audience at a rally organized primarily by middle-class members of Rochester's branch of the National Association for the Advancement of Colored People (NAACP). A crowd of six hundred to eight hundred people, an unprecedented turnout for Black Rochester, assembled in the auditorium of the Baden Street public housing project to protest several recent cases of police brutality, including one involving members of the Nation of Islam (NOI). Among those in attendance was Malcolm X. Although not scheduled to speak, Malcolm eventually took his turn at the podium. The speeches given that day emphasized the need for Black Rochesterians to unite across the lines of organizational affiliation, class, and religion that divided them, the better to face their common oppression, of which police brutality had become the most evident symptom.[1] Mildred Johnson, longtime Rochester leader and activist, summarized the sense of the meeting (see figure 2.1). Using fiery rhetoric not typically associated with members of the middle class, she offered support to all the victims of police brutality, whatever their religious ties, Muslims and non-Muslims alike, and urged her listeners to do the same. "We are Black folks first!" Johnson thundered.[2]

By the time of the 1963 Baden Street rally, several key developments had taken place among Rochester's Black community. First, the NAACP had secured a more radical president after Quintin Primo's departure. Second, and

FIGURE 2.1. Mildred Johnson leads Flemington protestors in song before picketing. Photograph, Flemington, NJ, ca. 1967. Box 119, folder 5, Kodak Historical Collection #003, D.319, Rare Books, Special Collections, and Preservation, River Campus Libraries, University of Rochester. Credit: Used with permission from Eastman Kodak Company.

perhaps more importantly, Rochester's Black middle class had come to see itself as sharing a common experience with its working-class and underemployed neighbors, segregated and distinct from white Rochester. Black Rochesterians, whatever their socioeconomic class, faced a series of unremitting inequalities, chief among them segregated housing. As white flight continued in Rochester, white taxpayers diverted considerable resources from city schools and neighborhoods that desperately needed rehabilitation to the construction of new schools in the outer city and suburbs. The children of the Black middle class then also had to make do with the same inferior schools as those of the working class, given their near complete exclusion from white neighborhoods. The undifferentiated racism imposed on the Black community fostered this collective sense of being "Black folks first."

The police were no less indiscriminate, and their heavy-handed and often brutal methods affected and outraged all within the Black community, as the Baden Street rally made evident. As the housing crisis in Rochester grew more disastrous, the city responded by increasing the number of police and patrols in the Third and Seventh Wards, now predominantly Black neighborhoods. Several specific altercations, including the attack on members of the NOI, as well as a collective sense of being under siege, both remobilized the local NAACP and attracted the attention of Malcolm X, who returned to the city repeatedly. The local NAACP welcomed Malcolm's support in their struggles to improve policing in their communities. In many instances, he brought the national media gaze to Rochester, though many would forget this shared campaign to expose conditions there by the time the uprising occurred in July 1964. Malcolm seemed pleased by the warm welcome he received from the Black community. He traveled to Rochester often and promoted Black Rochester's version of unity in his subsequent endeavors. It appears that he had been looking for just such an example.

The national NAACP, under the auspices of Roy Wilkins and Gloster Current, however, was less impressed with this new development. The duo worked diligently to divorce the NAACP from all Black nationalist organizations, especially the NOI, which had quickly risen to national fame under Malcolm X's tutelage. At the national level, Wilkins rightly believed that any association with such groups, perceived or otherwise, would curtail the flow of white money that supported the NAACP's work. In Rochester, Black leaders had to negotiate these seemingly irreconcilable national tensions while fighting grassroots battles that were less dependent upon white funding.[3] Current and Wilkins feared the publicity around the burgeoning unity movement in Rochester, and they used the situation to reassert control over local branches facing similar confrontations involving the NOI. Black Rochester's middle-class leaders ultimately refused to be drawn into the tensions playing out at the national level because it would have been destructive to local efforts.

At a moment when Black communities were navigating intense repression from the state and searching for effective organizational strategies to protect their communities, activists in Rochester provided the nation a powerful example for transcending socioeconomic and religious differences to unite. Rochester historian Adolph Dupree reflected on this dynamic: "Black Unity was punishable by banishment from middle class America. However, in the face of extinction, the most battered victims often find the courage and power to rise above the depths of despair and unite for survival."[4] Rejecting the divisiveness playing out at the national level between organizations such as the middle class NAACP and the more militant Nation of Islam (NOI), Black Rochester identified a shared problem and sought a common goal. In so doing, Black activists helped to politicize hundreds of new constituents who would ultimately change the face of Rochester. With as much support from the Black community as they could muster, they demanded an end to police brutality.

They successfully petitioned for a citizen police review board to ensure police accountability. Black organizers further drew national attention to their local yet universal condition, effectively calling for federal intervention to enforce their freedom rights.[5] Without such vigorous efforts to embrace those with ideological and economic differences, to include all and sundry, the nascent Black community could not have accomplished so much. Their numbers in Rochester were simply too small to have yielded such impressive results.

Imposing Boundaries and Behavior

Shared misery, in the same confined space, produced a race-first consciousness in Rochester. As longtime local historian Blake McKelvey explained: "In the forties . . . a new migration from the south had more than doubled the city's non-white population, with most of the newcomers settling in the Seventh Ward."[6] McKelvey failed to share with readers that few options existed for Blacks outside the Seventh Ward, whether in housing, schooling or recreation.

Though many larger cities had fought redline housing battles with some success by 1960, Rochester's smaller Black middle class could boast no such achievement. A report by the statewide Human Relations Commission noted, "In 1958 . . . Rochester had the most rigid barriers against the sale of houses in the suburbs to Negroes," even as the city's "economy was attracting a greater influx of non-whites, proportionately, than any city in the state."[7] Further, many white Rochesterians, who remained in the city and experienced the deterioration of these neighborhoods, blamed the newcomers, rather than city hall, for the conditions. At the same time, they objected loudly and bitterly—most often to William Lombard, the chief of police—to the increased presence of African Americans. Olive Le Boo was a local resident who shared her grievances so vociferously with city officials that the mayor opened a file specifically for her correspondence. She complained of these "transient undesirable Negroes" or, more pointedly, "this low down hoodlum negro element."[8] By 1963, these conditions in the everyday lives of Black Rochesterians had the effect of blunting socioeconomic divisions among them, of decreasing class tensions, and of heightening racial consciousness, thereby fostering Mildred Johnson's notion of being Black folks first.

Of all the obstacles that African Americans in Rochester faced, however, none caused a more immediate, visceral, and emotive response than police brutality. As always in oppressed communities, the police formed the vanguard of state repression. In early 1961, the local NAACP began to publicly protest police brutality against Black people.[9] As with housing, so too with policing, the local NAACP was new to confronting city hall. Here the Young Turks, that recently arrived group of agitators, placed themselves at the forefront of efforts once again. Journalist Desmond Stone took note, reporting the arrival in Rochester of a new breed of Black leadership. "One thing is certain," Stone wrote at the time, "the disappearance of the old Negro docility and the emergence of new, fiercely aggressive attitudes is bewildering to many police and citizens alike."[10] These new activists, individuals such as Walter Cooper, Constance Mitchell, and others, were behind the NAACP's growing frustration with business as usual, an attitude best expressed on the explosive issue of police brutality. But this issue lent itself to support by a wide cross section of Rochester's Black population, young and old, longtime resident and newcomer. Police brutality was one issue they all faced and could therefore get behind.

As policing Black bodies and movement became a constant source of contention for Black Rochester, local leaders proposed a multipronged counterattack. In the early 1960s, the Young Turks, under the leadership of Glenn Claytor and youth adviser Laplois Ashford, took it upon themselves to relieve some of this pressure on Black youth. They led teenagers on trips not only to explore nearby Letchworth Park and thereby to experience upstate New York's natural beauty and foster wonderment but also to escape the constant urban surveillance. A second undertaking involved leading these youngsters in picketing the skating rink in town where they spent time. The presence of Black teenagers seemingly drew police units with their K-9 or police dog units. After all, the police and their dogs did not patrol recreational venues in other (white) city neighborhoods.[11] The picketing eventually led to meetings with city hall to end the practice. This young group of activists did not yet, in the main, have children of their own. Their actions were not of self-interest but, instead, reflected a general concern for the well-being of their larger community.

But as the Young Turks's insistent demand for dignity and respect from the police grew, conditions worsened. Between 1962 and 1963, several cases of police brutality and harassment shook Black Rochester.[12] Three of these cases will serve to demonstrate the police terror and its total impact on community formation among African Americans at that particular moment. The first case involved an innocent gas station attendant harassed by police as he locked up the service center where he was employed. The second case had the police entering a religious service of the recently formed NOI, while the third involved a man beaten at a block party for moving his car from one side of the street to another while intoxicated. Together and separately, they showed the conditions that Black Rochester faced.

The first of these, the "Fairwell case," riled Black Rochesterians because they considered the working-class victim an upstanding and productive member of the community. One stuffy August night in 1962 after completing his chores, Rufus Fairwell got ready to close the service station where he worked. Importantly, Fairwell's uniformed employment at the station was a source of working-class pride for many in the community. Undoubtedly aware of this, two Rochester police officers pulled into the establishment and demanded to know what Fairwell was doing there.[13] Local residents report that this type of harassment was common in their communities, particularly by specific officers. Fairwell, clad in his uniform, replied that he was closing up and produced a key to further attest to his legitimacy. The unimpressed officers tartly responded, "What's a nigger like you doing with a key?" Fairwell likely responded in kind. The officers followed with a physical assault that left Fairwell with two broken vertebrae and confined to a wheelchair.[14]

The second case of police terror to infuriate Black Rochester involved members of the Nation of Islam, which had been operating quietly in the city for some years. In January 1963, several months after the Fairwell incident, two officers forced their way into the NOI mosque, reportedly acting on an "anonymous tip." In the process, they disrupted a religious service in progress, all in search of "a man with a gun."[15] Accompanied by police dogs, their seemingly ever-present companions when patrolling the Black community, the officers arrested two Muslim men on the spot and recorded the names of every man present at the religious service. That was only the opening salvo in a larger campaign of repression against the NOI in Rochester and across the state. Weeks later, a grand jury indicted an additional seventeen male Muslims from the disrupted service. The saga of the Rochester Seventeen, whose travails may be seen as something of a prelude to the more famous and searing case of the Wilmington Ten, had begun.[16]

The third case of police brutality came just weeks after the violation of the mosque and was particularly brutal. This incident left A. C. White, another Black Rochesterian, hospitalized for twenty-one days and shattered any illusion that justice existed for the Black community.[17] Although White was not regarded as a model citizen, as Fairwell or the members of the NOI were viewed, the community was no less furious about his case. White incurred the wrath of the police by moving a vehicle from one side of the street to another while a block party was in progress. Known for his hardworking ways during the week and his enjoyment of libations on the weekends, White was not entirely sober at the time.[18] Still, the block party was a joyous affair where families and children from the neighborhood celebrated together as a community, no accident occurred, and no one had requested police intervention. Unconcerned with such niceties, several police officers assigned to observe the block party arrested White, brutally beat him in front of the revelers, transferred him downtown, beat him some more, and then delivered his mangled body to the emergency room. White would live to tell the tale, but Black Rochester was beside itself. Minister Franklin Florence, a recent migrant from Florida who would cut his teeth politically on the White case, recalled, "It was as if the police were saying 'You don't have any control over your neighborhood.'"[19] With their gruesome brutality and disrespect, the police reminded Black Rochester of who ultimately controlled their neighborhoods.

For its part, the Black community acted in concert both to relieve the suffering of Rufus Fairwell and A. C. White and to defend them and the NOI members in their subsequent trials. When Minister Florence and others sought to locate White after the beating, their efforts took them first to the local jail. There they were told White was receiving medical care for his injuries. On what seemed a wild goose chase, they traveled to Strong Memorial Hospital, where they were told that no one by the name of White had been admitted. Frustrated, the men converged in the vestibule to discuss their next steps. As they did so, a Black maintenance worker perched above them on a ladder asked the men to continue looking at each other so as not to draw attention to what he was about to tell them. Florence and his companions did as they were asked but listened carefully to the janitor. The unnamed and unknown janitor directed the men to the basement of the hospital, where he said orderlies had taken White for treatment, out of the spotlight the hospital staff had anticipated. Florence thanked the man and then promptly found White and ensured continued access to him.[20]

The extent of Fairwell's and White's injuries and the violation of a sacred religious space sparked outrage and an outpouring of activism in Black Rochester because it spoke to a common experience. As a result, Black Rochester's organizing efforts rippled nationally. A united action committee, which included the now-veteran Young Turks and first-time activists, such as Minister Florence, alike, sprang up immediately following the attack on Fairwell. Groups such as the NAACP, the Human Relations Commission, and the Rochester Area Council of Churches were also well represented.[21] The coalition's aims were threefold: to raise money for Rufus Fairwell's legal and medical expenses, to pursue action against the arresting officers, and to end police brutality and harassment in Black neighborhoods. The group soon commanded some attention from city manager Porter Homer, who met with representatives of the coalition repeatedly over more than two months. Despite the activists' best efforts, Homer failed to resolve a total of nine cases of police brutality to their satisfaction and offered little to alleviate the problems. Eventually, the community activists turned to higher authorities, requesting an investigation of the Fairwell case by the Department of Justice.[22]

It was the second attack, the one on the Nation of Islam, however, that galvanized national attention around police brutality in Rochester. Though just a small fraction of African Americans actually joined the NOI, its impact outsized its membership. Many non-Muslim African Americans reported attending NOI meetings on occasion. Still more purchased the group's publications and kept abreast of its activities. Elijah Muhammad, Malcolm X, and the NOI offered a mouthpiece for widely held sentiments regarding American race relations nationally, even if African Americans did not rush to join the group.[23]

In Rochester, the NOI personified Black nationalism as the most readily accessible voice for Black militancy. Though numerically insignificant in 1962 and 1963, the NOI influenced a sizable portion of Rochester's Black community, including its Christian ministers, who appreciated Malcolm X and his racial, if not his religious, ideology. Testifying to its local importance, police officials reported their increased awareness of the local NOI and quickly put the organization under surveillance, which led to the attack on the mosque.[24] What is more, the Rochester Seventeen, arrested immediately following the police intrusion, were well-known and respected members of the Black community. So when police arrested these men, their African American, non-Muslim neighbors rallied to their support. Finally, police did not perpetrate this attack on a public street, where Black Rochesterians had come to expect harassment, but rather in a private, sacred space—a religious temple. The assault on the Muslims eventually brought Malcolm to Rochester, which was not his first trip; however, his engagement with the larger Black community became deeper and more self-sustaining at that point.[25] For these reasons, the story of police brutality in Rochester must be understood in the context of the state attack on the Nation of Islam across New York.

Anti-Muslim Hysteria in New York State

As an organization born and raised in adversity, state repression and hostile propaganda were nothing new to the NOI. Even by this standard, however, the NOI had a hard time in 1963 in New York State, where a cabal of police, prosecutors, and journalists seemed determined to crush it. The Rochester events were central to a larger statewide campaign of repression against the NOI specifically and Black activism broadly. Rochester became significant in that larger campaign to blunt the growth of the NOI in the New York State prison system. Attica state prison, which would gain national prominence after its 1971 prison revolt, had special importance to Rochester, to Malcolm, and to the NOI.[26] Many Black Rochesterians knew family or friends incarcerated at the nearby prison. Local ministers often traveled to Attica to serve former congregants imprisoned there. For the NOI, Attica too was a major recruiting ground.[27] For this reason and for its Black nationalist position, prison officials across the country loathed the NOI, refusing to acknowledge it as a religious organization. Consequently, imprisoned NOI members were denied the rights, considerations, and privileges granted other inmates who professed a religious affiliation. NOI members at Attica boldly challenged the discrimination. They sued in federal court, seeking to have their organization recognized as a legitimate and constitutionally protected religious body. This suit, combined with others filed by NOI inmates throughout New York State, would have national implications. If successful, they would open the door for imprisoned NOI members everywhere in the country to stake their own claims.[28] The NOI in Rochester was intimately connected to Attica and Buffalo because the same minister served Muslims in all three places, or would have been expected to, in the case of Attica. For multiple reasons, therefore, an attack on Muslims in Rochester, the event responsible for Malcolm's presence at the Baden Street rally, also threatened the NOI elsewhere in upstate New York, namely at Attica and in Buffalo.

With this case still undecided, it was as if the anti-Muslim coalition wanted to make a preemptive strike against the potential legitimization of the NOI in the prison system, a major source of recruits. The opponents of the Muslims seemed to strike especially hard in Rochester for three reasons: the NOI branch there was the most vulnerable in the state, it was in close proximity to Attica, and widespread agitation over the large Black migration to the city was widely shared by a broad cross section of the majority population. Eliminating the NOI could be read as a next step toward curbing the Black migration. The Muslim community in Rochester, like the larger Black community, was still in formation and so was more tenuous, for instance, than the NOI branch in Buffalo. As the forces of repression likely saw it, a fatal or crippling blow to the Muslims in Rochester would have larger consequences, demoralizing the NOI statewide and the anti–police brutality campaign then underway.

Given the close links between the NOI and the prison system, and the pushback to contemporary policing practices in Rochester, it was predictable that the campaign against the Muslims would be passed off as a war on crime in that city. In Rochester, the police and prosecutors needed the media to present their repressive tactics as necessary protection for the white majority. It was not coincidence that the following article, conflating Black migrants with the NOI and crime, appeared in a Rochester newsweekly on January 7, 1963, a day after the police barged into the Rochester mosque:

It hasn't become the talk of the town yet, but in some sections of the city and, fortunately, among some high police officials, there are strong suspicions that the crime wave that hit Rochester the past year can be laid at the door of some Black Muslims. . . . The truth of the matter is that in the first nine months of 1962 Rochester experienced the greatest crime wave in its history. Most of them were committed by the riff raff of the Negro race. Migrants have been blamed for many of these crimes, but in recent months there has been a growing suspicion that the real cause for this big increase can be traced to the Black Muslims, whose membership is made up largely of convicts and ex-convicts. This reporter talked to a high-ranking police official two weeks ago and was told that there were strong reasons to suspect that Black Muslims are responsible for the record crime wave in the city. . . . It became known two weeks ago that the Black Muslims of Rochester have a temple or meeting place on North Street, above Buddy's Casino. There they hold their meetings and sell copies of their official newspaper, published in Chicago.[29]

Precise numbers on the NOI presence in Rochester at that time are not available, but in all likelihood the nineteen men in jail represented a substantial number, possibly even a majority, of the male Muslims in Rochester. The attack was meant to decapitate the local NOI specifically, to derail the state prison lawsuit, and to discredit the anti–police brutality campaign then taking place in Rochester. The subsequent reporting aimed to connect Black migrants with criminality in the larger community.

Black Rochester was determined that a campaign of brutality against the Black community, including the NOI, would not succeed. Given the gross attacks on their community, they drew on all possible resources, including Malcolm X, with whom they had some familiarity, to fight back. For his part, Malcolm seemed more than ready to join the fray, accepting an invitation to speak at the University of Rochester in 1963. Members of the NAACP—recently regrouped under the presidency of the more radical but well-connected Wendell H. Phillips—approached the University of Rochester's College Cabinet Subcommittee on Civil Rights to provide a venue for Malcolm to speak publicly in Rochester.[30] An ordained minister, Phillips grew up in Pittsburgh but moved to Rochester to attend Colgate Rochester Divinity School. According to his son, Phillips "believed in God and religion, but he had grown weary of denominations and their doctrines" because "denominations did more to divide churches as opposed to providing cohesion."[31] If his presidency of the Rochester branch of the NAACP is any example of his stewardship, he felt too that organizations often served to divide the race in

FIGURE 2.2.   Franklin Florence, Malcolm X, and Constance Mitchell pose at the Cornhill Methodist Church. Photograph, Rochester, February 1965. Box 8, folder 6a, Franklin Florence Papers, Rare Books, Special Collections, and Preservation, River Campus Libraries, University of Rochester. Courtesy of Florence Papers, Department of Rare Books and Special Collections, University of Rochester Library.

their struggle for equality, and he worked against this. An invitation by an NAACP president to the NOI's chief spokesman demonstrated this desire to transcend organizational and religious affiliation (see figure 2.2).

Once in Rochester, Malcolm used his speech to connect the conditions of police brutality in that city to those across the country. Always the humorist, Malcolm "drew laughter when, after a dog howled in the audience, he remarked: 'That's probably a police dog—they're famous around here.'"[32] The audience was overwhelmingly white, reflecting the racial makeup of the Rochester NAACP at the time and the location of the event at the University of Rochester, a place where few African Americans would have gone. Among Malcolm's listeners that evening was an unlikely Black Rochesterian, recently elected Third Ward supervisor Constance Mitchell. She came to hear Malcolm upon an invitation from Dr. Freddie Thomas, a friend of Mitchell's, who spent a lifetime researching and writing Black history.[33] On Mitchell's reporting, Malcolm invited Thomas and Mitchell, two of the only African Americans present, to stay behind following the event.[34]

That night, after Malcolm's formal discourse ended, the trio began a discussion that increased Malcolm's presence in Rochester and brought him into their activist fold. As the auditorium closed and the janitor asked the three to leave, Mitchell, unconcerned with the political liability of fraternizing with Malcolm X, invited her interlocutors to her home, which had become the informal gathering place for socially and politically conscious Rochesterians during her election campaign. Though the hour was late, she immediately called friends and coworkers, many of them veteran campaigners who had assisted in tutoring migrants to pass the literacy exam necessary to cast a ballot in her election the previous year. It was the first of several informal invitations to participate in Rochester's community affairs that Malcolm would accept. The open and ongoing invitation enabled Malcolm to develop close personal relationships with members of many organizations and groups and to transcend the various racial, religious, professional, and organizational attachments that worked to divide them.[35]

Malcolm returned to Rochester in search of allies in western New York some months later when the NOI first came under severe attack. While Black activists viewed the persecution of the local NOI as an attack on Black Rochester, Malcolm, in his capacity as head of the NOI on the East Coast, came to defend the NOI. Black Rochester, for its part, was glad to have Malcolm's support. They believed his national prominence and his reputation for speaking truth to power would command the attention of city leaders, such as city manager Homer Porter, who consistently sought to deflect scrutiny and responsibility. In the struggle by Black activists to protect Black life, Malcolm's presence could only benefit Black Rochester. In any case, they had little to lose by consorting with Malcolm. It is noteworthy that Malcolm and the NOI met much less resistance from the Black leadership in Rochester than they did in many other cities, especially those with larger populations. Actually, Rochester was one of the few urban centers where mainstream African American leaders, not the Black nationalist or the radical element, openly embraced Malcolm both before and after he left the NOI. Malcolm returned the favor; he seemed partial to Rochester. From all accounts, no other city of Rochester's size received as much of his affinity and attention. Malcolm would further mention Rochester in a famous assessment of the potential for Black liberation in 1965, the year of his death. Significantly, he was in Rochester just five days before he died. This trip to Rochester may well have been Malcolm's last visit outside of New York City, and that at a time when he no doubt had many invitations to appear in much bigger and more famous places.

In any case, Malcolm had become a familiar presence in Rochester, something the local police department, among others, did not welcome or appreciate.[36] Referring to the raid on the mosque, Malcolm opined, "A similar situation would not have occurred 'if someone called and said there was somebody in another church with a gun.'"[37] Consequently, he formally lodged complaints, as had so many Black Rochesterians, with both the State Commission for Human Rights and with the Rochester public safety commissioner.[38] Not to be outdone by the anti-Muslim forces publishing stories about Muslim violence, Malcolm launched his own propaganda offensive, predicting that Rochester "may be a precedent-setting city for police hostility towards Muslims" and that it "will be better known than Oxford, Mississippi."[39] By comparing Rochester to Oxford, a place notorious for its hostility to the civil rights movement, Malcolm was directly connecting the struggles of the Muslims in the North with those of Black people in the South, politically and morally. It was time for Black folks, Muslims and non-Muslims, North and South, in and out of Rochester, to accomplish greater unity. In Rochester, the city fathers took offense to the comparison to Oxford. "Obviously he [Malcolm X] is a stranger to Rochester because he is not describing any condition that exists here," retorted Mayor Henry Gillette, sounding appalled.[40]

The mayor's dismay did little to relieve the repression of the Muslims, or Black folks in general, in Rochester. Despite his claims to the contrary, Mayor Gillette's actions mirrored those taking place in the South. Even his fire department joined the attack. Taking their cue from their counterparts in law enforcement, Rochester firemen, acting on the usual "anonymous tip," entered the same mosque previously raided by the police. The building custodian, however, reported no signs of fire. It only remained, in this formulation, for the media to chime in, which they soon did. Fed the usual "tips" by the police department, the local papers continued to paint a picture of violent and crime-prone "Black Muslims." One paper denounced the "Black supremacy organization" and the "secret sect preaching Black supremacy." Lacking any evidence that the Muslims were actually a threat, another daily informed readers that a pipe had been found in the hallway of the building where the NOI mosque was located, implying the Muslims had sinister intentions.[41]

Clearly the campaign against the NOI was a coordinated effort by state and local officials (possibly national ones too), with allies in the media. *Muhammad Speaks*, the NOI organ, reported on the connivance, singling out the situation in Rochester: "Political observers have linked both the police and fire department to a statewide attempt to create public hysteria against Muslims in New York State and to brand the followers of the Honorable Elijah Muhammad as 'subversive.'"[42] On one of his visits to Rochester, Malcolm called attention to the role of the media in the campaign: "The racists . . . use the press to get public opinion on their side. When they want to suppress and oppress the Black community, what do they do? They . . . make it appear that the role of crime in the Black community is higher than it is anywhere else. . . . It makes it appear that anyone in the Black community is a criminal."[43] In Rochester, Malcolm and *Muhammad Speaks* were preaching to the choir. But Black activists certainly appreciated the national attention that Malcolm's presence drew to their condition.

In his search for Black allies in Rochester, Malcolm cast a wide net. The result was sometimes surprising. Loftus Carson was one of those surprises. Some in Black Rochester viewed Carson, an African American member of the statewide Human Rights Commission, as an "Uncle Tom."[44] Carson, needless to say, saw things differently. True to his self-perceived role as mediator, he arranged a meeting between Malcolm and Rochester's city fathers. Malcolm emerged from the meeting to announce that a better understanding had been reached and that the talks "had been very, very fruitful."[45] However, the deliberations were not so fruitful as to persuade Malcolm to call off other forms of protest. As usual, he would pursue multiple tracks. On returning to New York City, he promptly organized a rally outside city hall that highlighted the anti-Muslim repression statewide, including in Rochester. Religious scholar Louis A. DeCaro Jr. describes a document distributed at the rally: "The flier also referred to the disruption of Muslim services in the Rochester mosque as 'gestapo-like,' and bore in its challenge to Black people Malcolm's own inimitable signature: 'We must let [the Rochester Muslims] know they are not alone. We must let them know that Harlem is with them. We must let them know that the whole Dark World is with them.'"[46] Another NOI rally in Times Square similarly "protest[ed] the arrest and indictment of 19 persons who attended a Muslim meeting" in Rochester.[47] Protestors at this event carried signs declaring, "America Is a Godless Government" and "We Demand Freedom of Religion."[48]

Mounting Pressure

Within days of those protests, Malcolm returned upstate for the Baden Street anti–police brutality rally, connecting Rochester to the larger anti–police brutality efforts underway across the state. The Baden Street event, which featured an inspiring lineup of Black activists, was formative in the struggle for African American freedom in Rochester. The attendees included clergy and members of the NAACP, CORE, the Monroe County Non-Partisan League, the Committee for Rufus Fairwell, and the Rochester Civil Rights Committee. In addition to African American churchmen, these committees included an impressive number of white clergy. While they played a secondary role in the Baden Street event, their support set a precedent for ministerial aid in Rochester's Black Freedom Struggle. But, importantly, although organized by the NAACP and supported by ministers, the rally was not held in a church or in an office downtown, as was generally the case in Rochester and across the nation with such NAACP events. The decision to meet at Baden Street, the site of a settlement house in the heart of the ghetto, seemed to signal a new dawn. If the poorest and most dispossessed could not come to the table, the table would come to them. Given the sizable crowd—more than six hundred attended—people from all walks of Black life took part.

Members of the Rochester NAACP prioritized the organization and advertising efforts required to pull off the Baden Street rally. In a press release, Rozetta McDowell, the NAACP secretary, informed the media of her hope that "a committee will evolve out of the meeting to unite local Negroes. 'This is what we need and this is what we're going to have,'" she confidently predicted. Graphically illustrating the kind of unity she had in mind, McDowell's press release included a picture of herself, Malcolm, the Rochester Seventeen and the other two Muslims facing prosecution.[49] As for the committee she hoped the rally would produce, McDowell noted, "It is quite possible that the Black Muslim nationalist movement will be represented on such a committee [as] 'they do represent a segment of the Negro community here.'"[50] It made perfect sense that this should be so, since Muslims were also part of the planning committee and were among those on the official list of speakers. The NAACP deliberately and explicitly sought to unite with all members of the community, the better to influence public opinion and dialogue on the issue of police brutality.

Malcolm was excluded from the list of speakers either because he was not expected to show up or because it was a Rochester event and the planners endeavored to feature local speakers. Still, after Mildred "We Are Black Folks First" Johnson and others had held forth, Malcolm was invited to the podium "amid shouts of 'speech, speech.'"[51] He did not disappoint. The local press reported that Malcolm "took a swipe at unidentified Negro factions 'too afraid of the white man to unite.'" The reporter apparently failed to realize that Malcolm was likely contrasting the unity rally in Rochester with events taking place in other cities and on the national scene. *Muhammad Speaks* would later report on the historic nature of the gathering: "Observers called the rally the 'most spectacular display of Negro unity ever witnessed in Rochester.'"[52]

Not surprisingly, the national NAACP was not impressed with this display of Black unity. Just two days after the Baden Street rally, Gloster Current, the NAACP director of branches who was based in New York City, announced that there was a "problem in Rochester." The problem, of course, was the Rochester branch's seemingly cozy relationship with the NOI and Malcolm. "Our problem in Rochester," Current informed Roy Wilkins, the longtime head of the national NAACP, "is how to protest police brutality and not appear to be supporting the Muslims on their program *per se*, a position into which Malcolm 'X' wants to push us."[53] Fearing that Rochester might influence other locales, Current issued a memorandum to every NAACP branch in the country. Entitled "NAACP and the Muslims," the memo provided strict instructions to govern future exchanges with the NOI. "If a community-wide mass protest meeting called by the NAACP involves other groups, *avoid*, if at all possible, having Muslim speakers at your rally," Current commanded. "Public meetings are, of course, open and the possibility is that Muslims will attend, ask questions and seek to get their viewpoint across." In that case, "NAACP spokesmen should reiterate our policy, stating clearly that in fighting police brutality we are *not* supporting Muslims." The Rochester folks had set a dangerous precedent in their unabashed support of the NOI, and the national NAACP strongly disapproved of the kind of unity advocated at the Baden Street rally. "*Avoid at all costs any inference* of a Unity Movement or that NAACP is calling for a 'common front,'" Current's directive to the branches concluded. "Point out clearly wherein our programs differ, although we uphold all citizens' constitutional rights."[54]

The Rochester branch, whose action had incurred Current's wrath, did not respond accordingly. Having brought some of the activist heart back to the organization, Wendell Phillips, the new Rochester NAACP president, acknowledged ideological differences with the NOI, but he did not seem repentant about the Baden Street rally. "While we are in total disagreement with their separatist philosophy, we do, however, vigorously uphold their right as citizens to the enjoyment of all constitutional guarantees of protections from police brutality," Phillips said of the Muslims.[55] Eugene Newport, a Rochester native, youth adviser for the local NAACP, and one of Malcolm's hosts, was even less compliant. If anything, Newport seemed to reject outright the directive from the national NAACP. He told the local press, "Ranting against the activities of these dissenting nationalistic groups are pointless. . . . The situation demands, without further delay, that this community recognize that our Negro citizens are entitled to all the rights and privileges of American citizenship. Failure to do this can only stimulate the growth of nationalistic organizations, and increase the vigor of their protest."[56] Evidently, by 1963, instructions to stay clear of the Muslims were not being received well in Rochester, even among the NAACP leadership. Mildred Johnson's "We are Black folks first" message seemed to have greater appeal.

The United Action Committee that formed immediately following the attack on Rufus Fairwell had accomplished each of its goals. When the Rochester police department refused at the last minute to release the results of its investigation into Fairwell's assault, and a grand jury ultimately found that "Fairwell did not assault the policemen; they did not assault him" despite the severity of his injuries, the group successfully pressed the federal Department of Justice to intervene.[57] The committee was instrumental in forging alliances and garnering support among a wide cross section of Black Rochesterians. They supported Fairwell financially, and this set the ball in motion to reign in the Rochester police. And while the committee's efforts did not immediately ensure a change, its unwavering determination generated tangible engagement around this issue.

The city leaders appeared eager to blunt this gathering momentum. Increasingly, they became less resistant to the idea of a citizens' police review board, a central demand of the newly energized Black coalition. Pressure was mounting from various quarters. Days after the Baden Street rally, the local clergy, including the Black Rochester Area Ministers' Conference, placed a full-page advertisement in the paper calling for the creation of a police review board. The declaration, signed by a hundred members of the clergy, announced, "We have investigated sufficiently to learn that there is a list of documented cases, gathered in a responsible fashion, which detail a story of difficult and bitter experiences undergone by many Negro citizens."[58]

Immediately the police chief took evasive action. He countered with an offer of a "police retraining program" aimed at producing kinder and gentler officers, meaning, in practice, kinder and gentler to Black Rochesterians. The police chief was not the only one trying to blunt the Black protest. So too were some of the newly converted supporters of a police review board, such as the Human Relations Committee of Monroe County, which includes Rochester. The committee hoped that the creation of a police review board would reduce its caseload while simultaneously draining support from the emerging Black coalition. With any luck, the members surmised, the review board would also blunt nationalist sentiment and drive Malcolm out of town. The Human Relations Committee finally put its support behind "an independent citizens' group to review complaints against police . . . [and] also hailed the non-violent committee for 'performing a valuable service by providing a focus for the concern of the entire community and an alternative to the leadership of Malcolm X and his Movement.'"[59]

Rochester City Council members apparently found this argument persuasive in the face of mounting militancy among a unified Black Rochester. In the face of strong and colorful opposition from the police department, they approved a police review board.[60] Rochester became the second city to have such a body, after Philadelphia, which had agreed to form one only months earlier. The police review board was one of the first concrete results of the new political momentum that originated at the Baden Street rally. Contrary to the wishes of the Monroe County Human Relations Committee, however, creation of the police board did not curb police conduct, nor did it blunt the burgeoning frustration within Black Rochester. Nonetheless, Black activists had done their best to raise the alarm locally and nationally. All was not right in Rochester.

CHAPTER 3

A Quiet Rage Explodes

The Uprising—July 24 to July 26, 1964

On the evening of Friday, July 24, 1964, Black youth attended a street dance in the heart of Rochester's Black community, a welcome relief from a summer night's oppressive heat.[1] Concerned adults hoped the dance would provide a productive outlet for neighborhood teenagers while simultaneously raising funds for much-needed recreational facilities. Near the end of the event, several dance organizers asked an inebriated and disruptive young man to leave. When he refused, the organizers called the police. As white officers arrived with dogs in tow (which was standard procedure in Black neighborhoods), a crowd gathered. In the midst of the excitement, rumors circulated that a police dog had bitten a young girl.[2] The aggressive police tactics and the dog-bite rumors proved to be explosive. Despite the creation of a citizens' police review board just months earlier, this arrest unleashed anger and animosity left unresolved in Rochester's Black neighborhoods. Bystanders hurled insults, bottles, and rocks at police officers and dogs alike. City officials and the media quickly labeled the event a "race riot." When the smoke cleared three days later, four people were dead and approximately 350 had been injured. The police had arrested nearly nine hundred people, and property damage totaled over one million dollars.

While the repression of the Black community had drawn some regional and even national attention with the police attack on the NOI and others in the Black community, it was the 1964 uprising that seared Black Rochester into the nation's conscience. The Rochester uprising was among the first in a series of Black rebellions that rocked the nation's urban centers in the 1960s. The Rochester events preceded the revolts in Watts, Newark, and Detroit that have garnered so much scholarly attention. Yet less attention has been paid to uprisings outside those major urban centers.[3] To fully examine Black insurgency in the civil rights and Black Power era, the inclusion of smaller cities such as Rochester is required, not just from a documentary but also from an analytical standpoint. Revisiting the rebellion in Rochester is not just a matter of filling a gap or adding to the existing literature; it is a question of reimagining and reconceptualizing the movement and the era as a whole. Far from being peripheral and isolated, or even quaint and colorful, the events in Rochester were central to the national drama of urban rebellions as it unfolded. In fact, Rochester was a bellwether. As the NOI-NAACP showdown and the creation of the citizens' police review board demonstrated, events and ideas originating there often became models that were closely followed by activists, government officials, and corporate managers nationally.

Though not the first northern center in this period to explode (Harlem went up in smoke just ten days before the Rochester uprising, with accompanying minor outbursts in nearby Bedford-Stuyvesant), the eruption in Rochester stood out. Harlem had been a volatile place since its emergence as a Black mecca in the early twentieth century. Indeed, the 1964 outburst was the third such event in Harlem in thirty years, following previous uprisings in 1935 and 1943. An uprising in Harlem was definitely unsettling, but it would not have come as a total surprise to government officials, residents, or observers from around the nation. The Rochester uprising was different, upending expectations and confounding assumptions, at least in official circles. Despite Black agitation around housing segregation and police brutality, local officials confidently asserted after the Harlem uprising and days before Rochester exploded that "Rochester is not Harlem. . . . Nothing like a riot could ever occur here." Yet Black activists had warned that tensions brewing in the city's Third and Seventh Wards would lead to such an outburst if not remedied. Still, officials maintained their line: the city's majority white population, low unemployment, and history of progressive politics, capped by its antebellum reputation as a bastion of abolitionism, rendered the city immune to this emerging form of Black insurgency.[4] Whitney Young, the Urban League's longtime president, was not so sure. On the eve of the Rochester uprising, Young warned, "Many a middle-sized Rochester sleeps today. We must not allow them to become the Birminghams of tomorrow."[5] The uprising underscored this point and catapulted Rochester into the national imagination. In the two months after the Rochester uprising, a number of second-tier and smaller cities also experienced uprisings, including Jersey City, Elizabeth, and Paterson in New Jersey; Dix-moor, Illinois; Seaside, Oregon; and Hampton Beach, New Hampshire.[6] Besides New York City, Philadelphia was the only other large metropolis to erupt in those months. Thus smaller cities dominated the 1964 urban uprisings, in practice, if not in historical memory. And among those smaller cities, Roches-ter by far had the greatest impact. Judged by its imprint on the national imag-ination, the Rochester uprising was arguably the iconic "race riot" of 1964.

In Rochester, as in other urban ghettos, living conditions in the period pre-ceding the uprising were acute. Housing segregation and police brutality were two of the more recognizable indicators of the Black urban plight. Slum houses were not just unsightly; they were also dangerous, and by 1964, 35 percent of Rochester's housing was classified as deteriorating and dilapi-dated, the vast majority of it in the nearly all-Black Third and Seventh Wards.[7] In these deteriorating neighborhoods, police brutality became a frequent occurrence from which few residents were spared. From the juvenile delinquent to the upstanding pillar of the community, ugly run-ins with the police were a daily reality for those living in and entering Rochester's Black neighborhoods. The ubiquitous police dogs made matters worse. One Black Rochesterian remembered, "In my entire upbringing the dogs were the number one subject that . . . most of the people thought about, talked about, wanted something to be done about, because that was a bad situation."[8] These conditions set the stage for a violent reprisal. Minister Franklin Florence, who would emerge as Black Rochester's most articulate voice after the uprising, recalled the feeling: "Everybody in our community, Black and white, knew that something was drastically wrong in this community. . . . There was a quiet rage."[9] Florence was in a position to know; he had worked on the A. C. White case and with several white ministers to advocate for the civilian police review board.

The rage, which was not always so quiet, extended beyond unscrupulous landlords and police to many storeowners in Black neighborhoods. Black dis-satisfaction with white merchants was so strong and so well publicized that within hours of arriving in Rochester, Thomas Allen had heard about it. The national field secretary of the NAACP, Allen reported to NAACP president Roy Wilkins, "Antagonism toward merchants for overcharging was a factor [in the riot]. Merchants were accused of taking more than two million dollars out of the Negro community each year and into the suburbs."[10] Residents complained bitterly about being overcharged for inferior goods. Another major source of grievance was excessively high credit rates. Allen was also told that the "mer-chants did not return any of this money to the community either in projects, in helping the community or in making their business establishments more attractive."[11] New York congressman Frank Horton heard similar complaints in the wake of the uprising. In addition to "asking for the city to cease using police dogs in Negro neighborhoods," the congressman said, "Negroes felt that merchants had not participated in the Little League efforts, and that the merchants there had refused to accept Coke bottles from Negro children who were returning them."[12] In the immediate aftermath of the uprising, Black Rochesterians would urge the mayor's investigating committee to "take concrete action to encourage the establishment of more Negro businesses" in the Black community.[13] This unholy trinity of housing, police brutality, and economic practices was at the root of every single uprising that took place in the long 1960s.

The Iron is Hot

The Rochester uprising began late on the night of July 24, 1964, just as order was being restored in Harlem from the outburst there days earlier. It seemed to the *New York Times*, with its big-city bias, that the events in Rochester were merely an extension of those that had begun in Harlem. But whatever inspiration they may have drawn from the flare-up in Harlem, Blacks in Rochester rose up in protest over grievances that were both long-standing and local. It had been an extremely hot week in Rochester, with temperatures rising above ninety degrees for several consecutive days. Crammed into housing without air-conditioning, residents sought relief from the day's heat in the cooler night air. People congregated on the steps and stoops with their neighbors for conversation; others shot dice, hoping to make a quick dollar. Meanwhile, youngsters gathered for an approved and chaperoned street dance sponsored by the Northeast Mother's Improvement Association, a local block group. The mothers hoped that refreshments sold at the dance would provide some wholesome fun for the community's teenage population while raising funds to build a playground.

As the chatter on the police transmission announced, however, this would be "more than a typical Friday night in July."[14] Things came to a head when the police, who had been called by the dance organizers, arrested twenty-year-old Randy Manigault for public intoxication. The organizers found themselves in a difficult situation. Manigault's behavior had escalated at the event, culminating in his groping of several young girls. He refused to leave when asked. Though organizers were undoubtedly aware of the ongoing conflict between the community and the police, they had obtained a city permit to hold the dance, which meant police officers were patrolling nearby. Unable to manage Manigault any longer, they enlisted the officers' assistance. Community residents reported, however, that the officers, supported by their K-9 unit, were overly aggressive and unnecessarily harsh in making the arrest—standard police practice in Rochester's Black neighborhoods by that point (see figure 3.1). What was unusual was the way community residents responded: they attempted to rescue Manigault from police custody. When that failed, residents picked up rocks, bricks, and bottles—retrieved from the garbage and debris left lying in the streets by a neglectful Department of Public Works—and turned them into missiles aimed at the officers and their dogs.

The police and the community quickly became mired in a state of war, as officers engaged in hand-to-hand combat in the streets with the rock-throwers

FIGURE 3.1. State police with batons take a Black man into custody. Photograph, Rochester, July 1964. Box 4, Photograph Album, Rochester Race Riot Papers, D.185, Rare Books, Special Collections, and Preservation, River Campus Libraries, University of Rochester. Credit: Staff photo, *Rochester Democrat and Chronicle.* Used with permission.

they were attempting to arrest. As the ranks of their opponents grew, the officers called for reinforcements. Police Chief William Lombard, believing his presence would cool tempers, soon arrived. Despite the unsavory reputation of many of his officers, Lombard believed he personally retained the respect of many Black residents, including Black leaders. On this occasion, however, Lombard got no respect. As he called for order, even agreeing to release those who had been arrested, Lombard's own car was overturned in the street and he too was bombarded with bricks and bottles.[15] Outnumbered and under assault, the officers retreated and formed a perimeter around the Black community. The strategy now became one of containment, that is, preventing the insurgency from moving into the prosperous and upscale downtown area. As the *New York Times* reported, "The melee became so intense that [the police] withdrew from the center of it and established a perimeter defense to contain it. The police said the situation was 'definitely out of control and critical.'"[16]

Government had disappeared from the Black community, if only briefly. Seizing the opportunity created by the power vacuum, the insurgents turned their attention to the hated retail establishments. One of the first targets was Kaplow's liquor store. The media would portray this particular attack as purely opportunistic, aimed merely at obtaining free liquor. In reality, the decision to single out Kaplow's was much more complex and strategic. Mr. Kaplow was well known and despised in the community. At his establishment, one could get liquor on credit. In exchange for engaging in this illegal practice, Kaplow charged hugely inflated rates of interest. John Mitchell, the husband of Third Ward supervisor Constance Mitchell and an activist in his own right, recalled Kaplow's methods for the purchase of liquor on credit: "He'd write it down in the book, and then if he wanted to charge you for two bottles, he'd charge you for two. If you got one and he wanted to charge you for two, you had to pay," on pain of being denied further credit.[17] Consequently, Mitchell was not surprised at the swift sacking of Kaplow's. "When they started the riot," he continued, "the first thing they broke into was Kaplow's. Man, they cleaned his liquor store out. That's why they brought ten cases of liquor over to my house, put it on my porch, and said, 'This is your share, Mr. Mitchell.'"[18] The sharing of liquor from Kaplow's, including with those who had not participated in the attack, even to highly respected members of the community such as John Mitchell, set the tone for the moral economy of the riot. Similar acts of redistribution followed the ransacking of food, clothing, and other establishments.

The pattern of attack throughout the uprising demonstrated that far from being opportunistic and capricious, as media depictions suggested, the participants deliberately and willfully chose their targets. In addition to Kaplow's liquor store, Peck's pharmacy was attacked and supplies seized on the first night of the uprising. This, too, was unsurprising. Lester Peck had long maintained a dual career as pharmacist and politician, using the one career to advance the other. As previously detailed, Peck's predominantly Black constituents finally ousted him as ward supervisor in 1961. Constance Mitchell, a recipient of some of the loot taken from Kaplow's liquor store, replaced him. Peck's crimes against the Black community were twofold. He maintained a practice of strong-arming his constituents for votes, threatening to restrict their access to necessary medication. Second, his pharmacy extended credit, although whether at the same usurious rates as Kaplow is unclear. The uprising apparently removed Peck from the Black community altogether. When queried by a reporter whether he would rebuild his looted pharmacy, Peck responded, "I doubt it; I think this will be the coup de grace; I think this will drive us out."[19] Peck's pharmacy and Kaplow's liquor store were not alone: the targeting of stores with questionable practices and of owners with unfavorable reputations continued throughout the uprising. At the same time, schools, churches, and community organizations, along with businesses with good standing in the community, all escaped unscathed.

City leaders took strong measures to quell the disturbance. After consulting state officials, city manager Porter Homer declared a state of emergency and ordered liquor stores throughout the city of Rochester closed. He also imposed an 8:00 p.m. curfew. The curfew not only failed to stop the upheaval, but it also outraged many who resented the curtailment of their rights. Buddy Granston, a veteran recently returned to Rochester from military service in Germany, recalled a series of events that increasingly fueled his anger at the curfew and the police charged with enforcing it. First, the police refused to let Granston (and other residents) off his porch. On the second evening of the uprising, officers pointed guns at his head as he returned home from work. The following night, Granston and his landlord were arrested for breaking the curfew. He remembered,

> We were goin' over to [a friend's] house to have a couple a' cold ones, and I'll never forget this: the police stopped us right around the Plymouth Circle. . . . They stopped us and they said we were breakin' the curfew and so they called the wagon and they put us all in the wagon. And that's when I, you know, I might have lost it some, here I'm a veteran just got home from servin' my country in the war and here I am in the Black Mariah, one of the names we used to call the wagon; you call it "paddy wagon" or whatever, we call it the Black Mariah. . . . Here I am goin' to jail with a wagon full of people that they had—were puttin' in jail because we broke the curfew.[20]

Granston and those with whom he went to jail had plenty of company, most of them also charged with curfew violations. An analysis by the city manager's office reported that of 893 total arrests, more than 50 percent, 451 people, were curfew violators.[21] In fact, the curfew increased the level of anger against the city and the police, thereby aiding the uprising, which became better organized after the first night.[22] Both residents and the police reported that bricks, rocks, and Molotov cocktails were made and stored on rooftops in preparation for the second night of the rebellion.

Those with inside knowledge of the Black community knew that the uprising would continue after the first night. Accompanied by other members of the clergy and the community, Arthur Whitaker, pastor of Mt. Olivet Baptist Church in Rochester's Third Ward, walked the streets of the Seventh Ward, where the uprising began, to survey conditions during the first night of the uprising. "Reverend," the ringleaders greeted Whitaker, "we're coming over to your side tomorrow night!"[23] Sure enough, after a daytime lull in events, the uprising did spread to the Third Ward on the second night, even as it continued unabated in the Seventh Ward. Typical of the era, television played a role in the diffusion of the uprising throughout Rochester's predominantly Black neighborhoods, almost all of them in the Third and Seventh Wards. On the day after the uprising began, film footage showed firefighters spraying African Americans in the face with high-power fire hoses and policemen beating Black women with nightsticks (see figure 3.2). Viewers could also see and hear white crowds chanting, "Send them back to Africa!" behind police lines meant to prevent the rebellion from spreading downtown.[24]

Roswald Graham was among those who experienced the heavy hand of the law as the police began the suppression on the second night of the uprising. Graham, an African American, left work with three white fellow employees in his car. He had already dropped off two members of the carpool at their places of residence when a police car pulled alongside his. Although the police had neither sirens nor lights going, Graham understood his predicament and immediately pulled over. One of the officers bounded from the car and fired a barrage of questions at the startled Graham, who offered a nervous smile. Even before the other three officers came around, Graham was already spread-eagled against the wall, as the first officer searched him. Suspecting he was carrying a weapon, the four officers bantered about where "they" typically hide knives and guns. Finding nothing, the first officer forcefully kicked Graham before allowing him to get up. He was later treated at the emergency room for injuries sustained when the officer kicked him. Graham's white passenger was more fortunate, escaping with a gentle search and polite conversation.[25]

FIGURE 3.2.   Police use vehicles and fire hoses to prevent the rebellion from reaching downtown. Photograph, Rochester, July 1964. Box 4, Photograph Album, Rochester Race Riot Papers, D.185, Rare Books, Special Collections, and Preservation, River Campus Libraries, University of Rochester. Credit: Staff photo, *Rochester Democrat and Chronicle*. Used with permission.

The evidence indicates that such scenes riled up Black Rochesterians and added fuel to the uprising as it spread from the Seventh to the Third Ward. As the uprising migrated, its moral economy remained unchanged. Loma Allen, the white president of the Baden Street Settlement, which at the time of the uprising aided residents with housing, finding employment, and responding to discrimination, remembered an "interesting thing that happened. . . . Not one thing at Baden Street was hurt." Likewise, she continued, "there was a strip of shops along Joseph Avenue of all kinds. The ones that had been good to the neighbors were not touched. [However] the other ones were trashed." As goods looted from targeted establishments were redistributed, and in some cases destroyed, schools, churches, community organizations and favored businesses were exempt. "It was fascinating," Allen continued. "They knew exactly who to pick off."[26]

With the police focused on containment, and apparently powerless to deal with the uprising inside the Black community, city officials appealed to the state. Governor Nelson Rockefeller was awakened at 3:00 a.m. the same night the disturbance began and told of the crisis. He immediately ordered state troopers to the scene, though it took them nearly four hours to arrive. Rocke-feller also promised to send the National Guard, if necessary, an action he did not take during the Harlem uprising. On arriving, the state troopers took com-mand of the situation, which the Rochester police resented. Despite public proclamations about the outstanding cooperation between the two police units, the evidence suggests that local police and local officials felt displaced by the state troopers. Certainly there were disagreements over the best course to pursue.[27]

Even with the arrival of the state troopers, the strategy for dealing with the uprising did not initially change. The authorities were still focused on con-tainment. As the day wore on, however, police presence in the Black commu-nity increased. Then the rebellion leapfrogged from the Seventh to the Third Ward that Saturday night, marking a second night of rebellion. It seemed to some that greater force would be needed to restore order, especially with talk circulating about a third night. Against the advice of the state troopers, Gov-ernor Rockefeller was requested to make good on his promise to send the National Guard if the situation warranted. Importantly, this request came not from city officials and the state police, who opposed it, but from an influ-ential group of private citizens—Black and white—led by Georgiana Sibley, better known as Mrs. Harper Sibley, Rochester's wealthy white matriarch and avowed racial liberal. Sibley, a board member of the Rochester Area Council of Churches and a proponent of the police advisory board, held constant meet-ings with various church and community leaders in her home throughout the uprising. At one such meeting, the public safety commissioner reportedly threatened to "line the niggers up like cordwood in the streets" if the rebel-lion did not end. Fearing a bloodbath if the local police were not restrained, Sibley and several ministers from the Rochester Area Council of Churches went over the heads of city officials and the state police, using backdoor chan-nels to appeal to Rockefeller to send in the National Guard.[28] It was the first time in this era that the National Guard was called in to help suppress an urban rebellion. However, the Guard never actually entered the battle. On arriving in Rochester, they paraded through the streets and then retired to their barracks in the local civil defense shelters. Still, the show of force convinced many that the Guard had quelled the disturbance.

Actually, the uprising effectively ended after the second night, before the National Guard came on the scene. For one, the protestors had run out of tar-gets to attack, having already looted or burned the most hated symbols of oppression in the Black community. Repression also took its toll. As authori-ties became more confident about the security of the downtown area, the city and state police abandoned the policy of containment and took the fight to the insurgents. The dragnet of the Black community resulted in some nine hundred arrests. For all practical purposes, the curfew placed the whole Black community under house arrest, and once they returned to the neighborhoods, the police aggressively enforced it. Most of those arrested were charged with curfew violation, as already noted, but many who took an active part in the uprising were also apprehended. The removal of such individuals from the streets and the increasingly heavy police presence served as a deterrent to others who may have considered joining the fray. In any case, would-be participants had fewer targets to attack. Sibley and her supporters may not have been convinced, but the uprising had indeed run its course by the time the National Guard arrived (see figure 3.3).

While officials lauded the police for their restraint and congratulated themselves on the small number of deaths during the rebellion (no one was actually murdered), those on the receiving end have different recollections.[29] Black victims of the police roundups report experiencing persistent and routine verbal and physical abuse. Ward supervisor Constance Mitchell caught a glimpse of the attitude of the police. After learning of the city's intention to impose a curfew, Mitchell visited the public safety commissioner's office in the company

FIGURE 3.3. Police attempt to enforce the curfew during the Rochester uprising. Photograph, Rochester, July 1964. Box 4, Photograph Album, Rochester Race Riot Papers, D.185, Rare Books, Special Collections, and Preservation, River Campus Libraries, University of Rochester. Credit: Staff photo, *Rochester Democrat and Chronicle*. Used with permission.

of eight ministers. Their purposes were simple. They requested passes to remain on the street, talking to their neighbors and cooling tempers, a role Mitchell had been playing for many years. As they waited in an outer room, a voice announced over the intercom, which had been left on accidentally: "Let those niggers do what they want to do, but the minute they step outside of [the prescribed] boundaries and head towards Main Street, shoot to kill."[30] Apparently the death toll was so low because the ruckus was confined to the Black community.

Black members of the police force were not immune from the repression. Charles Price was one of the few Black officers on the Rochester police force at the time of the unrest, having by then advanced to the rank of sergeant. Though quite tight-lipped regarding his perceptions of the uprising, his recollections of the event and his own interactions with the state troopers are telling. Given his ability to meld into the Black crowd, Price had been assigned to work intelligence in plain clothes. On the second night of the uprising, he came face to face with a state trooper, who ordered him, "Get off the street!" Price asked the trooper why and was promptly thrown into a paddy wagon. His fellow officers were in disbelief when he arrived at the police station downtown in handcuffs and explained to the state trooper that he had just arrested *Sergeant* Price, who was on duty that evening. The state trooper, only mildly embarrassed, blamed Price for not telling him he was an officer. Price rejoined that at no point did the trooper inquire about his identity or his mission. On Price's retelling of this story, his wife, Pauline, quietly murmured, "Typical."[31] Forty-five years after the fact, Price's convictions on the nature of the uprising remained the same: "The riot was an economic and, I would say, political [event]; people were tired of being denied things that they actually should have, that were their given rights."[32]

Riots Reconsidered

Many misconceptions about the uprisings of the 1960s persist, despite (or perhaps because of) multiple contemporary reports by local and national investigative committees.[33] J. Edgar Hoover's 1964 Federal Bureau of Investigation report sets the tone: "A common characteristic of the riots was a senseless attack on all constituted authority without purpose or object." The report continued, "They were not a direct outgrowth of conventional civil rights protest."[34] The mainstream media echoed such sentiments. An article in *U.S. News and World Report* mirrored this refrain. About the Rochester participants, the publication suggested,

They are the people who ran wild when a crowd of boozed-up Negroes attacked a couple of policemen. They weren't "demonstrating" for anything. They used the riot as an excuse to see how much they could get away with—wrecking and sacking hundreds of stores—but making sure they cleared out the liquor stores first. They got away with enough liquor to keep them drunk for six months. Fired up on the stolen liquor, police said, the Negro mobs raged through areas covering more than 50 city blocks. . . . The mobs broke into store after store.[35]

In fact, there is much evidence to suggest that urban residents used these disruptions to voice discontent with specific local conditions, particularly those conditions left unresolved by traditional civil rights struggles.

Historical scholarship, however, still has not fully come to terms with the Black insurgency of the 1960s. Although making great strides in reconceptualizing the Black Freedom Struggle, historians have yet to consider "race riots" as a legitimate part of "the Movement." The first generation of scholars to engage this era's urban race riots and rebellions tended to see them as disorganized responses to economic or social repression; race was generally a secondary factor in their analyses. Furthermore, these scholars focused primarily on the conditions that led to rioting, or the conditions that suggested riots may occur. They often looked at single factors (e.g., segregation or poverty) in an attempt to prove or disprove such notions as the underclass theory. Such works rarely historicized events or examined changes over time.[36] Moreover, many early scholars of the civil rights movement were former activists who were politically invested in separating themselves from the supposed senseless violence of the rebellions. They rarely looked closely at the organizations and movements the uprisings produced, much less placed rebellion in the context of the Black Freedom Struggle.

This historiographical lacuna is a direct result of the tendency to write about the civil rights movement as though it were solely a nonviolent phenomenon.[37] That scholars maintained this framework for so long has shaped the way that urban disturbances continue to be understood. The media take their cue from such entrenched perceptions, positioning "violent thugs" in opposition to "responsible Black leaders." If a Black leader is to remain "responsible" in the public eye, he or she is expected to condemn any and all acts against private property or state authority. Yet in committing such violent reprisals, those engaged in rebellions often bring national attention to the disturbing conditions in their communities in ways that have eluded "responsible" leadership. It is only recently that scholars have begun to make positive connections between the uprisings of the 1960s and the civil rights movement.

Far from engaging in senseless acts of violence against all authority, as Hoover and others claimed, participants in the Rochester uprising attacked specific conditions and sought tangible outcomes from their efforts. Black Rochesterians and their white allies had exhausted their efforts to mediate conditions in the predominantly Black wards as business leaders and city officials repeatedly dismissed their concerns. Loma Allen recalled that the Baden Street board had little success with city officials and so instead turned to business leaders. Allen set up a meeting with Monroe Dill, Eastman Kodak's industrial relations director. Allen recounted the conversation: "[Dill] said, 'Oh, Loma, don't worry.' I said, 'Monty, please get the people busy and do something about this housing, harassment, and so forth and so on.' 'Oh, Loma, now don't get excited. I'll take care of everything.' So I left him and he said, 'Nothing's going to happen anyway.'"[38]

Black concerns had been articulated before, during, and after the July 1964 uprising through the news media, in the bid for the civilian police review board, and through a series of demands submitted to the mayor's office. These concerns got lost in the binary juxtaposition of "violent thugs" and "responsible leadership."[39] For people not confined to respectability politics and tactics, violent reprisals to private property and state authority became a logical next step to ensure their concerns were acknowledged. In the midst of the uprising, one man declared, "Violence is one thing the white man understands." When asked whether he had taken part in the looting, he responded that he had taken "some things my wife and family need. And the white man owes me more."[40] Darryl Porter, who volunteered as a teenager in Constance Mitchell's election campaign and has worn many hats in Rochester, also participated in the 1964 uprising. He offered the following analysis of his actions:

> I was doing about what everybody else was doing, I was breaking the law, throwing bottles, breaking windows, robbin' places and things like that, because people in Rochester are getting tired of all these slum houses and the brutality from the policeman, the way they beat on teenagers, and the way they yell at ya if you stand on the corner, and the treatment they do to ya when they get ya down to the police station. When all the riot was going on, this made the mayor and the city get up [off] their high horses and wanted to come see what was going on and why it was going on. Since it happened, everyone is getting down to talk about it and I think there should be a little bit more change in this world.[41]

Still another young Black man offered, "Something have to be done. It have to be done. I mean, we can't get our rights, so I mean if you can't get your rights, you got to take some kind of risk now, ain't ya? Ain't ya?"[42]

Another misconception suggests that riotous mobs simplistically targeted white-owned stores while sparing Black-owned businesses. There is, indeed, plenty of evidence from Rochester and elsewhere that white establishments were looted or torched even as Black businesses were spared. The NAACP national field secretary reported on the Rochester uprising: "It is worthy of note that only white businesses were broken into and looted. It was obvious this was a form of retaliation and resentment."[43] City Manager Homer confirmed this: "The pattern has been one of containment. And a pattern of white stores looted, Negro stores missed. There is a high probability whites may take counteraction tonight."[44] African American storeowners got the point. As disturbances began in some cities, they posted signs indicating their establishments were Black-owned.[45] A confidential 1964 study by the Chicago Police Department concluded that such postings were effective: "It was felt . . . that such signs did protect the Negro store in most instances."[46]

Yet the participants in these uprisings were much more methodical than such reports indicate. In Rochester, Deputy Police Chief DePrez noted that there was order inherent in the chaos, though perhaps he misjudged its nature. "For the most part only stores operated by whites were smashed and looted," DePrez asserted. "Negro-owned places weren't touched. Someone had to point out which places to smash."[47] In fact, no one had to point out which stores to target. As Loma Allen contends, anyone residing in the community knew which stores had offended the community. Their decisions were not based solely on the race of the storeowners. While the few Black-owned business and stores were exempted, white store owners with solid reputations were also spared. Take, for example, the white-owned Mangione store in Rochester. Mr. Mangione lived and worked in Rochester's Seventh Ward, where the uprising began. His son, the famous jazz musician Chuck Mangione, remembered this:

> Papa Mangione had a grocery store on the corner of . . . Martin Street. The store was actually attached to our house, and so . . . my father would eat dinner and keep the door open so he could see who was coming into the store. And I don't ever remember him really having a complete meal without having to get up and go out to sell some kid some penny candy or somebody came in to get something.[48]

The elder Mangione, it seems, was kind to the youth of the community, extended reasonable credit to those who could not pay immediately, and made his home with the people from whom he made his living. As Trent Jackson recalled,

> The Mangione store was, you go in, and Mr. Mangione you know, looked like he had this feeling, you, it sounds funny, I'm dating myself but you

know you could get a donut for a nickel. And you could go in, and we would go in sometimes after practice and we would look at the donuts and then you look at a piece of cake, and then you look [making a decision between the two], well I'll take that. And well, then sometimes he would say, "you know, you're a good boy, you can get both for the price of one."[49]

Not surprisingly, the Mangione store was untouched during the uprising, even as other white-owned establishments were looted and destroyed.

The mob was neither headless nor heartless, and there were constant negotiations between participants and residents about which establishments to target and which to exempt. Again, the moral economy of the uprising can be seen in a case in Rochester, where the crowd changed course and spared a white-owned storefront at the request of a single mother. The woman heard people below her in conversation, discussing setting fire to the looted building where she lived with her children. Afraid for her family, she descended to face the crowd and pleaded for them to move on, leaving the building intact.[50] The crowd did so expeditiously.

There is further evidence that the resentment of participants was directed at specific targets. In Rochester, many of the items taken from looted stores, particularly televisions and appliances, did not end up in private residences but instead were smashed in the streets.[51] By contrast, food, always a prized commodity among the poor, was redistributed to members of the community. Even Constance Mitchell was offered some of the looted food, just as her husband John was offered looted liquor. She remembered, "People were bringing all the stuff—they come over and they brought a side of beef and set it on our porch and said, 'Here, Mrs. Mitchell, this is your share.'"[52] Evidently the looters were giving back a little to the Mitchells, who were revered for opening their home to the community for meetings, education, and counseling on a daily basis. Reportedly, if the door to the Mitchell home was open, there was a pot of food on the stove, and anyone was welcome to partake.

Yet another common theme in the literature is that the majority of participants in these rebellions were mainly young men. Various scholars portray the participants in the rebellions as both overwhelmingly male and overwhelmingly young. Thomas Sugrue is typical. In his highly regarded synthesis, *Origins of the Urban Crisis*, Sugrue is so convinced that youth dominated the urban uprisings that he frequently uses the term "teenager" as a stand in for "rioter." Additionally, he argues that in the course of an uprising "allegations of police harassment of women challenged Black manhood: Men should—indeed must—protect their women."[53] The emphasis on male participation continues throughout the chapter devoted to riots.

Sugrue is not alone. Matthew Countryman's important work on Philadelphia and Komozi Woodard's on Newark, New Jersey, also emphasize the role of teenagers. Countryman, like Sugrue, argues that confrontations with the police were a way for young males to assert their masculinity. Countryman argues that chants, which "promised violent revenge on the police," performed on a picket line in the wake of the Philadelphia uprising, "enabled the teenage protestors to symbolically resolve their anxiety that racism would prevent them from claiming the prerogatives of masculinity."[54] Writing of the 1967 riot in Newark, Komozi Woodard adds his considerable authority to this line of argument: "CORE members attempted to divert the crowd by leading a march on City Hall, but the attention of the Black youth in the streets was riveted on the precinct station house." Woodard continues—"Before long, a hail of bricks, bottles, and Molotov cocktails hit the side of the police station"—using "Black youth" as a synonym for young Black men.[55] Other scholars of the urban uprisings also place the male teenager front and center.[56]

These accounts do not comport with the evidence from Rochester, where women were active participants during every stage of the uprising. Police arrested at least seventy-five women during the course of the Rochester uprising; the charges against them mirrored those faced by men: curfew violation, felonious rioting, and various others associated with looting. Though women made up a relatively small proportion of total arrests, this is likely due to a police predilection to view Black men as more violent and dangerous than Black women. Other evidence suggests that women were entirely engaged in the rebellion and offered considerable support to the efforts. A Rochester police document entitled "Preliminary Report of the Riot Investigation" noted that during the uprising, "the police detail made several attempts to disperse the crowd . . . but were forced back by the barrage from behind buildings, roofs, *and the crowd of women and older people.*"[57] Reporters also noticed the presence of large numbers of women during the uprising.[58] Given the very public role of women in the civil rights movement and in local protests, it is unsurprising that they would join in this form of Black agitation as well.

In Rochester, at least, the uprising was far more than just a male youth rebellion, or even a youth rebellion. While young men and women certainly provided energy and voice, they did not have a monopoly on discontent. Rochester residents Gavin Huber Jr., age ninety, and Eva Dyer, sixty-three, were both charged with felonious rioting. Forty-two percent of those arrested in Rochester were over the age of thirty.[59] These statistics reflect widespread discontent rather than youthful rebellion. Even the Rochester police department took note: "The crowd swelled to about 500 people, and the older people were not assisting the police in their attempt to control the situation. They joined the youths in abusing the police and whenever the police tried to make an arrest they would interfere with the police and accuse the police of brutality." The police department's report added, "The older Negro citizens made little or no attempt to correct the riotous acts of the younger Negroes."[60] Indeed, they did not; they had joined them! Constance Mitchell remembered, "It was the young people that stole the televisions and you know stuff like that, but it wasn't just the young people that stole milk, pop, bread, meat."[61]

Reducing the Contagion

In ways large and small, the events in Rochester were a taste of the coming decade. Just two days before the Rochester uprising, psychologist and activist Kenneth Clark, renowned for his research on the impact of racism on Black children, declared, "Riots like those in Harlem could occur in any other city with a large Negro population."[62] A shaken Constance Mitchell echoed the warning after the eruption in Rochester. She declared that America "was in the middle of a social revolution. . . . And the same thing that happened in Rochester on Friday night can happen in any community in America."[63] The reverberations of the Rochester uprising would indeed be felt across the nation. In the midst of the uprising, an FBI agent visited Rochester with a blunt message for city officials: "The White House wants to know what's going on."[64] The president and his advisers were not alone. Rochester became, and remained for some time to come, a topic of conversation among government officials at the state and local levels, businesspeople, and activists.

For those charged with preserving law and order everywhere, Rochester would also become a place of note. Fearing a contagious effect, and seeking ways to combat it, police departments and public security officials across the nation turned their attention to Rochester. Rochester garnered such attention for three reasons. First, the timing of the uprising put Rochester at the forefront. Second, most cities had more in common demographically with Rochester than with Harlem. That Rochester exploded was unexpected and put a wider swath of urban areas on notice; they could experience such rebellions too. Third, Rochester had successfully quelled the uprising without any reported homicides. The police effectively contained the uprising to the Black neighborhood and prevented its spread to the prosperous downtown area. Thus, the prospect of such rebellions compelled cities and states to improve their response, communication, and recovery plans. After calling up the National Guard for the Rochester uprising, Governor Rockefeller took steps to increase the level of coordination among city, county, state, and federal officials in case of another emergency. In March 1965, the New York State Division of Military and Naval Affairs issued directives to all locales outlining "the authority and procedures for requesting the use of troops, equipment and armories of the New York State's Military Forces in an emergency."[65] This document would be revised several times over the next decade.

Other cities followed New York's lead. In October 1964, John Madl, chief of patrol division for the Chicago Police Department, visited New York City, Rochester, and Philadelphia to study the most effective means of controlling and quelling racial disturbances. Madl's confidential report stated that "the trip was most beneficial and that much of the material [collected] will be useful in strengthening our plans for riot control."[66] Around the same time, Lieutenant Colonel Rex Applegate, working for the Office of Strategic Services and an expert in hand-to-hand combat, published an article in *Ordnance* entitled "New Riot Control Weapons" in which he complained, "The spontaneous and directed demonstrations and riots now being encountered on the domestic scene are no longer restrained by the mere 'presence' of the uniform. The military as well as the police have recently had to confront civilian crowds and mobs that held none of the 'respect for the uniform' that once automatically was assumed to be present."[67] One of Applegate's most treasured new weapons for riot control was the long baton, which he found superior to both the bayonet and the gun because it could be used to "achieve the desired result and, at the same time personally perform in the kind of aggressive manner that maintains [its user's] morale and offensive spirit."[68] Similar articles appeared in various news outlets and were clipped and circulated among lawmen.[69]

Police officials nationally also paid close attention to the role of the media in rebellions. Here, too, they drew lessons from the Rochester uprising. While appreciating the media's ability to convey public information quickly, as in publicizing the state of emergency, the Rochester police accused the broadcast and print media of inaccurate and biased reporting. Police officials were also concerned that reporters had been given too much information. In his "Command Report" of the Rochester uprising, Colonel William F. Sheehan noted an incident "whereby [a] reporter was able to secure far too much information from a young 2nd Lieutenant. Serious consideration must be given to the isolation of troops from reporters unless accompanied by an experienced [public information officer]."[70] Some news managers agreed and suggested self-censorship. In 1967, the Northern California chapter of the Radio and Television News Directors Association drafted guidelines to regulate the coverage of rebellions, which it then disseminated throughout the country. The guidelines included this introduction: "The following are *suggestions for reporting of civil disorders* and other events that may reflect public tension. These reminders to newsmen in southern California are based on experience in various cities of the United States, including Los Angeles." The upshot of these recommendations was that news outlets should rely on the statements of public officials rather than "interviews with obvious 'inciters.'"[71] The California news directors also suggested that the media should restrict information about how to make the weapons used by rioters and the exact locations of the rebellions. These recommendations would have delighted Rochester's Colonel Sheehan, whose own suggestions for controlling the news did not go nearly as far.

As the 1960s came to a close, scores of Black uprisings had shaken the nation, causing many to claim that indiscriminate mobs engaging in senseless violence had brought the civil rights movement to an end. Civil rights activists, in turn, did much to distance themselves from the uprisings, in many cases denouncing them outright. Yet in Rochester, the Black Freedom Struggle blossomed in the wake of the rebellions. An independent report of six cities, released in 1967, rightly determined that,

> although numbers vary from city to city, sizable percentages of both whites and Negroes agree that "riots have brought about some long-delayed action by the city governments to help the Negro community." The benefits perceived by both groups range from such psychological matters as focusing attention on Negroes' needs and problems to the concrete steps of providing more jobs and better housing. . . . It would seem possible that though Negroes do not particularly like being the "squeaky wheel," they are coming to the conclusion that only intense forms of social protest can bring relief from social injustice.[72]

A full accounting of that squeaky wheel, and the intense forms of social protest it produced, is impossible without including the Rochester uprising and its consequences. Though historians and other scholars have long privileged the story of Black agitation in larger urban settings, there is much to learn by reconsidering the era in the light of events in the second-tier cities.

CHAPTER 4

Build the Army

Scrambling for Black Rochester after the Uprising

The wave of urban rebellions that struck many cities beginning in 1964 fundamentally altered the parameters and the possibilities for the Black Freedom Struggle in the United States.[1] The media, which had focused almost entirely on the civil rights struggle in the South, charting the movements of national organizations and leaders—the National Association for the Advancement of Colored People (NAACP), the Student Nonviolent Coordinating Committee (SNCC), the Congress of Racial Equality (CORE), and Martin Luther King Jr.'s Southern Christian Leadership Conference (SCLC)—turned its gaze (and that of the nation) rather suddenly to the North, where the Great Uprising had begun.[2] Many movement leaders, unwilling to accept the rebellions as an integral part of the Black struggle, criticized the "rioters." Joseph Lowery, chairman of the board for the SCLC, "dismissed the rioting as 'gang tactics' that had no connection with the civil rights movement."[3] Despite such critiques, Americans, white and Black, pondered the apparent contradiction between the movement's recent successes—Congress had just passed the Civil Rights Act of 1964—and what increasingly came to be seen as its failures. As Kristopher Burrell points out, American liberalism was facing a racial crisis.[4]

Shortly after the July 1964 uprisings in Harlem and Rochester, the *New York Times* asked, "Who speaks for the Negro?"[5] It was a salient question. Ultimately, the national journal determined, "there is already reason for doubt that any

Negro spokesman, however distinguished his record of accomplishment, can speak for—or even speak to—the Negroes who have been quickest to take up bricks and bottles in street fighting with the police."[6] For all its reactionary intent, this was an insightful statement.

In Rochester, the uprising alerted city leaders, corporate executives, and progressive white ministers that their traditional interlocutors in the Black community had been rendered ineffectual and that business as usual was no longer possible. Black Rochesterians were now seeking alternate voices to represent their concerns and new organizational structures that would pursue their aspirations—socially, politically, and economically. The traditional civil rights organizations *had* failed. Thus, despite successful mobilization around the issue of police brutality, the local NAACP could not maintain substantial numbers of African Americans. Conflict between the national NAACP and the local branch, for example, was exacerbated by the presence of a large white membership, which historically privileged the city's corporate and business desires over the needs of the African American population. Their dominance of the local branch made it all but defunct by the 1964 uprising.[7] Likewise, CORE's Rochester branch was dominated by white liberals. In fact, one Rochester insider reported that "it has a funny reputation in this town. [CORE is] looked upon by most Negroes as a white organization and their picket lines [at the local Woolworths] are generally about 65%-70% white."[8]

There were other organizations that one would expect to emerge in a growing Black community such as Rochester. The Urban League, though offering assistance to African Americans in most major U.S. cities by the 1960s (neighboring Buffalo established an affiliate in 1927), did not have a presence in Rochester. Wherever it emerged, the Urban League required startup capital. Until 1964, Rochester's business community and the Community Chest (the local version of the United Way) refused to provide it. Though not a traditional civil rights organization, Rochester's Nation of Islam (NOI) branch might have provided an organizational framework for those concerned with Black Rochester's economic ills, but the NOI was unacceptable to the establishment and had been severely hindered, organizationally and financially, by the 1963 police harassment and subsequent court cases.[9] Additionally, the NOI's most prominent spokesman, Malcolm X, who enjoyed a large following in Rochester, had separated from its ranks. In 1964, the SCLC and SNCC, both of which had southern roots, remained ambivalent about working in the North. Thus, the Rochester uprising demonstrated that existing traditional Black organizations had not served as effective vehicles for organizing many African Americans, and certainly not the poorest and most dispossessed in this northern outpost.

The *New York Times*'s inquiry about "who spoke for the Negro" thus captured the ethos of a changing era. While Stokely Carmichael had not yet seized the attention of Black activists with his declaration of Black Power, the liberal progression of the civil rights movement had been called into question.[10] Demands for unadulterated and unfettered self-determination were becoming louder and clearer in Black communities and certainly in the North, where white liberals had traditionally found it more palatable to focus their critiques on the Jim Crow South.

In Rochester, too, the early uprising commanded citywide attention to local conditions and forced a new conversation. As a result, major segments of the Black community felt emboldened to forge multiple, and sometimes competing, paths to attain their goals. Various factions developed, each staking a claim for the newly available resources and making a rhetorical case for the effectiveness of its proposed strategies. Ultimately, the factions were competing to determine "who spoke for the Negro."

The uprising also created conditions in Rochester favorable for recruiting new participants and leadership into the movement. Those Black ministers and activists, who had so diligently raised the alarm in the prerebellion years around police brutality, were now joined by a small group of white ministers, some of whom previously had worked to establish the police review board, under the auspices of the Rochester Area Council of Churches (RACC). The council, which had been unwilling to fund efforts in the Black community prior to the uprising, now sought projects to bankroll. Business executives, whose reputations took a hit during the rebellion, also showed increased willingness to fund ventures in the Black community, particularly if they would prevent future uprisings.

In this milieu, the veterans of Rochester's 1963 Baden Street rally— Walter Cooper, Constance Mitchell, Mildred Johnson, and Minister Franklin Florence—collaborated with white ministers from the RACC to find alternatives to the traditional civil rights organizations. The coalition members worked diligently to understand its strengths and weaknesses. The members knew the community possessed a strong indigenous black religious tradition. The white ministers, cut from the social justice cloth, understood the problems as economic. These ministers also admitted that traditional religious work could not placate Black Rochester. The coalition members sought an organizational structure that was going to truly organize and not just lead the people. In so doing, the coalition blazed a trail of its own. Over the course of the following year, this loose alliance of ministers and activists invited the SCLC to Rochester. The same group would subsequently travel to Chicago to interview the Industrial Areas Foundation's Saul Alinsky, a radical organizer who privileged social and economic transformation. The coalition would weigh in on the anti-poverty programs emerging from President Johnson's War on Poverty as a strategy for improving the lives of Black Rochesterians, and they would demand representation of the Black poor in every city agency and committee. As elsewhere in the nation, the call for Black self-determination grew stronger.

Rochester Gets Religion Anew

The Rochester Area Council of Churches, an affiliate of the National Council of Churches, had long pondered the "race question" in the city. While unwilling to fund Black-led initiatives in the prerebellion period, some of the council's members had grown increasingly invested in race relations and the civil rights movement. It was this white-dominated council that first organized educational and humanitarian efforts in the migrant camps and employed Black ministers to run the resulting programs after World War II. The council had also developed the Rochester Board for Urban Ministry, a new effort designed to bring together inner-city ministers and churches to address the rapid demographic changes taking place in the city. Once established, the Board for Urban Ministry put its resources into a full-time director, hiring Herb White, an up-and-coming white minister who earned his urban organizing stripes in nearby Buffalo and in Baltimore.

In Rochester, White had immediately set to work getting the lay of the land and building an organizational structure. He introduced himself to the Black ministers, serving as a bridge in many ways between white and Black churches.[11] One of his first encounters involved the Reverend Marvin Chandler, a young Black theologian studying at the Colgate Rochester Divinity School. While a divinity student, Chandler worked in the migrant ministry for the Rochester Area Council of Churches and served as a liaison between the migrant community, the Black churches, and the council. Chandler recalled these broader efforts "to move toward . . . more contact, cross-contact with African-American churches and so forth." He believed "there was this effort, I think, during those years in the churches to at least not so much integrate as to have some kind of . . . interconnection."[12]

Herb White also met Minister Franklin Florence, the fiery Church of Christ leader, who previously fought for the police review board during Rochester's prerising wave of police brutality cases in 1962 and 1963. Florence later recalled that his early encounters with White were somewhat disappointing. Florence implored White to devote resources to run recreational programs for Black youth, only to be told that White was unable to provide that type of financial assistance. The Board for Urban Ministry simply had not given him the budget.[13] While White attempted to forge relationships, he also began to develop small programs to build coalitions of citizens, churches, and businesses to address the spread of urban blight. He did all of this with meager resources. White's work was an important step toward exposing the urban crisis in Rochester, but he struggled to move beyond dialogue and discussion.

By 1963, the council had charged its churches with learning more about the urban crisis. The programs and organizations that the council and the Board for Urban Ministry hoped to build required congregational support and funding. In order to educate its lay and clerical members, to build support, and to fund its efforts, the council assigned contemporary texts for ministers and congregants to read. These included Harvey Cox's *The Secular City: Secularization and Urbanization in Theological Perspective* and Michael Harrington's *The Other America: Poverty in the United States.*[14] The most memorable and influential of these texts, however, was Charles Silberman's *Crisis in Black and White.* By capturing several important elements of the northern Black struggle, Silberman made that struggle accessible to a largely white, middle-class, liberal audience. Perhaps this was the book's appeal to the Rochester Area Council of Churches. Silberman described the collective powerlessness and so-called apathy of the urban poor. He also touted several movements for self-determination, such as those initiated by the Nation of Islam and the Industrial Areas Foundation. Here, he noted the success of those movements for rehabilitating African Americans' self-perceptions as well as the economic conditions of the Black urban poor. A relevant and significant strength of Silberman's text was its focus on the Black Freedom Struggle in the North. While northern whites were exposed nightly to the civil rights movement in the South, they remained consciously ignorant of the struggles taking place in their own communities. Silberman's book helped to contextualize the Rochester events for those who would later ponder how a "riot" could have taken place there.[15]

Perhaps more importantly, *Crisis in Black and White* admonished white liberals to support—rather than to lead—the Black community's efforts to organize for collective and economic power. Silberman effectively documented the consequences for traditional civil rights organizations when white liberals dominated the agenda and activity: "Negroes remained the junior, and usually silent, partner in the great liberal coalition, deferring to white judgment on strategy and tactics. However unavoidable, this relationship had unfortunate consequences for both the Black and white partners. . . . But Negroes always resented the relationship; their dependence on their white allies created an underlying animus that was no less real for being carefully suppressed."[16] For Silberman, then, African Americans taking "the initiative in action on their own behalf" became absolutely crucial to the success of any Black move-ment.[17] Armed with Silberman's insights, the Rochester Area Council of Churches set out to find a way to aid the Black community in organizing its ranks. After the uprising, Herb White turned in earnest to people like Frank-lin Florence and Marvin Chandler. David Finks, a white Episcopal minister, remembered, "Since 1960 several groups had been studying the church's role in the changing city, and the riots provided the occasion for action."[18] What could be done to support their efforts? Here, religious leaders sought new in-roads to existing movements.

The coalition of Black ministers and Black activists along with the Roches-ter Area Council of Churches realized they needed each other to make head-way in Rochester. The ministers and activists could galvanize the people, while the council had access to resources. Together they needed to decide on a course of action. Georgiana Sibley, better known as Mrs. Harper Sibley, who played an important role in bringing the National Guard to Rochester during the rebellion, would reappear as a key participant in these discussions. Born to wealth and privilege, Sibley led the life of a debutante, which provided her ac-cess to people in power, including Governor Nelson Rockefeller and Ethel Roosevelt, who served as one of her bridesmaids. At various points, she served as president of the Rochester Area Council of Churches and of the United Council of Church Women. Sibley was also widely regarded for her skills as a mediator and, having attended the Second Vatican Ecumenical Council in 1962, she believed in the responsibility and the power of the church to resolve so-cial ills. In the organizational frenzy following the 1964 uprising, Sibley's home "became a sort of headquarters where members of both factions could come together and the head of the Black Muslims was welcomed as graciously as the mayor."[19] It was in one such meeting that a member of the coalition sug-gested working with the SCLC. It was not a novel idea.

In the midst of the 1964 Harlem uprising, New York's Mayor Wagner had also invited Martin Luther King Jr., as the most recognizable face of the civil rights movement, to New York City.[20] Wagner, like white officials everywhere, frantically turned to national civil rights movement leaders and organizations to "control their people."[21] His invitation to King began a trend that would continue throughout the remainder of King's life. For his part, King resented these requests, arguing that by turning to national movement leaders, officials in riot-torn cities implied "that in some strange way, the Negro leadership is fundamentally responsible for the acts of violence and rioting which have oc-curred within these Negro communities."[22] Even so, King did travel to New York City and met with several officials. He ultimately declined the invitation to organize there, on the grounds that he had committed himself to "spending more time in the deep South working in communities that are involved in nonviolent direct action campaigns."[23]

Despite King's unwillingness to dedicate himself to the urban North, the uprisings in both New York City and Rochester marked a turning point for him and for the SCLC, even if it did not translate immediately. One historian of the SCLC has argued that until this point, "King had given little consideration either to the economic hardship which afflicted most Blacks or to the complex forces which created and perpetuated the ghetto."[24] Though not willing to go himself, King eventually sent organizers into rebellion-torn northern cities in hopes of finding a project north of the Mason-Dixon Line for the SCLC.

Georgiana Sibley was only too happy to use her national church connections to volunteer Rochester for that northern project. The SCLC, as a Black-led religious organization, fit nicely within the council's new effort to support Black-led organizing efforts. And so, with a donation from its national parent group and the blessing of the Black leadership, the council invited King's men to Rochester. They were hopeful that the SCLC's brand of social and political organizing might work to quell further disturbances. While "the Black ministers were interested," the white ministers were ecstatic when the SCLC sent two of its leading lights, Andrew Young and James Bevel, with a team of organizers.[25]

Once in Rochester, the SCLC facilitators engaged with the youth and the church people. The ministers joined young men on the basketball courts and in the alleys, hoping to win them over to the nonviolent cause. Young would later report on the games with a touch of arrogance: "Much to their surprise, these 'nonviolent' soldiers managed to beat them at their own games. The youth's humiliation was matched only by their respect and amazement when they discovered that half of the team were ordained ministers."[26] But beating the younger men at basketball and dice did not translate into a moral victory. Though Young did not advertise it in the SCLC newsletter, his men were verbally accosted outside Rochester's African Methodist Episcopal (AME) Zion Church after James Bevel finished speaking to a community group. Young men who attended the talk waited until Bevel walked out to challenge him. One explained, "I went along with the preacher until he started worrying about the white man's soul, until he said he was more concerned for a white man beating a Negro than for the Negro."[27] This young man was not alone in his rejection of southern nonviolent strategies. It was widely reported that "Jim Bevel's preaching and 'street raps' in the Christian rhetoric of M. L. King, Jr. were rejected by the young Black adults," even as "'What's all this Jesus shit?' threatened to become a battle cry."[28] While the young men rejected the turn-the-other-cheek language, their anger reflected a general impatience with

SCLC's strategies. One young man admitted, "I'm tired of waiting. I want to be free to live in Brighton [i.e., a white Rochester suburb] tomorrow."[29]

Though it went unreported in the papers at the time, Rochester's Black leadership was also dissatisfied with the SCLC men. While some viewed their presence as competition, others reported an inability to get in step with the SCLC contingent. Reuben Davis, the contrarian Black NAACP attorney who defended members of Rochester's Nation of Islam in their legal battle, recalled hosting a meeting at his home with local leaders, the SCLC men, and students from the Colgate Rochester Divinity School. He believed the problem to be a "personality" conflict: "I think that maybe . . . there was a personality thing that didn't click with the people who were active in the NAACP and the people from SCLC. And I don't know but it just never got off the ground . . . except for these couple of times, SCLC never came back so there was no opportunity to try and develop and create a good working relationship."[30] On the other hand, Constance Mitchell thought the conflict between the SCLC delegation and its Black Rochester hosts centered on a turf battle. Mitchell, who would later travel from Rochester to join King's famous march in Selma, believed "Rochester never bought into [the SCLC]." She also noted, "Rochester had an NAACP active at that time, and I think there was conflict between that group and a new group coming into town. Turfism—that's all it was, you know."[31] It is little wonder there was conflict between the various Rochester groups and the southern men. The SCLC approached Rochester as a teacher would a student, admonishing, "We're not here to tell you not to fight, we're here to teach you *how to fight*."[32] By all accounts, the SCLC contingent failed to appreciate the history of the Rochester struggle or the dedicated efforts of its leaders; in fact, they seemed downright oblivious to it. What is more, the SCLC rhetoric did not address the economic problems illuminated by the 1964 uprising that African Americans in Rochester felt were of the highest priority.

When the SCLC ultimately declined to organize in the city, the decision brought some relief to those in Rochester. As the SCLC's James Bevel explained, "Rochester's economic and social problems were not as clearly defined as those in the South and were ill-suited to SCLC's church-based organizing methods."[33] The SCLC's unwillingness to organize in Rochester was perhaps a missed opportunity for the southerners, though. In Rochester laid a model of the future of the northern movement and in many ways of the Black Freedom Struggle nationally. Adam Fairclough, who produced an organizational history of the SCLC, would remark that the SCLC "made little attempt, apparently, to assimilate and interpret its experience in Rochester."[34] For Rochester, however, the rejection led to further soul-searching and thus became a blessing. David Finks, scholar, activist, and Rochester insider, wrote that while the SCLC's visit was unsuccessful, "it raised the issue of bringing in trained organizers to assist the Black community in its leadership development."[35] The lack of "definition" to which the SCLC's James Bevel referred created an opportunity to define the parameters and the interrelatedness of the 'economic' and the 'social' in Rochester's struggle, again foretelling the direction the broader movement would take.[36]

Organizing the Poor

With the SCLC out of the way, the Rochester Area Council of Churches and the Black ministers who organized as the Rochester Area Ministers Conference went back to the drawing board. Through the auspices of the Board for Urban Ministry, Herb White asked that the Black ministers read Silberman's *Crisis in Black and White* as well. On White's telling, after reading the text, the Black clergy asked if the council would contact Chicago's Saul Alinsky and his Industrial Areas Foundation (IAF). The IAF came highly recommended. The SCLC had suggested Rochester leaders talk with Alinsky, while Silberman's book had promoted the IAF, even above the Urban League's economic efforts. At the time, the IAF's most impressive and well-known project was The Woodlawn Organization (TWO), a coalition of associations, religious institutions, and civic organizations on Chicago's South Side concerned with the economic condition of the Black neighborhood.[37] In many respects, then, the IAF's prior work mirrored what needed to be done in Rochester.

By contacting Alinsky, the Rochester Area Council of Churches took a provocative step. To begin, Alinsky's divisive reputation preceded his arrival in Rochester. A local man trying to make sense of Alinsky's efforts wrote, "Wherever he has worked, Alinsky has been the center of controversy. Few people who have had contact with him are neutral. They either admire him or hate him. He has been accused of being a Communist, a Marxist, and a Fascist, a tool of the Catholic Church, and a segregationist and an integrationist."[38] Further, leaders of the established social agencies in Rochester, namely, the white-led settlement houses, bristled at the thought of Alinsky's presence, believing "outside interference" unnecessary. They argued that Rochester could solve its own problems and that the ministers were simply meddling in affairs better left to local professionals, presumably the settlement houses.[39] The settlement house directors believed, as one observer put it, that the "poor and powerless people are clients to be cared for" rather than "citizens to be organized to wield a share of power in the metropolis."[40] This point was important. Sharing power would ultimately weaken the settlement house directors' influence. For others, rejecting Alinsky was pragmatic. They simply did not see that "such community-financed projects can become really effective in making drastic changes in the status quo, without antagonizing some influential community interests and jeopardizing their future financial support."[41]

Alinsky positioned himself as a defender of democracy for ordinary people and a radical organizer exposing class and race conflict for what it was. In so doing, he frequently made enemies with the keepers of the status quo, Black and white. He worked from the principle that all communities were organized and had indigenous leadership. The role of his Industrial Areas Foundation, then, involved locating the existing leadership and organizations to brainstorm strategies for assuming power in their communities. His approach made the poor and the powerless commanding agents capable of enacting necessary changes in their communities, not victims to be cared for. In response to his critics, Alinsky responded, "Do you think when I go into a Negro community today I have to tell them they're discriminated against? Do you think I go in there and get them angry? Don't you think they have resentments to begin with, and how much rawer can I rub them?"[42] He had a point, but not everyone in Rochester was ready to concede it.

Despite the hostility of some, the Rochester Area Council of Churches pressed on. In November 1964, a delegation of Black ministers accompanied by Herb White and Constance Mitchell went to Chicago to meet with Alinsky. Some remembered that at that meeting Alinsky played hard to get; he argued that the "entire country's in a mess" and in need of organization. He wanted to know what was so special about Rochester.[43] While Alinsky may have "acted like he didn't want to come to Rochester," nothing could have been further from the truth.[44] His understudy, Ed Chambers, later disclosed that the IAF had actually set its sights on Rochester generally, specifically Kodak: "It's one of the reasons we wanted to do this town, was to get them."[45] After the meeting ended, members of the Rochester delegation recalled a sense that their city would never be the same again. Alinsky warned that current leadership would be displaced by the new organization and that new—and sometimes unpopular—strategies would be implemented. But there was great hope among the group that Alinsky would provide the necessary "connection between the individual and the larger society."[46]

Back in Rochester, the churches and the Black leaders went to work organizing their various constituencies to meet Alinsky's demands. The IAF required $100,000 for a period of two years and an invitation from the Black community before setting up shop in Rochester. Herb White took the first request to the Rochester Area Council of Churches, which now consisted primarily of white ministers and Marvin Chandler. Finks later recalled that the council's proposal emphasized "the class unrest evidenced in the riots rather than merely the racial strife." Finks continued, "The 'have-nots' of Rochester's slum wards had legitimate grievances which the 'haves' were obliged to address."[47] Though not a unanimous vote, the members did agree to move forward, requesting funds from their churches and denominational boards.

In many ways, Rochester led the liberal and largely middle-class National Council of Churches (NCC) in new directions. Prior to the Rochester events, the NCC had done little to "think about specific responses to racial issues in northern cities." According to one NCC historian, "The predilections of these northern liberals, and of the nation at large . . . for so long . . . centered on the South and the struggle for equality there."[48] As the uprising in Rochester forced the city to face its racial ills, the NCC, which had long been active in the South, acknowledged the need to act in its own backyard. Shortly thereafter, the NCC became engaged in other riot-torn cities, Detroit and Cleveland among them. The NCC would ultimately commit considerable resources, political and financial, to bolster the movements for economic equality in the North.

Alinsky's other demand, procuring an invitation from the Black community, took a little more effort. For Black Rochester, the decision to invite Alinsky to town could not be discreetly couched in class rhetoric. Alinsky would later recall, "The Rochester Area Council of Churches, a predominantly white body of liberal clergymen, invited us in to organize the Black community and agreed to pay all our expenses. We said they didn't speak for the Blacks and we wouldn't come in unless we were invited in by the Black community itself."[49] Alinsky was right to be wary. Many in Rochester's Black communities were opposed to the plan. In fact, Herb White recalled that two young Black men came to his office at one point issuing veiled threats that "it ain't safe for you . . . as long as you're going to be supporting all of this."[50] Like the settlement house directors, though for different reasons, some longtime Black residents, such as Eugene "Gus" Newport, believed the Black community could organize its own people and did not require white outsiders to teach them how to do it.[51] Given that Black Rochester *had* failed to build an organization capable of meeting the community's various needs, Newport's sentiments likely reflected his own interest in organizing. Newport had assisted Malcolm X in starting the Organization of Afro-American Unity, thus beginning a long career of leadership and organizing, which culminated in his ascension to mayor of Berkeley, California, in the 1980s. Still, Newport's organizing aspirations aside, he did raise a troubling point for many in Black Rochester: Alinsky was white, and he had no history with that city.

Few were more troubled initially by Alinsky's whiteness than Minister Franklin Florence. But in time, Florence would come to see Alinsky as an organizational genius. He recalled that two important events persuaded him—and much of Black Rochester—that Alinsky was an acceptable man for the job. After the Rochester Area Council of Churches agreed to raise the funds, Alinsky began a talking tour in the city's two Black communities. Florence recounted the wisdom and honesty he saw in Alinsky's vision:

> We got this meeting at Mt. Olivet Church, and Saul [Alinsky] came in . . . just irreverent, vulgar, anti-establishment, but . . . on point about dig-ging . . . the sense of one's worth, and man's sense, the manhood, and the sense of who you are as a person, as a man, to take control and charge of your responsibility and yourself and there were all these things. One thing that stayed with me, with Saul, he said, "Never mind my being in-vited here by the Council of Churches. I refuse to come into Rochester unless *you* invite me." But here's . . . the genius of Saul and organizing—he said, "You would have to get about three thousand names of people in your neighborhood . . . before I come in, that they would agree that I come in to work with you." . . . "Now—" We'd raised with him, "Well, who's paying you?" He said, "That wouldn't be your business, but I'm going to tell you." He said, "Our contract with the Council of Churches is to come in and offer a service, providing that *you* invite me." I said, "Well what about their money?" He said, "Well, I'm going to take their money, but I'm not taking their money to do *their* bidding. I'm taking their money because they won't give it to *you*."[52]

For Florence, a light came on; Alinsky was offering to teach them a skill. He had also addressed honestly a plain truth about all of the planning and organ-izing the council had done. Despite its willingness to assist and raise money, the council had not offered to turn the funds over to any existing Black organ-ization or local leader. Having consulted both Marvin Chandler and Constance Mitchell, the council likely believed the key to preventing further uprisings dur-ing the coming summer was to organize the Black community quickly. Here, they believed that *trained organizers* rather than *activists* would prove immedi-ately successful. It also seems likely that those churches footing the bill pre-ferred a white national organization with a proven track record. For starters, it was easier to raise the money among their membership on these grounds. Nonetheless, Florence appreciated Alinsky's honesty. Still, he needed to have one other conversation before he was completely persuaded.

In February 1965, the debate over Alinsky raged in all quarters of Rochester. About that time, another so-called radical made his way back to the city. Mal-colm X returned for what would be his final visit to Rochester—just four days before he was assassinated in New York City. Organizers from Colgate Rochester Divinity School requested that Malcolm speak at a conference on world religions, and with some prerequisites, Malcolm agreed. This event, which required incredible collaboration between the religious community and the Black activist community, signaled once more the reemergence of the religious-activist alliance. But for Florence, who had helped to arrange Malcolm's visit, it was an opportunity to discuss the possibility of Alinsky's organizing in the city. Malcolm, they knew, had experience in Chicago and would surely be familiar with Alinsky's organization. Further, Florence and others believed that Malcolm, who had considerable history with Black Rochester, would make for a good sounding board to discuss Alinsky's whiteness in the local context.

At the close of Malcolm's formal talks that February day, he retired to his hotel room with various members of Rochester's Black community. The group engaged in heated debate over Alinsky and the IAF. Florence recalled that despite the intensity of the discussion, Malcolm quietly offered his point of view. "Look, all I can tell you," Malcolm reportedly said, "is that they have done a terrific job in organizing the south side of Chicago. . . . He's supposed to be the best organizer in the country, and one in the world."[53] Still, there were those present who balked: "Alinsky was a Jew," they argued. Malcolm admonished them that Blacks should always be willing to learn, regardless of the teacher: "One must never turn their minds away from learning a skill, whatsoever, and taking that skill and coming back to work for the good of our people."[54] It was the last piece of wisdom that Rochester would take from Malcolm, though long after his death, he continued to be an "absent presence" in the city.[55] For Florence and many others in the Black community, Malcolm's endorsement settled the matter. The signatures of Black residents were obtained, and a contract between the Industrial Areas Foundation and the Rochester Area Council of Churches was signed in March 1965.

Within days of the contract signing, the IAF worked alongside a temporary steering committee, initially consisting of several Black ministers and the ubiquitous Mildred Johnson, to identify the community's existing organizations. Believing that all communities were already organized, Alinsky counseled that they simply needed to be coordinated to act in concert. Thus, he charged the steering committee with identifying the various organizational units in the community. The new organization would not be comprised of individuals, but rather of existing member organizations: block clubs, employment groups, informal youth organizations, churches, barbershops, and the like. The umbrella organization would further have four structural layers of leadership and decision-making authority. First, each member group would elect representatives to serve on the Delegates Council. Then the Delegates Council would elect a steering committee to determine organizational priorities and actions. Thus, members of the steering committee were accountable to the Delegates Council through a yearly election. The steering committee, while holding ultimate decision-making power for the organization, would appoint various committees to investigate and make recommendations to the steering committee. They also would advise and hear suggestions from area vice presidents, who represented various geographic regions, generally specific wards. Any individual from a member group would be able to serve on any committee; however, in practice the steering committee generally appointed the chairs of each action committee based on prior service and area of expertise.

The community members who first interviewed Saul Alinsky, with a few additions, formed a temporary committee and began holding meetings. Though most of the members were skillful activists, few of them had experience establishing a large-scale organization. At their first meeting, then, temporary steering committee members recognized the need for, and then established, three guiding principles. For the benefit of the community, they clarified the intended role of the IAF in the formation of their new organization. Second, they established parameters for negotiating with Rochester's power structure. Third, they provided an organizational tone that they based on three values: discipline, respect for authority, and self-respect (see figure 4.1).

FIGURE 4.1. Minister Franklin Florence and the Industrial Areas Foundation's Saul Alinsky discuss strategy at FIGHT headquarters. Photograph, Rochester, ca. 1965. Box 172, folder 742, image ID IAFR_0172_1742_006, Industrial Areas Foundation Records, Special Collections and University Archives, University of Illinois at Chicago. Credit: Werner Wolff/Black Star. Used with permission.

Having been chosen temporary chairman of the committee, Franklin Florence's first public statements clarified the role the IAF would play in the new Black organization. Florence and the temporary committee addressed their immediate concern: mollifying those in the Black community who initially rejected Alinsky and the IAF. They further hoped to win over longtime Black community members, such as Gus Newport, who rejected Alinsky specifically and outside interventions generally. The committee hoped to assure Newport and others that Black leaders would be calling the shots. The IAF, Florence explained, would "consult with the temporary committee," "aid in the development of the Negro staff organizers," and "carry out all policy *as directed by the temporary committee.*"[56] The IAF would not direct the Black community. Florence's message was clear: the Black leaders ran the show; the IAF assisted. After announcing this policy at its meetings, the organization publicized it in the local papers: "This is a Black organization to be directed by Black people for the betterment of other Black people." Florence counseled, "We call the shots. Mr. Chambers [i.e., the white IAF organizer] and Mr. Alinsky are not in it. Mr. Chambers will only be used as consultant as needed."[57] Apparently the strategy worked; the new organization attracted more African Americans to its initial meeting than any other organization in Rochester ever had.

A second order of business established an organizational practice that leaders would follow for years to come. In advance of the organization's first meeting, Rochester's commissioner of public safety, Harper Sibley Jr. (Georgiana Sibley's son), extended a meeting invitation to Minister Florence. Despite his relationship with Mrs. Sibley, Florence was slow to accept the son's invitation. While the burgeoning Black leadership recognized a need to meet with Rochester's "power structure," they resisted any efforts to elevate or single out one representative from the Black community to occupy that role. A long history of Black organizing in Rochester (most recently in efforts to negotiate the placement of public housing under the NACCP president, Father Quintin Primo) demonstrated the perils of this practice. Instead, the steering committee aimed to privilege "cooperative action in meetings with [the] power structure."[58] Thus, it was decided that the entire committee would meet with Sibley at a mutually agreeable time. The decision was important for the new organization for two reasons: First, it established communal organizing and decision making as a central tenet of the group. Second, it made it difficult for the white establishment to recruit any one Black leader to a cozy relationship at the expense of the Black community.

While the temporary committee fostered a spirit of communal organizing, they remained mostly churchmen brought up in traditions that honored discipline and order. For this reason, two speakers presented back-to-back speeches at their first organizational meeting privileging unity and discipline. The Reverend Herbert Shankel spoke on "strength in unity," while the Reverend Murphy Greer emphasized discipline and respect for authority.[59] These themes addressed the two central concerns in the community at that time. In advance of the 1964 uprising, the Black community had established a strong sense of unity around the issue of police brutality. In the absence of a specific and galvanizing issue, the committee hoped to continue Mildred Johnson's call, "We are Black folks first." Not surprisingly, Mildred Johnson served on the temporary committee and spoke at its initial community meeting. Though women would rarely serve as spokespersons for this newly galvanized movement, they were central to its organizing efforts and played a critical role in defining issues and setting agendas for the nascent group. Publicly, however, men served as the voice of the organization. While Johnson's unity plea continued to be an organizing principle, the minister leaders believed that discipline and respect for authority had diminished during the uprising. They hoped the two—discipline and respect for authority—would foster self-respect, a key component for membership in the new organization, and would aid in the prevention of future uprisings.

Once the temporary committee—which was comprised almost entirely of Black ministers, Johnson notwithstanding—established these organizing principles, it set out to choose a name for the nascent organization. The name, the members felt, would establish them as a new presence in the community. Several suggestions of undefined acronyms floated among them—LIGHT, LOVE, and others. But despite their desire to instill discipline, the group maintained a certain respect for the rebellion and for those who had risen up. They were also cognizant of the constituency that had rejected the Southern Christian Leadership Conference and its nonviolent strategies. The organization's name, they felt, ought to reflect the spirit of the event that birthed it. A temporary committee member, Herbert Shankel, suggested the name FIGHT. Florence recalled his suggestion: "Well look, why [don't] we just fight the good fight of faith? That's a term different than the scriptures second Timothy."[60] Once they had decided upon FIGHT, the group sought to define the acronym. The "F" they agreed stood for "freedom." The "I" was for "integration," a concession made by the more militant members of the group to the more moderate. The group struggled with "G" and so left it for last. The "H" was for "honor," an attribute they took seriously, and the "T" was for "today"—there would be no more waiting for rights to come in due course. Their deliberations had been lengthy and at times stressful. Exhausted, they decided to leave the "G" until their convention in June. Alinsky, the atheist of the group and a latecomer to the meeting, suggested the obvious to a group of ministers: "Why

not 'G' for 'God'?" For Marvin Chandler, at least, the inability of the ministers to locate God in the formation of a Black Power organization represented
a larger struggle between the secular and the sacred. He remembered asking
himself,

> How did I locate myself as a clergyman and a Black man? What were
> the theological themes . . . being experienced: Humanity? Sin? Repen-
> tance? The Cross? Salvation? How was God operating in all this—in all
> of us? Each morning, as I left my office, I would look at a cross that an
> artist friend had given me. I felt that the goals towards which we strug-
> gled were proper and right, but I also knew the ambiguity that was pre-
> sent in the situation, and that I might be very wrong, so I prayed for
> honesty, humility, and the strength to face my private fears.[61]

God, they ultimately decided, was for Black Power. Having decided upon the
acronym, the group unveiled the name FIGHT to its membership and to the
community. Not surprisingly, there were those who felt the name should reflect a more positive or conciliatory tone. Yet Florence defended the name and
its meaning for the organization: "Why 'FIGHT'? But, you know, the history
here—the riots, or the rebellion, gave birth to FIGHT. Nothing else would have
caught the sense of our feeling, that the righteous indignation that we had,
that would express the other drivenness that we held for what was going on,
and the sense of power that that word gave us to relieve all that . . . this expressed, not *what* we will do, but *who* we are."[62]

With an operating ethos established and having declared themselves FIGHT,
the group began to recruit additional members. Once again, they owed a great
deal to a timely intervention by Mildred Johnson. In her typically unapologetic
fashion, Johnson abruptly interrupted Florence in a meeting with Ed Chambers and several other steering committee members early that summer. She
brushed past the secretary at the door and barged into Florence's office. She
demanded their immediate attention to a community issue. When Florence
and others suggested she bring it to the community meeting that night, she
scoffed. The issue had to be addressed expeditiously. As Johnson explained, a
young Black woman had attempted to use the restroom at the New York State
Department of Labor in Rochester, where she had an appointment. Employees there had denied her access to the restroom, indicating that it was for employee use only.

Chambers counseled the group to raise this at the meeting. He failed to
appreciate the immediacy of the issue for Black Rochester and was roundly
rejected. Florence recalled that as soon as they understood the issue's severity,
the Black ministers aborted their meeting: "We get in our cars, get down to

St. Paul. We go into the room, into the huge room they were in, Blacks around here, whites around there, but a sister was over here."[63] Johnson demanded to know why the man at the counter had denied access to this Black woman, who was no different than the white women who worked in the office. The supervisor attempted to explain that it was not a *public* restroom when Florence cut him off: "This is in Rochester, not Camilla, Georgia. . . . New York State don't—you don't let her use that restroom, so tomorrow we're going to be back here, close this place down."[64] On Florence's reporting, a group of thirty or forty people organized overnight, then turned up at the Department of Labor the following morning to demand a change in policy. They were shocked to find that the state agency was so anxious about conflict with FIGHT that by ten o'clock that morning, the office building had been reconstructed to include a public restroom. It was a significant victory for the burgeoning FIGHT organization. Once the story gained currency throughout the community, membership expanded exponentially.

That experience at the Department of Labor served as a lesson to Chambers, the outsider of the group. If simply declaring that the IAF would take direction from FIGHT and not the other way around was not enough, Johnson single-handedly transformed that assertion into practice. Mildred Johnson was a community mainstay. Her ability to attract attention, her unfailing desire to speak truth to power, and her insistence that action be immediate made her a natural leader and a voice for the community. Johnson understood an old saying of Alinsky's that *leaders* had *followers*, whether or not they belonged to an organization. Chambers found her natural abilities and her insistence on immediacy disconcerting initially. She was beyond his reach and control, and worse, the people responded to her. Johnson was a thorn in his side. After lengthy discussions with Alinsky, however, Chambers acknowledged the folly of fighting the tide in Rochester. He offered Johnson a paid position in FIGHT and put her organizational and leadership skills to use for the community group.[65]

Johnson was not the only woman to serve a leadership role in the early development of the FIGHT organization. Rochester women, married and single, consistently made up one-third of the steering committee, with ministers contributing another third, and nonclerical male leaders making up the remainder. Women also served as chairs of various committees, spoke at public meetings, and served as recruitment liaisons for the organization.[66] Hannah Storrs, president of Rochester's CORE branch, participated as one of two speakers at an early meeting in 1965. Women such as Ruth Tyler and Joan Smith served as delegates to the Delegates Council representing the National Negro Women's Association and the Clarissa Street Block Association, respectively. Alma Greene served as chair of the housing committee, investigating landlords and organizing actions when appropriate. Still another FIGHT mover and shaker, Mary Davidson, gave speeches on FIGHT's behalf to potentially supportive organizations.[67] While a great deal of the Black Power studies scholarship cites an ongoing tension for Black women in Black Power organizations, Rochester women navigated this space, providing their expertise in effective ways.

Women also took charge in the more traditional organizing roles. Constance Mitchell, now Third Ward supervisor, also devoted time to grassroots organizing on FIGHT's behalf. She and her husband, John, spent weeks pounding the pavement to organize block associations, which were then eligible to join FIGHT. John Mitchell recalled,

> We went to people and talked to 'em about joining up as a block association, but joining up primarily to be concerned about the living conditions that they had in their immediate residence. Then we started getting flower seeds and things like this. And we started planting flowers and when the flowers came up in the yard, the people saw what the block association could do. And they says, "Ooh, you got nice flowers in your yard." And we said, "Yes." And then the next thing you know, we were able to get 'em more involved in the other things. And then we got 'em involved in politics and we got 'em involved in education and we got 'em involved more in the schools, and, you know, being concerned about their children. And how much their kids was learning in the schools, and the kind of teachers that the kids had. And so, you know, you build on things like that. And you have to start small, in order to build those things up to those kinds of things that you want to.[68]

Organizing city blocks into associations became an important component of Black organizing in Rochester and particularly for women, for two reasons. First, the associations became politically involved in the most basic concerns of each particular block; for some this was trash removal or filling potholes. Still for other block associations, the urgent concern remained the creation and maintenance of appropriate and safe recreational facilities. It was at a block dance to raise money for recreational facilities that the 1964 uprising touched off, after all. These independent groups thus addressed specific neighborhood concerns with unity.

The block associations served a secondary purpose. Once organized into a block association, the group of individuals could become a voting member of the FIGHT organization, able to send delegates to the annual conventions. This strategy was a signature of Alinsky's IAF. The IAF's mode of operation had been the "organization of poor communities including all classes and religious groups within these communities; operationally, this [consisted] mainly of the poor with the militant potential and the activist clergy."[69] Each group had equal sway in FIGHT. The method was ingenious; organizations whose membership possessed less cultural, economic, or educational currency were no less valuable than churches, the highly educated, and the like. *Washington Post* reporter Nicholas von Hoffman explained, "They must pool their power to form an instrument for taking charge in an affirmative sense. By coming together in larger and wider unity they can consecrate leaders of sufficient power and backing to force recognition. Moreover, a larger and wider union permits the leaders to conceive and promulgate specific concrete and affirmative programs."[70] FIGHT, with its member organizations, set out to do just that.

Once organized at the supralevel, the newly created FIGHT organization held its first annual convention in June 1965 (see figure 4.2). The block associations were not the only groups to report; churches turned up, businesses such as George Cunningham's Service Station collected its employees into an official FIGHT member organization, and women's groups such as the Marian Anderson Federation, the Ernestine Burke Federation, and the Booklover's

Figure 4.2. Community groups prepare to caucus at the first FIGHT convention. Photograph, Rochester, 1965. Box 172, folder 742, image ID IAFR_0172_1742_003, Industrial Areas Foundation Records, Special Collections and University Archives, University of Illinois at Chicago. Credit: Werner Wolff/Black Star. Used with permission.

Federation attended in full force.[71] Each member group was allotted voting delegates and seats on the floor. Here, for the first time in Rochester, the Black community would elect its own leadership, adopt its own constitution, and vote to prioritize its policies and issues. With an audience of more than fifteen hundred people, five hundred delegates representing 136 community organizations—many of them recently formed—met to adopt FIGHT's first constitution.[72] Not since the days of the Baden Street rally had an organized Black meeting turned out such numbers in Rochester. White observers, the press, and nondelegates were relegated to the bleachers to watch as delegates held their convention and formally adopted the constitution.[73] Appropriately, Section 4 of that document declared, "Blackness is a color of honor which is to be worn with pride." In Rochester, an indigenous Black Power organization supported by a wide and varied swath of the Black community and funded by white churches came to fruition in 1965.

Choosing a Leader

In addition to adopting the constitution, the FIGHT organization proceeded to formally elect a leader to replace its temporary committee. Perhaps the most logical figure to be elected was Minister Franklin Florence, FIGHT's new chairman. Florence, a Southern transplant from Miami, was first and foremost a man of the cloth known to many in the community. His status as a migrant, though not of the agricultural variety, likely convinced the vast array of Black newcomers to Rochester that he understood their experiences. He was also a veteran of the police brutality cases that had shaken Rochester in the prerebellion years. Florence had attended the Baden Street rally and had demanded access to A. C. White, one of the victims hospitalized after a police beating. Florence was also a young, no-nonsense minister in the Church of Christ, who had developed a relationship with Herb White and the Board for Urban Ministry. Despite Florence's displeasure with the board's early refusal to fund Black initiatives, he was prepared to work with them in the months after the uprising. At the same time that Florence worked with Christian ministers of all stripes, he maintained a close relationship with Malcolm X. In fact, Florence traveled to Harlem on a monthly basis to visit with the former Nation of Islam leader, confessing that at one point he even considered joining the Nation of Islam.[74] As a result of these internal conflicts, Florence occupied incongruous, though not entirely incompatible, roles in the community. His relationship with Malcolm X would have been viewed as something of an anomaly for most Church of Christ leaders. On the one hand, he was an upstanding churchman committed to a conservative theology. On the other, he appreciated—harbored even—a more militant and radical worldview. He certainly advocated immediacy in his approach to rights.

Constance Mitchell recalled that initially they looked for someone "who had the leadership qualities, that could really take the helm, and who had the respect within the community." She continued: "We looked at certain criteria that were built in, that this person needed to have. And could take the helm immediately and get that ship to rollin. So, Minister Florence's name came up with everyone."[75] Local NAACP attorney Reuben Davis recalled that Florence had a reputation as a "forceful personality," one who understood that things needed to change expeditiously.[76] Darryl Porter remembered the sense that "when we started talkin' leadership, we were talkin' about people who had been in the community, who been doin' things out in the community—didn't show up today and decide they wanted to be a leader."[77] Gus Newport concurred with that position. Like many of the young Black people who grew up in Rochester, Newport was tired of organizations the he viewed to be led by white people and overeducated African Americans emulating white people. He believed in the Black community's ability to produce indigenous leadership. Once FIGHT was established, Newport supported Florence's election. He explained, "I'm not suggesting that we knew Florence that well. But, Florence got right in there with the radicals right away, you know—and he played a role."[78] Florence's credibility in multiple parts of the community made him a consensus choice.

Early on, Florence straddled the line between a Christian civil rights orientation and the burgeoning militancy of Black Power. He began his activist career negotiating a space between the more traditional, conservative members of the community and those who advocated self-determination and immediacy. In many ways, Florence had his finger on the pulse of the Black movement, and Rochester residents recognized this, even as some sought to fight it. Addressing a crowd in neighboring Buffalo a few years later, Florence demonstrated his oratorical skills: "Blacks are determined to take charge of their own destinies. We intend to have Black run organizations, based in the Black community, run by the grass-roots people of the Black community, speaking in the terms that make sense to the Black community." Florence declared, "They will not be the polite language of the middle class conference or seminar; nor will the tactics be the polite tactics of a gentle resolution or request." He continued: "We will picket, sit-in, shop-in, mill-in, mess-in, demonstrate and do whatever is necessary to bring our adversary to the conference table."[79] Florence's ability to "talk tough" drew recruits to him and to FIGHT in ways that the SCLC leadership simply failed to do.

As Minister Florence's presidency progressed, he increasingly delineated the FIGHT approach and tactics from those he identified as "middle class." In order to organize those most in need, and therefore considered most likely to engage in rebellion, Florence and FIGHT were determined to create an independent organization that, in many ways, became an antithesis to the civil rights organizations that remained unsuccessful or unviable in Rochester. In so doing, they fostered what scholar Angela Dillard has described as "oppositional consciousness." Dillard argues that in Detroit,

> activists joined the more militant factions of the city's Left community not only in sympathy for what the civil rights community represented but also in opposition to the ideas of their racial and ethnic compatriots. Generating an "enemies list" and defining one's position as more militant than that of groups such as the NAACP and JCC were important organizing actions that produced and sustained an oppositional consciousness. Indeed identifying the individuals and groups that the civil rights community defined as external adversaries is a helpful step in understanding how this community constructed its own identity and particular commitment to civil rights and social justice.[80]

This was precisely Florence's approach.

In its first year, FIGHT became something of a grassroots political machine. Steering committee members actively sought out and encouraged the creation of new member groups. Each steering committee member was responsible for distributing squad sheets to recruit actively for FIGHT. Among the targets for additional recruitment were barbershops, public housing complexes, and organizations such as the Elks, the Masons, and the Knights of Pythias.[81] Once members had recruited all potential member groups, they began to organize new groups. Young people, they instructed, should form social groups in order to become member groups with voting delegates. Though recruitment occupied a great deal of time in that first year, it benefited the organization immensely. Aside from the excitement FIGHT generated in the Black community, its organizational structure provided something of a clearinghouse for community issues. In 1965, during FIGHT's first year, those issues spanned housing, media reporting on African Americans and the Black community, and job referral and creation. Some of FIGHT's efforts were immediately visible to the public. Others were transmitted through member groups to the larger constituency.

By the end of 1965, FIGHT had earned a reputation for acting effectively on community concerns. It was a reputation well deserved. One example proves instructive. In April, FIGHT picketed two known slumlords at their own residences. A group of approximately one hundred African Americans arrived at each landlord's home, located in an all-white suburb, armed with signs and placards. Once there, they marched on the sidewalk for hours, all the while drawing the neighbors' attention and embarrassing the landlord. A member of the housing committee had notified the media of the events in advance, the better to provide citywide coverage of the action.

That particular action drew new member groups, initially encouraged by FIGHT, to join the Delegates Council. Groups such as the Edward Vose Neighborhood Association formed and approached FIGHT's steering committee for assistance. Apparently unable to sway their landlord, Mr. Gray, to respond to concerns about a property at 31–33 Thomas Street, the tenants brought a list of more than thirty issues to FIGHT. In response, the FIGHT housing committee organized an action plan consisting of several steps. First, they facilitated a meeting between the tenants, the housing committee, and the city's building bureau to investigate the tenants' concerns and the building's condition. Second, FIGHT housing committee members secured a copy of Rochester's housing code so as to serve as an informed assistant to the tenants' association. Third, they invited the landlord to meet with FIGHT representatives. Should he fail to meet with the group, members of the committee would organize additional action against him. Their plan was flawlessly executed. A building inspector cited twenty-three violations, and the landlord agreed to turn up at a FIGHT housing committee meeting to address tenant concerns.[82] Plans to continue picketing Mr. Gray's personal residence were aborted.

Immediate action, such as that taken in the case of Mr. Gray, convinced community members that FIGHT would amplify their voices on all matters. At the same time, evidence suggests that FIGHT increasingly took an active role in mediating and adjudicating their housing concerns. Like the tenants at 31–33 Thomas Street, residents of Hanover Houses, a local housing project, formed a tenants' association under the tutelage of Mildred Johnson. In trying to resolve "violations existing on apartments in the projects [and] tenants dissatisfaction with Hanover Houses Management," the tenant association's spokesman, Mrs. Hampton, approached FIGHT's steering committee. In turn, FIGHT proposed a solution that would "unite the thinking and efforts of all groups concerned—all to the benefit of the tenants of the project." Mrs. Hampton took the proposal back to the tenants for approval, and FIGHT turned the matter over to the housing committee to follow through should the tenants agree.[83] It is unsurprising that one of FIGHT's foremost concerns at its inception was housing, particularly given Black activists' loud calls for housing reform in the prerebellion moment.

While housing proved a central concern to residents and FIGHT alike, the various committees, from steering on down, acted upon other issues of local concern. Representatives from member groups registered matters that were raised at their individual meetings. For a particular group, a traffic light at an intersection might be needed, so the issue was brought to FIGHT. In turn, FIGHT would use its collective might to lobby city government to provide the necessary improvement. All FIGHT actions were driven by suggestions, feedback, and concerns of member groups.

Having become the conduit for all things Black Rochester, FIGHT's steering committee began to tackle larger, systemic issues. Media coverage of the Black community remained unsatisfactory, despite the hiring of the well-known African American reporter Earl Caldwell a few years earlier. Urban renewal plans continued, often without any input from the residents affected. Corporations failed to hire Black applicants despite a labor shortage. For each of these issues, the steering committee formed an issues committee. Each issues committee was comprised of a cross section of delegates or representatives from member groups, with a chair appointed by the steering committee. The chair and his/her committee members identified a specific problem, secured the necessary materials for making an informed decision, debated and agreed upon a course of action, and then made a recommendation to the duly elected steering committee before acting upon the proposed plan. In its first year, FIGHT's success was threefold: First, the group grew its membership by organizing people into small member groups, encouraging a sense of belonging that many had never experienced. Second, as this brought various groups together, FIGHT's membership multiplied its strength and magnified its voice. Third, FIGHT's impressive numbers convinced landlords, city hall, and corporations to sit down at the table with the organization to negotiate its demands.

Countering FIGHT

FIGHT would emerge as the loudest and brashest response to the 1964 uprising, but it was hardly the sole organizational effort in the works. Given the hit that Rochester's corporate reputation had taken as a result of the rebellion, many in the city explored "riot prevention" strategies. However, city leaders and corporate executives sought organizational vehicles that would remain under their control. They looked to the Economic Opportunity Act of 1964 (EOA), passed by Congress and signed into law by President Johnson shortly after the Rochester uprising. A central component of Johnson's Great Society and the War on Poverty, the EOA provided funds for development and implementation of locally run programs such as Head Start, Job Corps, Work Study, and Adult Basic Education. In addition to creating and funding such programs, the EOA legislation called for "maximum feasible participation" by the poor. The curious and unprecedented phrasing continues to be shrouded in mystery, one scholar noting that "even among those who framed the Economic Opportunity Act, there is little consensus about how the phrase 'maximum feasible participation' was formulated or about its intended meaning."[84] If the framers of the legislation were unclear about its intended meaning, local communities wasted no time in defining it. This particular requirement became at once a source of contention and a powerful weapon for the poor across the United States.

In Rochester, the EOA legislation prompted the formation of Action for a Better Community (ABC) to serve as a conduit for the federal EOA funds. Walter Cooper—Constance Mitchell's campaign manager, Baden Street Rally veteran, and research scientist at Eastman Kodak—was chosen to serve a six-month stint as the interim associate director. A skilled organizer, he abandoned his scientific research for a period to establish the various policies, procedures, and committees that would make up ABC. For Cooper, economic poverty was rooted "generally in a lack of educational achievement." He noted, "Earning power today is closely correlated with education."[85] As children, Cooper and several of his running mates had escaped abject poverty through educational attainment.[86] It is no surprise then that the major thrust of his ABC efforts created educational opportunities for both children and adults in Rochester's ghettoes. He apparently met with some success. Within a year of ABC's inception, Congressman Frank Horton, representing Monroe County, would proudly boast at congressional hearings, "The private nonprofit agency which was created last year to carry out the various community action programs of the Economic Opportunity Act . . . ABC, Inc., draws its membership from a considerable cross section of Rochester and Monroe County. Public and private social welfare agencies, educational institutions, business, labor organizations, religious faiths, civil rights movements and government are all represented and all participate actively in the formulation of policies and programs."[87] Despite the glowing recommendation provided by Congressman Horton, his lengthy list of participants made no mention of the poor themselves, a crucial component of "maximum feasible participation."

A second crucial dimension of ABC's efforts turned on its Neighborhood Services Committee. This particular committee was charged with creating neighborhood service centers for one-stop, social-service shopping. Once established in a neighborhood, community members could find childcare, physical and health services, and education and tutoring services, in addition to job referrals. Each of these services reflected the committee's position that "the major problems faced by people living in poverty . . . [are] housing, education, employment, discrimination, cultural deprivation, etc., as well as the more subtle problems of hopelessness, apathy, lack of motivation, etc. Concomitants related to all of these problems are family disorganization and break-up, delinquency, crime, illiteracy, mental and physical health breakdown, plus many others."[88] By June 1965, less than a year after its inauguration, ABC received $900,000 in funds from the federal government for programs ranging from daycare to training centers to Head Start. By August, its budget had increased by nearly $3 million in federal grants.

At the same time, FIGHT had begun its campaign for the hearts and minds of Rochester's Black communities, building its reputation on self-determination. Poor Black people should decide what they needed, who should get it for them, where it should happen, and how to go about getting it, FIGHT boldly declared. That ABC's board of directors—consisting of corporate officers, settlement house directors, and members of city hall—selected Cooper and others to head the antipoverty organization without consulting FIGHT or its member organizations smacked of paternalism. ABC was not an indigenous operation and therefore became a foil for building FIGHT's oppositional identity. The Citizens Advisory Committee, especially, became a target of FIGHT's ire.

The Citizens Advisory Committee attempted to meet the requirement for maximum feasible participation by choosing members from among those who lived in the designated poverty areas. FIGHT argued, however, that ABC's directors handpicked the members, leaving the poor no opportunity to choose their own representatives. Therefore, FIGHT concluded, ABC spent federal antipoverty funds without meeting the stipulation of maximum feasible participation. In typical fashion, FIGHT members stormed the first public meeting of the Citizens Advisory Committee. With only six committee members present, the FIGHT contingent of forty to fifty people overwhelmed the meeting.[89] The FIGHT supporters listened patiently for thirty-five minutes to reports on ABC programs. When the session was opened for questions, FIGHT pounced. They demanded of the new director, "How much money do you make?" Rather than answering, as Ed Chambers described it, "he came charging down the center aisle saying, 'What's behind that question?'"[90] What lay behind that question, of course, was an assertion that poverty funds created more jobs and revenue for middle-class professionals than for the poor.

The neighborhood community centers, which were slated for discussion at this meeting, came under specific attack. FIGHT's criticism was twofold. Some members of the community felt the centers were poorly constructed and poorly run. An official from the 4-H Club, a youth development and mentoring organization, agreed that ABC's first neighborhood service center was open, functioning, and had appropriate funding, but that the "roof leaks . . . [and] floors are in dire need of repair. . . . There are no shades or curtains of any sort for the windows, and there is 'minimum' equipment in the way of tables, chairs, etc."[91] For this individual, the center, intended to be a beacon for advancement and self-respect, was not up to the task. Likewise, members of FIGHT charged ABC with negligence in creating the centers. That a white woman directed the first such neighborhood center compounded FIGHT's anger and backed its claim that ABC only created jobs for middle-class professionals. While the neighborhood community centers would eventually employ some poor Black women as nursery aids and cooks, ABC readily admitted that they did not "have many jobs to give to the poor."[92]

FIGHT's second criticism dispensed with the center's operations to address its purpose. ABC advertised that neighborhood community centers brought together "all kinds of services, including medical, mental, welfare, employment, and legal."[93] The Reverend Marvin Chandler, now a FIGHT vice president, scolded ABC: "I'm saying to you that we are neither sick nor crazy. We don't need physical examinations. We need job[s] and money."[94]

At a second meeting of the Citizens Advisory Council, FIGHT continued its critique of ABC. The mild-mannered Chandler said, "Those of us who represent the poor are saying that ABC ought to be more *of* the poor than *for* the poor. . . . I ask you, who chose you to represent us?"[95] Another FIGHT vice president chimed in, invoking the federal legislation. He stressed "that the law calls for maximum feasible participation of the poor and asked that boards representing the poor, and appointed from the poor, be set up to establish programs and policies for antipoverty neighborhood service centers."[96] FIGHT's mouthpiece, the *FIGHTER*, would identify the community centers as "another example of thinking for Negroes, without asking us what we want before anything is done. After all, we only live there, we are not supposed to know what's best for ourselves and our children."[97] Desmond Stone, a local reporter sympathetic to the Black struggle, noted that at that meeting, "there were several further exchanges between FIGHT and ABC spokesmen on whether the centers should be run by the poor or by qualified professionals."[98]

Walter Cooper, now head of the ABC nominating committee, sought to mollify FIGHT. He informed the group's president, Franklin Florence, that he and two other FIGHT members had been nominated to the ABC board of directors.[99] Cooper clarified, however, that the nominees would be appointed "specifically as individuals and not as members of any organization."[100] Apparently viewing Cooper's condition as a distinction without a difference, the FIGHT members joined the ABC board and promptly sought to change its operating procedures. Among other things, they argued that meetings held in the middle of the day for the convenience of businessmen and government officials discriminated against the working poor, who were at their jobs, thereby violating the maximum feasible participation clause. If meetings were held in the evening, more of the poor would be able to attend to voice their concerns, the FIGHT members countered. They also asserted their right to hold up any plans for community centers in their neighborhoods and asserted the right of residents to determine how the centers would be staffed and where they would be located.[101]

FIGHT's goals in attacking the antipoverty program were twofold. First, in order to be successful, FIGHT believed it needed to be *the* voice of the Black poor in Rochester. Florence and others understood that if a more moderate Black organization existed in the community, the "power structure" would always use that alternative organization to subvert FIGHT's efforts, while at the same time extolling its racial progress. FIGHT's aggressive tactics were intended to expose ABC as a tool of the establishment. According to FIGHT, "many of the ABC programs now in progress generally embody the paternalistic philosophy of existing social welfare programs and heavily reflect the so-call 'zoo keeper' attitude, the attitude that the poor, like animals have to be taken care of and given enough to keep them quiet. . . . Such programs provide temporary relief but do not attack the causes of the poverty problem."[102] Second, FIGHT rejected any practice that made poverty more endurable by resisting ABC programs that simply provided escape routes to a few, insisting instead on structural changes to eradicate ghetto poverty more broadly.

FIGHT and ABC were not the only two competitors in the scramble for Black Rochester. The settlement houses, long providers of social services, viewed the conflict between FIGHT and ABC as an opportunity to reestablish their dominance in the afflicted wards. The settlement houses had long served the wards in which African Americans now lived. When European immigrants of various stripes resided in such wards, the settlement houses aided their transition, focusing on education and job training. As Black migrants replaced the white immigrants, the settlement houses increasingly came to focus on the "cultural deprivation" of the residents.[103] In 1967, the settlement house executives, chomping at the bit, used FIGHT's ongoing attack on ABC as a way to discredit the Black Power group in certain circles and to bolster their own influence. In fact, a statement drafted by three settlement house executives boldly tagged ABC and FIGHT as competition to their agencies and asserted the settlement houses' right to control the funding stream: "We Settlement executives feel that for any program to work to the best advantage of the community it must be a program developed in a cooperative, coordinated way with Agencies that have had the know-how for many years in terms of many types of services that people require."[104] This was the language FIGHT decried. The antipoverty programs were created to meet the needs of the poor, not for "the best advantage of the community."

At FIGHT's prompting, in 1967 the federal government interceded. The *Rochester Democrat and Chronicle* reported that the Citizens Advisory Council's appointment of people to sit on the board of ABC "does not qualify as 'democratic,' because the council members are not themselves chosen by the neighborhoods they are supposed to represent."[105] Here, a federal ruling vindicated FIGHT's position. The council—consisting of corporate officers, settlement house directors, and members of city hall—could not appoint the representatives of the poor. Rather, the poor would choose their own representatives. It was an important victory for the FIGHT organization. Even so, FIGHT continued to confront resistance from Rochester's power structure. Thus, in response to the policy change mandated for the ABC board, the editor of the *Rochester Times-Union* maintained, "There are some competent people on the ABC board who know how to get things done for the poor. But those whose only qualifications for a directorship are their personal poverty and obstreperousness should get out of their way."[106]

Less than a year into its existence, FIGHT was everywhere in Rochester, criticizing and opposing anything that did not lend itself to Black self-determination. It had taken on the poverty program. FIGHT members had also successfully picketed the suburban homes of white absentee landlords, embarrassing them in their own neighborhoods, to powerful effect. When the city's Human Relations Commission hired a white secretary, FIGHT demanded to know why a Black candidate had not been considered. As the city enacted stricter code enforcement in a Black neighborhood recently abandoned by white people, FIGHT demanded answers from the city government. Florence recalled, "This was during the formative days of the organization and we were, you know, we were fighting *everything*. I mean, to just, you know, to get out there."[107] In essence, FIGHT made it impossible for others to operate in the city of Rochester without considering how the organization would respond.

Perhaps no other event signaled FIGHT's rise to prominence more effectively than the rapid funding and formation of an Urban League branch in Rochester. To curb FIGHT's dominance in the new political landscape, the corporate community and city leaders sought a more moderate and tractable alternative. The Urban League was known for its work to assist African American migrants in the urban North. As such, it would have been ideal to help facilitate the post–World War II Black migration to Rochester. But rather than welcoming it, for years Rochester's industrial powers dissuaded local residents from forming a branch of the Urban League. It was not until FIGHT established itself as a controversial organization willing to challenge the pillars of the community that the city's industrial leaders and its Community Chest agreed to fund a branch of the Urban League.[108]

The Community Chest was Rochester's version of the United Way. It was "the major reservoir of charity funds and the pride of the city establishment. Its directors each year include[d] the chief corporate officers of such firms as Xerox, Eastman Kodak, Bausch & Lomb and the banks."[109] Walter Cooper, the architect for much of Rochester's antipoverty program, recalled approaching the Community Chest for funding to establish an Urban League chapter. "They came forth," Cooper recalled, "with forty-nine thousand dollars."[110] The Community Chest and many of the city's industrial leaders hoped an Urban League chapter would blunt FIGHT's popularity.

Yet not everyone in Black Rochester felt the need to choose between the newly formed Urban League chapter and FIGHT. One person who sought to split the difference was John Mitchell, at once a founding member of the Urban League chapter and a FIGHT supporter. Mitchell, however, was something of the exception. He recalled the class distinction between the two organizations: "The Urban League . . . picked up the banner and started comin' in and bringin' in more of the middle or professional Blacks into the Urban League." Such cleavages in turn served to fuel the oppositional consciousness of FIGHT and its leader, Minister Florence. Marcus Alexis, a professor of economics and one-time president of the Urban League, noted that some FIGHT members disparaged the educational attainment of many in the League: "You know, the same old names: [Drs.] Knox, Lee, Cooper, Woodward, and Alexis. And we were known as the Ph.D.'s. . . . And then of course, three of the Ph.D.'s worked at Kodak."[111] These African American PhDs working at Kodak felt their skills and experience with the business community offered them an opportunity to fulfill the Urban League's mission. The question was whether the business community would actually fund the Urban League to bring real change to Black Rochester, or just use it as a foil in the fight against FIGHT.

CHAPTER 5

Confrontation with Kodak

Corporate Responsibility Meets Black Power

During its 1966 annual convention, the FIGHT organization prepared to increase its profile in the city of Rochester. The organization's leaders recognized that to remain a powerful force, they must tackle the problem of the so-called hard-core unemployed. Largely ghetto-bound, the hard-core unemployed lacked the required education and training, skills, and prior experience to work in industrial settings; for some, criminal records and spotty employment histories further plagued them. Despite evidence to the contrary, many in Rochester—and across the nation—believed it was this population that was most likely to incite and participate in urban unrest. To prevent further outbreaks of "rioting," local, state, and national government, along with many in business, believed the hard-core unemployed needed incorporation into the mainstream economic systems. Certainly in Rochester, where unemployment was at 1.8 percent (the lowest of the thirty-nine major industrial areas in the United States) and ten thousand jobs went unfilled, this should have been a reasonable task to accomplish.[1] Yet in the midst of the now-famous urban crisis, many in business and government believed the hard-core unemployed were "unreachable." To be worth their salt, then, self-professed "ghetto organizations" such as FIGHT needed to demonstrate they could reach and sustain this population, turning them into "productive" members of society. No longer an upstart organization struggling to be recognized, FIGHT dedicated itself to assisting the urban Black unemployed. In the ensuing process, it demanded that Rochester's largest employer, the Eastman Kodak Company, the international film conglomerate headquartered in Rochester, share this responsibility by partnering with FIGHT and supporting its program for training and job creation.

For its part, the Eastman Kodak Company had been operating successfully in Rochester for nearly eighty years and had earned admiration locally and in the larger business world. By 1966, Kodak ranked thirty-five on *Fortune*'s list of America's largest corporations and was climbing.[2] Kodak was nationally known for its philanthropic support of arts, education, and healthcare, and for providing cradle-to-grave insurance and care for its employees. For its continuous ability to circumvent labor unions, Kodak was something of a corporate anomaly in the postwar era, making it a likely partner for FIGHT's job creation program.[3] Certainly in Rochester it had no industrial equal, employing a full 13 percent of the city's population, with several local sources estimating that nearly 40 percent of the city was either employed by Eastman Kodak or had a family member in the company's service. Driven by several consecutive years of record sales and growth, the company's influence in Rochester grew alongside its sizable donations to community institutions. But these great contributions came at a price to the community. Kodak enjoyed and expected the deference that accompanied its annual giving and had for some time asserted its right to rule the city by paternalistic philanthropy. Kodak directed; it did not take direction from others.

Still, as one reporter put it, "Kodak is considered both a good place to work and a good corporate citizen. The first to be asked to contribute to any cause, Kodak knew Fight [*sic*] would be calling."[4] Indeed, FIGHT did come calling. Envisioning an exchange between equals, FIGHT's president, Minister Franklin Florence, asked for a meeting with Kodak president William Vaughn in September 1966. Kodak accepted the request, but evidence suggests its executives expected to handle FIGHT as it handled other community organizations. Kodak was accustomed to asserting its own objectives and implementing its own plans and projects while directing the community to gratefully rally behind its efforts. "But in Minister Florence," *Business Weekly* would later report, "they did not precisely get a little old lady holding out a slotted collection can."[5] FIGHT was not another community group coming to the Eastman Kodak Company in search of a contribution to a worthy cause. Instead, its members desired a reciprocal relationship in which the two organizations realized the potential benefits of working with one another. As FIGHT envisioned it, Kodak would acknowledge that FIGHT was an integral community player and that the Black community had a right to expect and demand jobs. In exchange, FIGHT would create a direct line for Kodak to the hard-core unemployed.

Second, under FIGHT's guidance, the Black community would abandon rioting as a means to political, social, and economic advancement, sparing Kodak and the city of Rochester the embarrassment that accompanied the 1964 uprising. While Kodak relied on decades of community goodwill and successful business practices to legitimate itself, its reputation had suffered as a result of the rebellion. FIGHT, on the other hand, had only the promise of its organizing strength and its ability to keep peace in the streets of Rochester to offer.

The resulting negotiations between FIGHT and Kodak lasted some ten months, were mostly unpleasant, and would ultimately rewrite the rules of corporate responsibility in the United States. In fact, James Farmer, writing about Rochester, asserted, "It is a different ballgame now and the rules are new. . . . What happens to paternalism when the child grows up? What happens to the formulae which have traditionally governed race relations in the nation when the factors in each equation have been shattered and reassembled in a constantly shifting pattern?"[6] As the nation watched the Rochester row, corporations around the country took note of FIGHT specifically, the emergence of Black Power organizations in the operation of urban centers more generally, and changing public sentiment about both. Around the country, those invested in business, in civil rights, and in the church debated the role of each in assuaging the urban ills in the communities in which they operated. The media asked its readers to decide to whom corporations were responsible and in what ways. Kodak would argue that it "[has] a social responsibility; but that since Kodak is a private business, it best helps society by being successful. [Kodak] did not feel there was any special obligation to take extraordinary measures to solve Rochester's particular ghetto problem."[7] FIGHT would argue to the contrary, "The establishment feels it can plan for us and not with us. The only thing the white paternalists want to know about Negroes is whether they will riot again this year. And that all depends . . . on how soon the whites learn Black men are human beings. They are not their simple children."[8] For nearly a year, Rochester asked the nation to decide if "the right to a job transcends the right to profits."[9]

Rochester's Remuneration Rebuked and Reproved

The twentieth century witnessed Rochester's grand entrance into the national business arena. A relatively small but innovative city, Rochester had impressive unemployment numbers that were the result of the Eastman Kodak Company and its subsidiaries. The camera and film behemoth continued to grow and hire even amid the Great Depression. In 1931, the company reported net earnings of $20,353,788, "surpassing all previous results except in the record-breaking year of 1929."[10] The city's economic growth and attendant wealth enjoyed by its companies and their employees was a source of envy to many in the nation. Eastman Kodak developed a reputation for sharing its phenomenal affluence with its workers. Those same workers also benefited from Kodak's pioneering labor-management conflict resolution strategies. To dissuade its employees from unionizing, Kodak offered employee stock options, improved health and retirement benefits, and provided recreational facilities to its employees, in addition to paying cash dividends as profits allowed. In the middle of the Great Depression, as employees lost their jobs all across the nation, Eastman Kodak continued to hire and paid handsome employee bonuses to boot.[11] "Bonus Day," the actual day Rochester employees received their wage-dividend checks, became an eagerly anticipated holiday of sorts. Parents allowed their children to stay home from school, and retail stores extended their hours, while furniture and auto dealerships planned their yearly sales to correspond with the Kodak distribution. In short, Rochester was feeling flush.

Kodak shared its wealth with its employees to be sure, but the corporation also donated significant funds to the University of Rochester, Strong Memorial Hospital, and other local institutions.[12] In exchange, Kodak exacted a toll from the city of Rochester. One scholar aptly compared Kodak to "the benevolent Puritan father who, while making sure of his children's welfare, does not hesitate to discipline them should they fail to measure up to his standards and values." He continued: "Keeping its employees happy with generous bonuses, good working conditions, and other benefits, the company has remained free of unions and has carefully guarded the established prerogatives of management."[13] Given that many of Rochester residents were either employed by Eastman Kodak or had a family member who worked for the company or one of its beneficiaries, its control over the city was pervasive. When Kodak made its wishes clear, local government, churches, and residents jumped to do its bidding.

This twentieth-century windfall made Rochester something of a model city for the nation's business world. Corporations that seemed constantly engaged in labor disputes watched Kodak closely. As President Franklin Delano Roosevelt drafted antimonopoly labor legislation, his emissary Robert Jackson toured the nation, touting "the growth of the Eastman Kodak Company, . . . saying 'there is no better illustration of the kind of business which this nation ought to foster than the kind of business you have fostered here. . . . The biggest threat to the enterprise and sound business of a city such as you or I live in is the threat of the speculating financiers, who grab these locally developed industries for exploitation.'"[14] This locally developed industry, however, was no small-town venture. Kodak continued to grow during World War II, unabashedly declaring itself "a veritable arsenal of photography."[15] Success generated during the war years earned Kodak officials the attention of the nation's presidents from Roosevelt to Dwight Eisenhower, who frequently recruited staff from Kodak's ranks.[16] If Rochester, through its economic success, had made its mark politically, it only remained for it to become culturally relevant. In the summer of 1957, with the advent of television, Kodak edged out Lincoln Automobiles for corporate sponsorship of the popular *Ed Sullivan Show*.[17] Rochester had indeed arrived on the national scene.

Between 1900 and 1930, in what scholar Juliet E. K. Walker has deemed the "Golden Age of Black Business," the relative peace and tranquility brought to Rochester by Kodak's success also bolstered the city's miniscule Black community, which comprised less than 1 percent of its total population of 305,000.[18] Despite the small number of African Americans, white affluence drove a demand for Black labor, not in the city's highly skilled, technical industries, but in the service industry: the kitchens, the cars, and the caravansaries of upwardly mobile white Rochester. Black porters, messengers, maintenance workers, and stockmen joined the city's chauffeurs, maids, service employees, and those who found employment in nearby mills, gypsum mines, and, during World War I, an ammunition factory. These workers and their income provided the basis for a Black economy and drove a short-lived proliferation of small Black businesses.[19] A 1926 city directory reported no less than forty such establishments.[20] Many of these were small family-owned shops. The Gibson family, for example, operated both the Gibson Hotel and Apartments and the adjacent Gibson Dining Hall, which served "meals at all hours" and offered dancing every night. Fred and Horace Jentons ran both a realty corporation and a "cash grocery," the former likely operated out of the latter.[21] But as with Black businesses everywhere, the Great Depression took its toll on the Jentonses. "A tightening economy," Rochester historian Adolph Dupree asserted, "squeezed out many of the smaller Black business enterprises through decreasing capitalization and stiffer competition from white business owners."[22] The Jentonses, who had purchased their real estate by using one piece of property as collateral for another, lost everything and moved to Washington, DC. Their story was not unusual in Rochester; a vital Black economy would not reemerge there until the latter half of the century in a frenzy of Black organizing. In the meantime, Black Rochester struggled to make inroads in the white-dominated industrial and corporate community.

The 1964 uprising served as a watershed moment, dramatically altering the reputation and success of Rochester's business community. Having wet their feet in Rochester's political well, FIGHT's leaders set their sights on Kodak. As previously indicated, FIGHT's targeting of Kodak was not random. Kodak was a company to be watched and modeled. Where Kodak led, other corporations followed.[23] But Kodak's national reputation, once a treasured asset, became a colossal liability in the wake of the uprising. Rochester's Catholic bishop Fulton Sheen would later note of Kodak and Rochester: "The whole world looks at Rochester . . . but it does not see the city's beauty; it sees the blemish on its face."[24]

Despite the hiring of men such as Walter Cooper, Kodak had developed a somewhat different reputation for refusing to hire African Americans in all but the most demeaning of jobs. As early as 1939, it will be recalled, a previous generation of Black leaders had challenged Kodak's founder George Eastman to hire graduates from the Black colleges and universities that benefitted from his philanthropy.[25] Evidence of Kodak's racism—institutional and otherwise—persisted into the post-riot period. The company's director of industrial relations, Monroe C. Dill, announced in the wake of the 1964 riot that Kodak was not "in the habit of hiring bodies. We seek skills. We don't grow many peanuts in Eastman Kodak," suggesting of course that African Americans were not fit for employment there.[26] Despite the negative response that Kodak engendered with Dill's remarks, future Kodak president Louis K. Eilers would reportedly inform one of Rochester's most respected Black ministers, "You know, we did your folks, we did you an enormous favor. We took you out of Africa where you were eating worms and things."[27] Given the personal sentiments of Kodak's top executives, it is easy to see how corporate policies discriminating against African Americans would follow. Several Black Rochester residents recalled applying for jobs at Eastman Kodak in the 1950s and 1960s only to be told, "We don't have any colored jobs. [We] got some jobs, but nothing for you."[28] One African American who did work for Kodak recalled his experiences there:

> Well, I started out as, just as everybody else back in those days—Blacks, colored, Negro, whatever area, age, you were in. The only jobs you could get is either running the elevator, moppin' floors, or "trucking," as they called it—taking material from one machine to another. . . . They had a gentleman there who didn't go to the service, went to RIT, got the management degrees and his salesman's and everything else there that they would teach him. When he came back to Kodak, there was no job for him.[29]

For his part, the same employee recalled that to secure a better position at Kodak, he leveraged his athletic ability. Kodak, like most Rochester corporations, played basketball in the intramural company league. Charles Price remembered, "I told them, 'Well if you want me to play on your team, you know, give me a little better job than pickin' up papers or moppin' floors.' They gave me a job in an experimental lab."[30] Kodak's competing reputations, nationally and locally derived, made it an ideal target for FIGHT. FIGHT's president, Minister Franklin Florence, felt "that if [they] could get Kodak in line, every other business [in Rochester] would follow."[31]

Paternalism Meets Black Power

To get Kodak in line, Florence led a small delegation of FIGHT officers to the company's headquarters in the fall of 1966 and demanded to see the president. Once an audience was gained, FIGHT proposed a program in which Kodak would hire and then train five to six hundred African Americans who could not meet Kodak's regular standards (which required a high school diploma) for entry-level positions across the board in the film and camera industry. Florence passionately argued that he was "not talking about the man who can compete. We're talking about the down-and-out, the man crushed by this evil system, the man emasculated, who can't make it on his own. He has a right to work."[32] Though Florence's rhetoric privileged men, FIGHT's job training committee also sought jobs for women.[33] In exchange for Kodak's hiring the hard-core unemployed, FIGHT offered to provide recruitment and counseling to the trainees, and advice, consultation, and assistance to Kodak for the duration of the project. Kodak president William Vaughn politely declined FIGHT's proposal but agreed to another meeting to discuss ways in which FIGHT could support existing Kodak programs. At that next meeting FIGHT arrived with its proposed demands in writing. Apparently Kodak was no more swayed by the written word than by the spoken. Again, Vaughn and his men said no but persisted in their attempts to redirect FIGHT's attention to Kodak's programs.[34]

For several months, meetings continued between the two entities without substantial progress; their engagement, however, became increasingly ugly. The underlying conflict was simple. FIGHT demanded the power to negotiate with Kodak as an equal player, while Kodak refused to share the helm with any organization, particularly a Black Power organization that made labor demands. All the while, their progress—or lack thereof—was followed closely in the local newspapers. Rochesterians, Black and white, watched with bated breath. Having learned something about the power of media, Minister Florence held a press conference after each Kodak encounter to present FIGHT's position and to expose Kodak's. Despite its inability to move Kodak with this strategy, FIGHT kept the issue alive in the local papers and by putting constant pressure on Kodak. Florence and his Industrial Areas Foundation counterparts Saul Alinsky and Ed

Chambers were also busily converting potential sympathizers to their cause on a national scale. Florence traveled to the 1966 Black Power Conference in Washington, DC, to tell the tale of FIGHT and Kodak in Rochester, while Alinsky worked the Jewish circuit, contacting national Jewish organizations to hear FIGHT's story.[35] Both were building support for a national campaign against Kodak should their confrontation come to that. Alinsky prophesied, "I tell you this, Eastman Kodak has plenty to be concerned about, because this kind of an issue . . . if it ever develops . . . and it may well develop . . . will become a nationwide issue across the board to every negro [sic] ghetto in America."[36]

Back in Rochester, the issue became increasingly divisive. Rather than implement FIGHT's proposal, Kodak hired the Indianapolis-based Board of Fundamental Education to "institute a program of remedial studies for illiterate and near-illiterate" potential employees. It was an obvious attempt to earn goodwill in the community while cutting FIGHT and Minister Florence out.[37] In response, FIGHT stepped up the attack on Kodak, no longer asking for a joint job-training program, but demanding one. No one had ever made demands of this kind on Kodak. Many believed that FIGHT's undertaking—to affirm Florence's assertion that "the right to jobs transcends the right to make money"—held the potential to turn that tide.[38] As summer became fall and fall turned to winter, the city's institutions and population split in their support; some believed FIGHT was out of line, while others hoped Kodak's smugness could be checked. Animosity gripped the city. Local news editor Paul Miller sided with Kodak and took every opportunity to lambast FIGHT and Florence in his editorial pages. But in the pulpit, if not across the pew, FIGHT found support in the city's churches. The Rochester Area Council of Churches and many of its denominations supported FIGHT and its attempts to remedy the ills of urban poverty. The laity, however, found themselves divided. Some were members of Friends of FIGHT, the white auxiliary formed to support the Black Power organization. Others were Kodak employees who had greatly benefited from Kodak's largesse and wholeheartedly supported their employer. Still another group belonged to the ranks of both Friends of FIGHT and Kodak. In fact, the conflict would fracture Rochester so deeply that before it ended, local lore would be established. A white minister, by all accounts unaccustomed to the harassment faced by Movement activists, hung himself in his basement to escape the constant barrage of angry phone calls he received for supporting FIGHT; a Black minister reported finding the lug nuts on his tires loosened after a FIGHT meeting; and new Kodak president Louis Eilers had installed a device to intercept abusive calls to his personal phone line.[39]

As the impasse continued, a major stumbling block became the negotiators involved. Neither side approved of the other's negotiating team. In fact,

Kodak was disinclined to use the term "negotiating team" at all, as it smacked of a labor conflict. At one point, Monroe Dill, the industrial relations director, reminded a reporter, "The officials [working with FIGHT] should not be designated a 'negotiating' team. We think of these talks as discussions, not negotiations."[40] Nonetheless, many believed if the spokesmen were replaced, a resolution could emerge. Here, members of the suburban Third Presbyterian Church interceded. A well-positioned member of the church connected John Mulder, both a member of Third Presbyterian and an assistant vice president at Kodak, with the Reverend Marvin Chandler, a member of the Rochester Area Council of Churches and a FIGHT vice president. The two discussed the Kodak-FIGHT impasse that continued to dominate the pages of the local papers. Both parties agreed they might work together and approached their respective sides to gain organizational permission to continue talks. Mulder proposed that he head a new team to meet with FIGHT; this team would consist of men directly responsible for Kodak's hiring and training, men who understood what was possible within the company. Vaughn, who was about to leave his position as president to become the chair of board and who was tired of the negative media attention surrounding his inability to successfully negotiate with African Americans, agreed to Mulder's proposal.

Led by John Mulder, the new Kodak team met secretly with FIGHT leaders for two days in Rochester's Downtowner Motel, which was no small feat given the media interest in the controversy. During that time, the two sides made progress in multiple ways. First, and perhaps most importantly for the players involved, they began to develop a relationship of trust. Chandler recalled that while "John Mulder didn't understand [the Black church experience], he didn't understand all that," he "really honored me by giving me *his* trust to try to make these connections, which we did."[41] Second, on December 20, just days before Christmas, the two sides emerged with a gift in hand, a peace offering for Rochester. They had signed an agreement providing for the "recruitment and referral" of six hundred hard-core unemployed "over a 24-month period, barring unforeseen economic changes affecting the Rochester community."[42] The agreement also called for the two organizations to familiarize each other with their respective operations, to share information on referrals, and to continue semi-monthly meetings to increase the program's effectiveness.[43] These were terms that Mulder believed Kodak could agree to. Both teams were jubilant; both returned to their people to share the news and expectantly await their holiday celebrations. According to FIGHT's standard operating procedure, Florence called a press conference to announce the agreement. It appeared that Rochester would enjoy a peaceful holiday.

But that was not to be. The next morning, unbeknownst to FIGHT, Kodak's executive committee met to discuss the accord. They unanimously voted to rescind the agreement. Later that day, Kodak's board of directors seconded the committee's decision. Publicly, the company would declare that John Mulder lacked the authorization to sign such an agreement. Kodak's chair of the board reportedly described this period of negotiations as the "Mulder Misadventure" at the annual stockholder's meeting in Flemington, New Jersey.[44] Secretly, the executives disliked the preferential hiring of African Americans, particularly those supported by a Black Power organization, and they feared anything that smacked of a labor contract, a trap Kodak had avoided for nearly a century. Mulder was immediately called to account in Louis Eilers's office. Eilers was set to replace Vaughn as Kodak president on January 1, and Eilers was not pleased that the FIGHT controversy had become one of his first responsibilities. He forbade Mulder to discuss the matter publicly, a command that Mulder has honored ever since. In the press, which was unable to detail Mulder's version of the events, Eilers would later describe Mulder as well-meaning but overzealous and liberal. Mulder would lose his post as an assistant vice president at Kodak before the misadventure was over.[45]

When Mulder realized that Kodak would not honor the agreement he had signed, he immediately called Chandler to ask if he could stop by his home. Chandler received the call in the midst of a holiday/victory celebration with Rochester's Black ministers and invited him to join them, given that Florence was also in attendance. When Mulder walked into the living room, "his eyes . . . full of tears," everyone present understood from his demeanor that the agreement would not come to fruition. Florence recalled that Mulder "looked like Christ must have looked when Peter denied him."[46] His delivery of the information in person, however, further endeared him to the FIGHT contingent.[47] Kodak's repudiation of the signed document led local reporter Desmond Stone to declare the December 20th agreement "the most controversial piece of paper in Rochester's history."[48]

The fallout from the repudiated agreement was catastrophic, as recrimination replaced disappointment. Both sides staged press conferences, took out full-page advertisements in the local papers, consulted with their constituencies, and prophesied the outcome for Rochester if the struggle continued. Kodak claimed it was not being racist; on the contrary, preferential hiring of African Americans, it claimed, "violated anti-discrimination laws."[49] Kodak simply could not "discriminate by having an exclusive recruiting arrangement with any organization."[50] Its executives assuaged their having reneged by pointing to a recent history of training initiatives and hiring practices benefiting, among others, African Americans. Eilers would later deem these programs "the white hope for the poor of Rochester."[51] FIGHT, the company claimed, was simply engaging in corporate harassment and failed to work with existing Kodak programs. Kodak's resistance to the agreement was most likely the result of several decades of anti-union labor policy. "We will not sign anything," Eilers clarified, "that gives a third party a voice in the formulation of industrial relations policy to do with hiring and placing."[52] Florence, however, had no interest in labor unions, an exclusive arrangement, or harassment for the sake of harassment. His concern lay with the Black poor: "When [Kodak] tore up that agreement, they tore up the hopes of the poor people of Rochester. The issue is, they have signed an agreement with us—are they honorable men? Do their signatures mean one thing to white men, another to Black?"[53]

With the repudiation of the agreement, FIGHT pulled out all the stops. Minister Florence warned of an impending "long hot summer," rekindling fears of another revolt. "What happens in Rochester in the summer of '67," he cautioned, "is at the doorstep of [the] Eastman Kodak Company."[54] Florence's prediction was seconded during the timely visit of Stokely Carmichael, that "high priest of 'Black Power,'" who descended upon Rochester to offer FIGHT his support.[55] The chair of the Student Nonviolent Coordinating Committee (SNCC), Carmichael was affiliated with Saul Alinsky and IAF projects in Detroit, though in true Black Power fashion, he indicated to his audience that "his organization was supporting only FIGHT, not Alinsky-organized groups in other cities."[56] Carmichael was followed into Rochester by national television crews from NBC and CBS that were only too happy to broadcast his statements to a national audience.[57] With the spotlight on him, Carmichael warned Kodak and its supporters that SNCC had "been looking for a fight against a big company to show Black people across the country about institutional racism. You've got everything we're looking for. . . . We're going to bring them to their knees if it's the last thing we do. When we're through, they'll see him [indicating Florence] and he'll say, 'Jump,' and they'll say, 'How high?'"[58] WNYR, a local station, became nearly hysterical at the presence of Carmichael and the national media in Rochester. Its fear that Rochester would be portrayed negatively across the nation mirrored Kodak's: "And now the television film will be taken to studios far from Rochester, edited and probably sent into millions of homes across the U.S. The nation will get a look at what they have no choice but to believe is our city."[59] Kodak remained silent regarding Carmichael's threat of an international boycott, but clearly FIGHT had raised the stakes.

FIGHT's leaders began to recognize their next step; little more would be accomplished if they continued to wage their battle in Rochester alone. If Kodak was to be persuaded, they realized, it would happen in the national spotlight. This prompted an abrupt change in course and two new strategies. For the first time, FIGHT directed its appeals that the December 20th agreement be honored not to Kodak executives, but directly to the company's shareholders. FIGHT also sought to maximize its local church-based support by enlisting assistance from the National Council of Churches and its various national affiliates. Both strategies were new to the Black Power movement and, therefore, garnered increased media attention.

Given Kodak's repudiation of the December 20th agreement and FIGHT's advertisement of that repudiation as a double-crossing of the poor, church groups rallied behind FIGHT's efforts. In January, the National Council of Churches' Commission on Religion and Race, the Board of National Missions of the United Presbyterian Church in the USA, the United Presbyterian Church's New York Synod, and the Board for Homeland Ministries of the United Church of Christ (Congregational and Evangelical & Reformed) and the Unitarian Universalist Association led the national church effort to support FIGHT by sending a joint telegram to Kodak president Louis Eilers, informing him that they were "gravely concerned about employment opportunities at Eastman Kodak." The telegram continued: "Believe good faith negotiation with FIGHT should continue. Urge that Dec. 20 agreement be honored."[60] Once on board, these national bodies continued their efforts by lobbying their respective churches and affiliates to investigate the Rochester situation further and support FIGHT. They sent passionate letters to their various memberships outlining the work that FIGHT was doing to alleviate poverty in Rochester, the need for effective leadership to represent the poor, and the preordained role of the church in poverty struggles.[61] The Rochester controversy thus became a frequent topic in both church newsletters and sermons.

With the churches largely supporting FIGHT's position, Florence and Alinsky implemented the next phase in their campaign to force Kodak to honor its signed agreement.[62] "Keep your sermons," they requested of the churches. "Give us your stocks!"[63] Florence and the FIGHT leadership implemented a tactic that activists in organizations such as Carmichael's SNCC had recently begun to explore.[64] FIGHT asked national church bodies to withhold their shareholder proxies at Kodak's annual meeting. Every shareholder of a publicly traded company has the option of attending the annual shareholders meeting and the right to vote on corporate matters, including the election of officers. Frequently, stockholding organizations (such as churches) will simply sign a proxy form authorizing the company's president or the chair of the board to vote on their behalf. Instead of following this course, FIGHT asked these churches to transfer their proxy forms to FIGHT, or at the very least to withhold their proxies from Kodak officers. In so doing, the church leadership would be expected to attend the shareholders meeting to publicly question Kodak's reneging on the December 20th agreement. *Presbyterian Life* reported, "There followed the unprecedented refusal of boards and agencies . . . to entrust their proxies to company management at the annual stockholder's meeting. The questions raised at that meeting may make a national issue of Kodak's employment practices."[65] The strategy was an immediate success. The national bodies of the Episcopal Church and the Church of Christ not only signed over their proxy forms to FIGHT, but sent an evaluation of the Rochester situation to each of their churches across the nation. The National Council of Churches asked its members to give Christian assistance to FIGHT in the struggle against Kodak, prompting discussions in the pulpit and the pew.

All You Need Is One Share

FIGHT stopped or slowed all other organizational efforts in preparation for the annual Kodak meeting. Minister Florence and Ed Chambers, the IAF staff person, reassigned all staff members to maximize their manpower for "Focus on Flemington."[66] In addition to asking national church bodies to withhold their proxies, FIGHT purchased ten shares of Kodak stock; with those shares it gained access to the annual meeting in Flemington, New Jersey, for ten members of FIGHT's executive board.[67] Once there, FIGHT hoped to disrupt the meeting and then force Kodak to recognize and honor the rescinded December 20th agreement. Planning began in earnest to recruit large numbers of supporters for the Flemington event.

By far the most damaging aspect of FIGHT's new campaign, however, was the national media attention both Kodak and Rochester received. All of a sudden, the Rochester struggle jumped from church bulletins and local papers to the pages of *Business Weekly*, *Fortune*, the *New York Times*, and the *Wall Street Journal*. A *New York Times* front-page headline announced, "All You Need Is One Share," while *U.S. News and World Report* offered "New Threat for Employers? What a Negro Group Seeks from Kodak." The *Washington Post* poked fun at the film company, offering its own headline, "Picture's Fuzzy as Kodak Fights FIGHT." From Kansas City to Cleveland, Washington, DC, to New York City, all eyes were on this new potential hazard to business. An Associated Press correspondent rightly summarized, "The Rochester struggle offers a study in microcosm of racial complexities facing large cities across the land: On the one hand, a militant 'Black Power' organization that purports to speak for the restless and exploited poor. On the other, a prestigious corporation that reflects, as few others, 'the establishment.' Caught in the crossfire are the churches, which helped give birth to the city's new Negro militancy; traditional civil rights groups, which find in Black Power an uneasy alliance; civic and social leaders, watching in anguish a wedge of discord knife through the community."[68] The outcome of this new strategy would reach far across the nation—indeed, *Fortune* magazine warned that Kodak's troubles "may be a portent of confrontations to come between other companies and other Negro organizations."[69]

As an unexpected outcome of the national media attention, FIGHT received proxy forms from individual Kodak shareholders far and near. Many individuals sent their proxy forms to FIGHT with heartfelt messages of support. One such note read, "Enclosed please find a proxy for my 56 shares signed over to you . . . to vote as best you see fit. I wholly approve of this approach to get action. MORE POWER TO YOU!!!!"[70] Still another read, "I would like very much to support you in your effort to induce Eastman Kodak to abide by its earlier agreement with your organization. I own some shares of Eastman Kodak and wonder whether it would help if I turned the proxy over to you. I don't think I shall be able to attend the stockholders meeting myself."[71] Though the *New York Times* would later report that "these expressions of stockholder discontent were too scattered to have much influence on management," most business journals and corporations acknowledged that "their potential influence is immense if the nation's growing ranks of stockholders could be mobilized to support them."[72] The potential had grown exponentially in the previous fifteen years. Between 1952 and 1967, during a postwar boom, the number of individual shareholders in the United States increased from 6.5 million to 20 million.[73] In addition to individual proxy contributions and the support of national church bodies, organizations such as the Young Women's Christian Association (YWCA) also withheld their proxy status. The NAACP's labor secretary, Herbert Hill, brought the Office of Federal Contract Compliance to bear by requesting that Kodak's federal contracts be canceled. For its part, Walter Reuther's Citizens Crusade against Poverty also promised to investigate Kodak.[74] FIGHT's plan was well underway.

As FIGHT and Kodak prepared for the annual meeting, tension and pressure continued to mount in Rochester and thus in Flemington, New Jersey, as well. As the Episcopal and the Methodist Churches added their shares to those that would be withheld from Kodak management, an interdenominational task force formed to pressure Kodak further. Its spokesperson warned that Rochester

is being talked about in Harlem, Boston, St. Louis and in all other ghettos from Chicago to Texas, and along the coast to Florida. The use of power is an essential ingredient in our country's economic position. Corporate power is very strong and there is some question about the way

Kodak used corporate power in this situation. There are a lot of anti-poverty people in churches who are interested in what is happening and who want to make sure this issue is not kept to Rochester but is raised in other communities to make certain other corporations do not do the same type of thing.[75]

The task force also took it upon itself to arrange transportation for concerned college students wanting to support FIGHT at the Flemington meeting. Robert Maurer, a student at New York's Union Theological Seminary, took the lead in organizing these student groups. He expected to enlist "busloads of students from about 15 colleges, including the University of Rochester, Princeton and Cornell."[76]

Aware of this massive organizing effort, Kodak executives prepared to defend themselves at the April meeting. In Rochester, William Vaughn, now Kodak's chairman of the board, practiced and rehearsed his role in the confab by answering questions aggressively delivered by his executives role-playing as "angry militants."[77] There was good reason for his preparation; the *New York Times* reported of the event, "When Eastman Kodak Co. President Louis K. Eilers takes the microphone tomorrow at the annual meeting here he'll be living a corporation president's nightmare. In the audience will be angry civil rights workers and ghetto organizers, intent church officials, and private citizens—all stockholders of Kodak and supporters of a militant Rochester Negro Organization."[78] Kodak's preparations were not limited to formulating answers to shareholder questions, but were also devoted to developing a full-fledged security and public relations campaign. In advance of the meeting, reported the *Rochester Times-Union*, "copies of Vaughn's remarks along with statements about Kodak's employment programs were packaged for distribution to guests as they left the meeting. Kodak guarded them ahead of time for fear they might be used against the company by its critics during the meeting." The company also "augmented its usual staff with extra public relations men and 21 security guards from its 250-man force in Rochester."[79]

Meanwhile, FIGHT continued both its organizational planning and its bluster. Florence declared that the civil rights movement was dead and that something new was needed to replace it.[80] He, along with the FIGHT leadership, believed the proxy strategy in the hands of Black Power organizations was just that something new. Once again, this posturing—asserting that FIGHT was on the cutting edge—drew the national television crews to FIGHT events. Bob Schackne of CBS assured the FIGHT organization that he would cover the events at Flemington and that perhaps some premeeting filming in Rochester was necessary. FIGHT too prepared for the upcoming meeting. Staff and vol-

unteers made placards and posters; bus captains were assigned and given instructions for keeping order en route to and in Flemington; and perhaps most
importantly, opportunities for resolution with Kodak were continually considered. Most of the parties involved, and some that were not, hoped for a
pre-Flemington resolution. Even New York Republican senator Jacob Javits
tentatively entered the fray, asking the Justice Department to intervene and
mediate. Though tight-lipped about how such a resolution might come about,
Javits and his team announced they were working on it. It is unclear whether
Javits had an inside track to the FIGHT organization, but the local papers reported that he scheduled a meeting with Kodak executives in advance of the
Flemington event to discuss the ongoing dispute.[81] While FIGHT had prepared
mightily for Flemington, the organization realized it was "in a situation . . .
where the threat of a demonstration is greater than the demonstration itself."[82]
Nonetheless, without a satisfactory resolution, FIGHT pressed on.

Buttressed by all this ballyhoo, FIGHT did not fail to deliver. With bus-
loads of supporters, all equipped with placards and signs, and proxy forms in
hand, FIGHT descended upon Flemington. In tightly disciplined ranks, the
FIGHT supporters, who came from Rochester, Chicago, Boston, and New
York City, carried signs warning, "Industry AVOID Rochester, NY" and "Broken Promises—Hot Summer." Others announced, "K.K.K. Kindly Kodak
Klan," "Kodak 61,000 Employees, Token Negroes," and "The Right to a Job
Transcends the Right to Profits."[83] Supporters also identified themselves geo-
graphically, educationally, and professionally by carrying identifiers such as
"Princeton on Principle," "Priest for FIGHT," and simply "Jersey City." They
marched from the Kodak offices downtown to the high school auditorium
where the annual meeting was set to take place. The demonstrators did not
speak, did not answer questions, and did not deviate from their instructions.
FIGHT leadership brought with them from Rochester a sound truck with
speakers, microphones, and a platform for addressing the crowd that gathered (see figure 5.1).

Awaiting the coming commotion, Flemington officials took several precau-
tions on the day of the event, canceling classes for the high school's students
and scheduling the town's full police force for duty. Kodak, too, brought its own
security forces to patrol the meeting and the grounds. The *World Journal Tribune* reported, "Heavy security was in effect as the meeting opened in an atmo-
sphere of tension. All persons entering the school had been stopped twice—once
to show their credentials and register, and again while waiting for a guard to
escort them inside in small groups."[84] The effect on this small, rural, New Jersey town was impressive, with the *New York Times* and news outlets across the
nation running multiple photos of the spectacle the following day.

FIGURE 5.1. Members of FIGHT picket at Kodak's shareholder meeting. Photograph, Flemington, NJ, 1967. Box 119, folder 1, Kodak Historical Collection #003, D.319, Rare Books, Special Collections, and Preservation, River Campus Libraries, University of Rochester. Credit: Used with permission from Eastman Kodak Company.

Amid the reporters and camera crews, FIGHT president Franklin Florence stormed into the shareholders meeting, interrupted the proceedings as soon as they began, and demanded to know if Kodak would honor the signed December 20th agreement. Without allowing Vaughn or Eilers a chance to answer, Florence gave the leaders two hours to discuss their response before he returned. This time frame also provided sympathetic shareholders an opportunity to question Kodak on the agreement and the company's labor policies. As Florence exited the meeting, portions of his supporters followed him out, while others stayed to question Eilers, Vaughn, and Kodak's legal team. Having thoroughly organized and rehearsed their actions, FIGHT came prepared with color-coded flags to indicate to supporters what their next step should be.[85] There was little disorder or hesitation as Florence left. The meeting continued with shareholders addressing pointed questions to Kodak's leadership. The leaders repeated the standard line—they could not legally or in good conscience honor the December 20th agreement, but they had implemented many other programs to address the labor needs of the hard-core unemployed in Rochester.

Outside, Florence and Alinsky were in their element, both making passionate speeches to the crowd and the media (see figure 5.2). Alinsky announced to reporters, "Eastman Kodak is going to make Bull Connor look like an integrationist."[86] He further "called upon all groups interested in civil rights to sell their stock in companies not favorable to civil rights and invest their money in those firms that are friendly to the Movement."[87] Meanwhile, Florence reminded the nation that temperatures (and tempers) were cool in April, but that soon "the long hot summer" would be upon them. His now famous refrain that "what happened in Rochester this summer lies at the foot of Eastman Kodak" garnered the media attention that FIGHT had come to expect. Newspaper headlines the following day from Kansas City to Boston reported "the threat of racial violence" if Kodak continued its present course.[88]

At 2:00 p.m., Florence returned to the auditorium, interrupting the shareholders meeting a second time to demand an answer to his previous question:

FIGURE 5.2.   Franklin Florence (center) with other ministers. Photograph, Flemington, NJ, 1967. Box 118, folder 8, Kodak Historical Collection #003, D.319, Rare Books, Special Collections, and Preservation, River Campus Libraries, University of Rochester. Credit: Used with permission from Eastman Kodak Company.

"Would Kodak honor the agreement?" In an equally loud and clear voice, re-portedly to the great cheering of Kodak employees and loud, angry boos from FIGHT supporters, William Vaughn repeated his answer: "No." Expecting no less, Florence exited the meeting to reveal FIGHT's next move to the crowd outdoors and, of course, to the national media gathered nearby. He promised to organize a national Black Power pilgrimage to Rochester. The date of this event, he announced, would coincide with the third anniversary of Roches-ter's 1964 uprising, arousing latent fears that further outbreaks of racial vio-lence were on the horizon. Florence, of course, only alluded to the possibility, but nearly all parties jumped on the reference.

Not to be outdone, Kodak also announced its next steps in the wake of the shareholders meeting. It seems management understood that the problem was largely one of public opinion. Their proposed solution involved making a $15,000 donation to the Flemington high school, where it had held the con-troversial meeting, and hiring Uptown Associates, a Black-owned advertising company to "explor[e] methods of giving better service to all our markets, including the ethnic market."[89] That the *New York Times* covered this develop-ment suggests just how tarnished Kodak's reputation was at the close of the shareholders meeting (see figure 5.3).

Whether or not Kodak executives feared Florence's threat of a Black Power pilgrimage to Rochester on the anniversary of the 1964 uprising, others in the state certainly did. New York had suffered disproportionate losses financially as well as in reputation during the early rebellions, both in Rochester and in Harlem. State officials could not in good conscience watch another one in the making. Senator Javits already had a failed intervention on his hands. Daniel Patrick Moynihan, famed sociologist responsible for the 1965 "Moynihan Re-port," interceded in the months that followed, imploring Kodak to go back to the bargaining table.[90] As director of the Joint Center for Urban Studies at Har-vard University and the Massachusetts Institute of Technology and a reputed expert on urban turmoil, Moynihan was as likely as any to intercede. He was acquainted with Kodak's assistant counsel, who reportedly asked the future senator to come to Rochester to discuss conditions.[91] By June, just weeks be-fore the pilgrimage was scheduled to take place, Kodak quietly made a working agreement with FIGHT to implement job training and employment for Roches-ter's hard-core unemployed. Despite the limited gains in the agreement— Kodak only agreed to a generic commitment to work with FIGHT in devising joint projects for Black employment and training—FIGHT claimed the victory.[92]

The immediate struggle between FIGHT and Eastman Kodak came to an anticlimactic close in June 1967, at FIGHT's annual meeting, a year after the Black Power organization decided to approach Kodak with a proposal for jobs.

FIGURE 5.3.   Franklin Florence picketing at Flemington. Photograph, Fleming, NJ, 1967. Box 119, folder 5, Kodak Historical Collection #003, D.319, Rare Books, Special Collections, and Preservation, River Campus Libraries, University of Rochester. Credit: Used with permission from Eastman Kodak Company.

The local outcome of this struggle cannot be overstated. Constance Mitchell recalled that in Rochester,

> it stood for opening the door to employment. And I think what opened the door to employment was going to Flemington, and bringing Kodak to its knees. And then when Kodak was brought to its knees, all of the sudden, General Motors and Strong and everybody else said, "You know, if they can bring Kodak to their knees, they can bring us to our knees. So maybe we need to open this door a little bit wider and offer some more entry level jobs." So I think that the manufacturing community came together and said, "Let's make sure that this door stays open, now that it's open." . . . I think that FIGHT forced their hand in Flemington, and I think the Kodak and the manufacturers decided to open up that door afterwards.[93]

The focus on jobs and training for African Americans, the sense of communal obligation for employment opportunities, and the realization that corporations needed to adjust their sense of responsibility began a series of marked changes in Rochester. As Mitchell noted, entry-level jobs opened to African Americans at a never-before-seen rate. But perhaps more importantly, the economic thrust of Black Power had been established. This victory for FIGHT established the organization as a formidable, if not entirely respected, player in Rochester's power structure. That victory also led to the further implementation of Black economic opportunities and development.

The exchange in Rochester, however, had implications well beyond that Northern city. The extensive coverage in the *Wall Street Journal, Business Weekly*, and the *New York Times* prompted a national debate over corporate responsibility and racial equality. FIGHT provided an opening salvo in a struggle to force corporations to act responsibly toward the poor and unemployed in the communities in which they operated. *Business Weekly*, perhaps more than any other publication, grasped the national significance of the FIGHT-Kodak conflict. In a summary article, the journal gave credence to Minister Florence's earlier boast that the civil rights movement was dead and that FIGHT's strategies would replace it: "The Kodak situation dramatically reveals that today's ghetto-bound, militant urban Negro may generate even more problems for business than the civil rights struggle in the South created. . . . Kodak's dealing with Fight [*sic*], in fact, starkly dramatize the clash of modern, radical Negro tactics with well-meaning but traditionalist business attitudes."[94]

That business corporations had a responsibility extending beyond traditional philanthropy to the communities in which they operated was significant in and of itself. But the implications of FIGHT's accomplishment extended beyond new visions of corporate morality and responsibility. The proxy strategy adapted by the FIGHT organization became a staple in the arsenal of activists over the next forty years. As students and antiwar activists came to challenge corporate underwriting of the war in Vietnam, colonialism in the third world, and apartheid in South Africa, the Rochester strategy would find new audiences.[95] Further, well-meaning church groups now possessed a successful example for supporting social and political causes across the globe. The same churches that supported FIGHT involved themselves in South African protests and refused to purchase supplies and services from companies that would not affirm equal employment opportunities. Buoyed by the Rochester success, these groups went so far as to create pamphlets for purchasing agents that listed companies with responsible hiring practices.[96] A new age in Black Power, corporate responsibility, and church involvement in economics and politics had dawned.

CHAPTER 6

FIGHTing for the Soul of Black Capitalism

Struggles for Black Economic Development in Postrebellion Rochester

By 1966, the Rochester uprising, the subsequent organizing frenzy, and FIGHT's confrontation with the Eastman Kodak Company highlighted the urgent need for economic development in the nation's ghettos.[1] In this new era of Black rebellion, Rochester emerged as a pioneer in the quest for Black economic development, which became something of a buzz phrase in the late 1960s. As urban uprisings swept the nation, the idea of Black economic development acquired wide appeal; it emerged as the latest effort by African Americans to enter the economic mainstream. But in practice, it proved to be a contentious and contested concept. For many, economic development of the ghetto would come to mean employment training and nondiscriminatory hiring practices, leading to job placement in existing, predominantly white-owned businesses. For others, economic development was synonymous with Black ownership, of which two approaches predominated. The first revolved around individual entrepreneurship, usually of small service or commercial-type businesses. The second approach to Black ownership presupposed a separate Black economy, an undertaking in which African Americans, cooperatively and collectively, would own and control the means of production in Black communities. Both approaches were capitalist, in that ownership would be vested in individuals or groups of individuals, although the collective approach also drew inspiration from various socialist economic systems. Proponents of the two approaches, the entrepreneurial and the cooperative, drove the contest in Rochester to define Black capitalism, where myriad national stakeholders—activists, politicians, entrepreneurs, corporate chiefs, and, not least, the federal government—closely watched and studied the various models emerging from that city.

FIGHT would not be the only organization to enter Rochester's contest to define Black capitalism. The Urban League, previously excluded from the city, quickly set up shop and got to work. Rochester Jobs Incorporated was also born in the aftermath of the rebellion to provide training and skills to unemployed workers, while the Rochester Business Opportunities Corporation competed to shape the parameters of Black capitalism. Black economic development emerged incrementally, but rapidly, in Rochester. While their ideologies and paths varied, each of these organizational efforts sought to break down racial discrimination in hiring, train Black workers for positions from which they had been excluded historically, and aggressively place them in factories and other industries. As might be expected, FIGHT would diverge from the pack by 1967, seeking additional opportunities to develop Black-owned, community-held businesses wherein profits and wealth would be returned to the larger Black community in the form of worker benefits, housing, childcare, and educational opportunities. This struggle to define Black capitalism in Rochester represented, in miniature, that larger quest for Black economic development, making Rochester both a national model and a symbol in the fight for the soul of Black capitalism.

The quest for Black ownership and control of the means of production may have assumed novel forms in the era of Black Power, but the fight for Black capitalism was not new in Rochester or elsewhere. As Malcolm X endeavored to build his Muslim Mosque Inc., he toured the nation's industrial cities in 1964, making the case for Black economic development:

> The economic philosophy of black nationalism means in every church, in every civic organization, in every fraternal order, it's time now for our people to become conscious of the importance of controlling the economy of our community. If we own the stores, if we operate the businesses, if we try and establish some industry in our own community, then we're developing to the position where we are creating employment for our own kind. Once you gain control of the economy of your own community, then you don't have to picket and boycott and beg some cracker downtown for a job in his business.[2]

Of course, Malcolm's ideas were not original. Debates over the success and failure of Black business in the United States frequently surface as a means to measure Black progress and advancement. The historical connections between

Black economic development and the project of racial uplift offer one measure of that progress; thus, developments in Rochester must be contextualized in the larger history.

Scholars have approached this history from three distinct positions. One argument posits that African Americans have a long tradition of business acumen that is based in their African past. This position is perhaps best articulated by Juliet E. K. Walker, who traces more than four hundred years of Black business activity in the United States, highlighting individual businessmen and businesswomen who have had exceptional success.[3] Walker refutes arguments that Black business has not prospered at the same rate as white business because African Americans failed to develop a capitalist ethos during the period of their enslavement.[4] Accepting capitalism as a legitimate goal, she argues that if Black capitalism has failed, it is due in large part to racism and uneven government support rather than Black failure.

A second set of scholars and activists, not entirely distinct from the first, celebrates Black business and its history as a fundamental means to Black advancement. This school credits businessmen-activists such as Booker T. Washington and Marcus Garvey, the Nation of Islam, buy-Black campaigns, and the creation of all-Black business institutions with promoting racial uplift. Rather than approaching Black business as a means to achieve integration, many of these scholars and activists laud the creation of a separate Black economy and all-Black institutions as a foundation for Black advancement and the development of race pride.[5]

Still a third set of scholar-activists is critical of the Black capitalist project. This critique typically takes two forms. The first represents a general distaste both for capitalism and for those who seek economic advancement as a means to emulate bourgeois white society.[6] These naysayers point to the reliance of many Black businesses and institutions, and Black capitalism more broadly, on white philanthropists for their success—a success that they argue is fleeting and permanently dependent upon the continuation of the white capitalist system. The second critique posits that Black capitalism purports to serve the race but instead benefits the Black elite at the expense of the Black masses.[7] These debates among scholars and activists reflect the historical relationship between Black business and racial uplift and advancement, a burden that white capitalism has not shouldered.[8]

Walker's 1998 seminal text, *The History of Black Business in America*, has spurred new interest in the field, most notably Robert Weems's *Business in Black and White*. Weems examines African Americans' insistent engagement of the federal government in the arena of Black business. But if, as Weems has posited, "inherent tensions, related to the African-American consumer market and what can and should be done for African-American entrepreneurs by the federal government, represent one of the major themes of twentieth-century African-American business history," then so too does the relationship between corporate America and Black communities.[9] Black Power activism in the late twentieth century decisively altered the theory and practice of corporate responsibility, the premise that companies were accountable to the communities in which they operated and should proactively address inequality. Relegated to footnotes and brief sidebars, the story of corporate responsibility in the age of Black Power has yet to be told.[10] In addition to agitating nationally for Black economic development, aspiring Black entrepreneurs and community leaders seized this particular moment to expand their political and social reach. In so doing, they secured a position of power that commanded the attention of major corporations, marking the long 1960s as distinct from earlier periods of Black economic development. It was in this context that industry leaders and African Americans in Rochester—both integrationists and Black Power advocates—struggled to redefine corporate responsibility and economic citizenship, oftentimes rejecting notions of governmental responsibility, a feature that delighted state and federal officials alike.

Do for Self in Rochester

Working at the crossroads of the FIGHT-Kodak conflict, which stretched over the winter of 1965–1966, the religious community intervened. The local council of churches, which had raised the funds to bring the Industrial Areas Foundation to Rochester, hoped to restore civility between FIGHT and the business community by forming Rochester Jobs Incorporated (RJI). RJI emerged as a collaborative endeavor intended to remedy the perceived mismatch between corporate needs (skilled workers) and Black needs (stable, well-paying jobs). RJI simultaneously sought to provide training and recruiting and to curtail the racist hiring practices traditionally employed by Rochester's corporations. More significantly, RJI's proponents hoped the new organization would quell the discord in the city and repair its image nationally.[11]

Initially presided over by the Reverend Gene E. Bartlett, president of Colgate Rochester Divinity School, RJI became an all-encompassing community project, bolstered by the divinity school's legitimacy locally and nationally.[12] Under Bartlett's commanding presence, RJI brought together forty local employers into a coalition RJI hoped would serve more than fifteen hundred hard-core unemployed in its first eighteen months of existence. Each of these employers would hire a percentage of the targeted fifteen hundred employees based on its relative size, and each would require its managers to attend retraining programs to prepare them to work with this population. Implementing quota employment, as demanded by FIGHT, and requiring "sensitivity training," RJI leaders felt, would satisfy the Black Power organization. RJI simultaneously ameliorated Kodak's irritation at being singled out by FIGHT. That Kodak chose to participate voluntarily in RJI alongside other Rochester corporations allowed Kodak to demonstrate, once again, its leadership and benevolent paternalism.

As happened so frequently in the twentieth century, RJI's creation thrust Rochester further into the national imagination. Michigan governor George Romney traveled to Rochester in September 1967 just months after Black Detroit erupted in another of the era's "race riots." Romney spent a day surveying RJI projects, visiting the city's settlement houses, and touring FIGHT's headquarters. Unable to ignore the connection between urban rebellions and poor economic conditions, Romney and New York governor Nelson Rockefeller collaborated on this trip to use community programs for self-promotion. Nonetheless, they found in Rochester private efforts to mediate urban poverty. Romney pronounced that in New York he learned that "things can be done at the local and private level."[13] Governor Romney all but expressed relief that the city government's responsibility to blunt Black agitation was alleviated by a clerical and industrial call to cooperate with community organizations.[14]

But Rochester claimed more than the attention of self-interested officials hailing from cities in rebellion. A year into its existence, RJI also became a model for the National Alliance of Businessmen (NAB), the creation of which "was the ultimate voluntary response to the ultimate act of pressure—rioting."[15] The NAB, a voluntary association of businessmen who professed a willingness to assist Black entrepreneurs, desired to restore tranquility and improve profitability in the nation's urban centers simultaneously. Rochester, having experienced one of the first uprisings of the era, was ahead of the curve in forming an industry-driven, voluntary job recruitment and training program, and therefore it became a model. In 1969, Richard Nixon reported that the NAB "concentrated the attention of the business community on the high unemployment rates in . . . inner cities, and . . . mounted an impressive attack on the predicament of the hardcore unemployed." Their success was substantive: "Some 15,000 participating companies [placed] 102,000 formerly hardcore unemployed persons on the job. The NAB has pledged that by June 1970, it will have found jobs for 218,000 persons, and the hope is that over 600,000 will be generated by June 1971."[16] The NAB would later return the favor to Rochester, providing additional staff to hire and train more hardcore unemployed to become entrepreneurs and capitalists.[17]

RJI represented progress. It also highlighted the potential of uprisings to trigger corporate-driven rather than government-driven economic development in the nation's urban centers. As such, FIGHT worked alongside clergy, business, even Kodak, to create opportunities for African Americans within RJI and to keep the spotlight on Rochester, but the process was not without continued controversy. RJI did not offer community control or self-determination. Rather, it kept African Americans and other hard-core unemployed in a system of begging and groveling for jobs from white corporations.

Bolstered by the attention to Black employment, however, FIGHT pressed for more. Members revisited their prior engagement with Malcolm X. As he once counseled, they wanted to create their own enterprises, which they believed would result in economic self-determination, increased Black control over Black economies, and real power to negotiate in the business world. The struggle for Black capitalism in the new era had begun.

After years of lengthy discussions among themselves and with collaborators such as Malcolm X, many FIGHT members began to follow the work of organizations around the nation, including that of the Reverend Leon Sullivan in Philadelphia, whose Zion Corporation introduced innovative job training programs and community development projects.[18] The Zion case was instructive for a number of reasons.[19] First and foremost, Sullivan drew on past experiences of successfully combining buy-Black campaigns with boycotts of businesses that would not hire Blacks. More importantly, he made inroads to white investors, namely, First Pennsylvania Banking and Trust, and to local corporations Coca-Cola and Boeing. Philadelphia, which also experienced an early uprising just one month after the Rochester rebellion, built upon national programs from welfare reform to Johnson's War on Poverty by forming local coalitions and programs that met the needs of Philadelphians.[20] While the Black community in Rochester had never been large enough to institute buy-Black campaigns effectively, FIGHT understood it could certainly target white investors.

Along these lines, FIGHT eagerly proposed a company it would call Fightronics, akin to a successful plan implemented in the Watts section of Los Angeles.[21] Watts Manufacturing, a "ghetto operation" training the hard-core unemployed, attracted FIGHT's attention because it "plan[ned] to offer an employee stock option plan allowing them to buy up to 51 per cent of the company."[22] Immediate divesture was a crucial component of FIGHT's vision for Black capitalism; it meant the Black community controlled the company, rather than the white parent corporation—a demand made by many in the Black Power movement.

While Fightronics did not come to fruition, the organization's pursuit of collective Black capitalism would ultimately guide their plans. In this way, FIGHT's struggle against white corporate power was not driven by an aversion to the capitalist system.[23] On the contrary, its approach to development mirrored the economic plans of the Nation of Islam, which urged Blacks to "pool their resources and techniques in merchandising, manufacturing, building, maintenance—any field in which unity and harmony will contribute to efficiency and effectiveness."[24] While some historians have viewed the Nation of Islam's approach to capitalism as "ideological[ly] incongruent" because it "denounce[ed] white capitalism while at the same time demanding Black Capitalism," they fail to appreciate the nuance—the sharp contrast between individual entrepreneurship and a cooperative capitalism for the sake of community uplift and advancement.[25] Taking seriously Malcolm X and the Nation of Islam's call, FIGHT, too, wanted to "do for self."[26]

On the whole, FIGHT was not among those in the Black Power movement who rejected Black capitalism outright. Repeating a longstanding critique of capitalism, there were those who rejected *Black* capitalism as a means for advancement and uplift. James Forman, a member of the Student Nonviolent Coordinating Committee, "denounced those Blacks who supported Black Capitalism" and "described Black nationalist supporters of Black capitalism as 'Black Power pimps.'"[27] While some members of FIGHT may have shared such criticism, having come of age amid Rochester's period of plenty, most members hoped their vision of Black economic empowerment and their pragmatic embrace of capitalist programs would offer the same economic security to the Black community that it had for Rochester's white population.[28] They readily believed that Black capitalism *could* avoid the ugliness and exploitation inherent in white capitalism. Indeed, Minister Franklin Florence, who was deeply influenced by his relationship with Malcolm X, argued that capitalism could have a human face, a Black face. In one of his many perorations on the subject, he declared, "We are not going to repeat, lockstep, the process that white companies went through. Whites have been so obsessed by profits they have created an insane society. We want economic development, drastic improvement in [our] living standard—but at the same time, our people intend to remain human beings."[29] In order to create a "sane" society, Florence envisioned "an industry where revenue will be turned back into the community for neighborhood improvement and services. Every Black man, woman and child, will benefit."[30] This was, in a way, Black capitalism with Rochester characteristics, an approach FIGHT defended against other models. These new Black freedom practitioners then embraced Black capitalism as a means to gain power, to define their economic rights, and to assert their economic citizenship. Rochester's stable business environment, relative wealth, progressive reputation, and fear of future rioting made it not only possible but imperative that industry respond to these demands from the Black community.

"Do for Self" Meets Corporate Responsibility

In order to "do for self," FIGHT sought allies. In the process, it partnered with the emergent Xerox Corporation. For FIGHT, a joint venture with the white-owned and controlled corporation would offer financial resources, expertise, and credibility in the larger community. For Xerox—Kodak's poorer cousin in Rochester's corporate world—a partnership with FIGHT provided important national publicity. Whereas Kodak had paid a heavy price in the media for its failure to embrace the Black movement, Xerox could capitalize on the new momentum generated by Black Power's interest in economic development. The mutually beneficial relationship lasted for some five years, established one of the nation's first Black-owned community development corporations, and shaped emerging notions of corporate responsibility.

Xerox began as a family business called Haloid that sold photographic paper to professional photographers and dabbled in emerging photographic technologies.[31] In the 1950s, however, Haloid's early investment in xerographic research began to pay off. After producing the world's first successful copier machine, the company underwent a face-lift, changing its name to Xerox and increasing its profile in Rochester's business world by taking the company international. As profits soared, Xerox's annual giving, and thus its influence, began to rival Eastman Kodak's legendary patronage. It was at this crucial moment in Rochester's business history that the city erupted.

FIGHT sought to capitalize on both the turbulent moment and the friendly rivalry developing between Kodak and Xerox. Disillusioned with Kodak, FIGHT turned instead to Xerox to launch FIGHTON.[32] Nationally, FIGHTON would mark both an economic and a political breakthrough: it was one of the nation's first Black-run community development corporations (CDC). Its mission was not only to provide employment opportunities to the hard-core unemployed in Rochester, but also to create ownership opportunities for the Black community. FIGHT argued, "We must construct Black-controlled capital-generating institutions." Being "producers, not just consumers" was crucial to its effort.[33] Indeed, for this reason FIGHTON would become a model for Black Power–inspired CDCs across the United States.[34]

As community-based, nonprofit organizations seeking to assert local control over local politics and economies, CDCs were among the most notable and visible institutional expressions of the Black Freedom Struggle between 1965 and 1975. Minister Florence claimed for FIGHT a place in the history books, articulating a well-understood truth in Rochester: all power—political, social, and civil—derived from economic power. Florence said, "This is a first for the nation. . . . FIGHT has introduced to Rochester and the nation Black

Capitalism, which means an influence that Blacks have never had before." He continued: "The profits from FIGHTON will be turned back into FIGHT and the Black community for housing programs, education, rehabilitation, jobs, day care and all those things the Black community needs."[35] It was this sense of community welfare that gained the attention of Xerox CEO Joe Wilson, who would later determine that his company could benefit from a partnership with FIGHT, perhaps economically, but most assuredly politically.

Wilson's developing interest in FIGHT and in the Black community more generally was an outgrowth of his relationship to the city of Rochester, where he was born and bred. Wilson transcended the traditional corporate executive role in that he invested not just in profits but in the community. His grandfather and namesake, J. C. Wilson, started the Haloid Company with three partners in 1906 and went on to serve as mayor of Rochester in the 1920s, an example of the close relationship between economic power and political power in that city.[36] J. R. Wilson, Joe Wilson's father, took the reins and grew Haloid while raising a family. After graduating from Rochester's West High School, Joe Wilson stayed close by, attending the University of Rochester. In fact, the longest he ever endeavored to be away from Rochester was the two years he attended Harvard Business School, where he graduated with high distinction.[37] Given his family's history, Wilson was well connected in Rochester. He was smart and driven, but above all else, he constantly sought ways to improve his community. Biographer Charles D. Ellis writes that in addition to his business acumen, "Wilson's creative commitment to social leadership included innovations in labor relations, commitments to advancing education; distinctive aesthetic style in product design, graphics, and advertising; pioneering public-affairs programming on television; and effective early initiatives in race relations."[38] These traits and Wilson's firm grounding in Rochester's soil combined to make him one of the greatest philanthropists in Rochester's history. In addition to giving money, which he did generously, he also gave of his time. The University of Rochester, acting under Wilson's guidance as chair of the board of trustees, for example, expanded to include new colleges in business, engineering, and education. Wilson outlined what he believed to be the role of industrial leaders: "Businessmen today . . . must think of functions beyond profit . . . must expand their vision beyond the limits of making maximum profits. . . . Each one must help solve, if he can, the social problems that wash the edges of his island."[39]

Yet prior to the 1964 rebellion, Wilson seemed oblivious to Black Rochester or its problems. His engagement with and employment of the city's Black community began only after the political mobilization fostered by the uprising. Lifelong Xerox employee Horace Becker noted, "At the time of the riots,

Xerox actually—not knowingly, but in actual fact, certainly not intentionally, had about, approximately two employees who were Black."[40] FIGHT's efforts to make Rochester take equal employment seriously led Joe Wilson to drive to FIGHT headquarters late one night to ask, "What do Blacks in Rochester really need?" The answer of course was immediate: "Jobs."[41]

Shortly thereafter, FIGHT and Xerox set out to determine what kind of economic development would best serve their respective needs. The first effort resulted in a program called "Step Up." The plan offered participants—the hard-core unemployed—paid training, tutoring in reading and mathematics, eighteen weeks of instruction in hand tools, and a guaranteed entry-level industry position upon successful completion of the training. FIGHT's jobs committee provided clear guidelines for what constituted "hard-core unemployment." Those considered high-risk hard-core had been arrested with confinement three or more times, had been confined as juveniles, and had performed poorly in school, culminating in their dropping out prior to the tenth grade. Those at medium risk had been arrested but without confinement, had dropped out of school after the tenth grade, and had a limited employment history or demonstrated no ability to sustain employment. The jobs committee determined that those deemed low risk had had no police contact, possessed an average academic record, had completed eleventh grade or higher, and had indicated success in previous jobs.[42] Though Xerox insisted that it was "not really a new idea, rather, it [was] an extension of our beliefs at Xerox that social responsibility in the communities in which we reside is a central concern,"[43] it was FIGHT that articulated what that social responsibility ought to be, insisting that Xerox guarantee Step Up trainees a job after completing the training course. Local and federal training programs offered no such guarantee.

Step Up was only a first step, though. The new project between FIGHT and Xerox—which came to be called FIGHTON—emerged in 1968, allowing FIGHT to showcase the kind of economic self-determination it envisioned (see figure 6.1). Demonstrating that which Joseph Schumpeter termed "creative capitalism," FIGHT developed a business plan and then investigated Rochester's industrial climate for an appropriate product.[44] With Xerox, FIGHT identified products that local businesses needed and that would require relatively little technical training to produce. They settled on industrial vacuum cleaners, low-voltage electrical transformers, and metal stampings, all of which would ultimately mean cheaper products for existing Rochester industries. FIGHTON, it was hoped, could fill a much-needed niche locally. In that same year, FIGHT secured a $400,000 federal grant from the Department of Labor to supplement training costs. In the true spirit of community development, FIGHTON would be located in a building in the heart of the affected Third

FIGURE 6.1. Bernard Gifford looks over machinery at FIGHTON. Photograph, Rochester, ca. 1970. Xerox Corporation, Xerox Historical Archives, Webster, NY. Credit: Xerox Corporation, Xerox Historical Archives. Used with permission.

Ward, a relic from the days when European migrants to Rochester could find ready work in the city's booming clothing industry. After a great deal of renovation and updating, training began.[45] Once up and running, FIGHT maintained "responsibility for the overall ownership and management with the development of a future plan for the eventual minority ownership by the company employees," providing recruitment and management of the employees and doing the "necessary job grooming and industrial orientation."[46] In exchange, Xerox agreed to guarantee FIGHTON one million dollars of business in the first two years of operation and to provide training and technical know-how. It was important to both Xerox and FIGHT that this was not a subsidy but rather a business arrangement.

The union of FIGHT and Xerox was the product of great effort and planning that produced tangible results for both organizations and for Black capitalism more broadly. Martin Skala, a business and financial correspondent for the *Christian Science Monitor*, would later report with great accuracy that FIGHTON, the ultimate project between the two entities, "was the climax of almost four years of collaboration between the Black self-help organization and Xerox on job training programs for the disadvantaged."[47] Of this union, FIGHT's Minister Florence pointed out, "It took us a year and a half before we were laughing at the same jokes. You can not wave a magic wand and say 'Black Capitalism' and expect it to be as easy as that."[48]

Given the deep commitment on both sides, FIGHTON offered more than training and jobs. It would also return an estimated two million dollars in income per year to the community.[49] As FIGHTON grew and turned a profit, the proceeds were slated for low-income housing, daycare centers, and additional job training. In answer to capitalism's critics, FIGHT announced that FIGHTON would be "the beginning of Black Capitalism for the Black man in America. Blacks ha[d] always been the victims of white capitalism—exploited, none of the big revenue turn[ed] back into the underprivileged community for improvement programs."[50] For Florence and others in FIGHT, Black capitalism in this iteration could work because Blacks, not white executives, would both control and own the industry from its inception.

"Despite everyone's high spirits," local NPR affiliate WXXI remembered in a 2003 broadcast, "the first couple of years were rough at FIGHTON. The company did not turn a profit. There was a turnover problem; many workers would come in, get training, and leave for better-paying jobs."[51] Though an obstacle for FIGHTON, this "problem" was not without its virtues; the training, whether used at FIGHTON or elsewhere, provided many African Americans with skills to make a decent living. The company also served as an inspiration to many in the Black community. Millicent Hartzog, a FIGHTON employee who continued to work for the company, remembered, "There were no other thriving [Black] businesses in Rochester. We had a lot of small business, mom and pop stores and small businesses, but they didn't last very long and our business seemed to last; we were profitable, we had a service or product that people needed."[52] Darryl Porter recalled, "When we heard that we were going to have our own company and they were going to be able to hire us, and we didn't have to worry about being discriminated when we got to the door, I mean, it was, it was overwhelming joy."[53] While FIGHTON had its share of struggles, it inspired the Black community (see figure 6.2).

FIGURE 6.2.   FIGHTON trainee at a machine. Photograph, Rochester, ca. 1970. Xerox Corporation, Xerox Historical Archives, Webster, NY. Credit: Xerox Corporation, Xerox Historical Archives. Used with permission.

FIGHT's version of Black capitalism went a step further than job creation, Black ownership, and community pride. The community organization approached Black capitalism as a covenant, a reciprocal relationship between FIGHTON and the community, binding one to the other for their mutual benefit. As the FIGHT organization approached its fifth annual convention, Florence sought to capitalize on the benefits of turning out large numbers of FIGHT supporters. The greater the show of support at the convention, the greater the media coverage would be. And as in the past, media coverage often spelled increased power for the FIGHT organization. Minister Florence laid down the gauntlet to FIGHTON employees. In order to be able to showcase its strength before the nation, Florence counseled that "staff should be pushed hard for the Convention." He continued: "Every employee at FIGHTON must produce at least one relative. . . . Every employee of FIGHTON must have friends signed up on credentials for the Convention. The success of our people making a good showing will depend on [this]."[54] Black capitalism, FIGHT style, did not allow an employee to do his/her job and then return home. Each employee was expected to reach back into the community and bring another along; it was indeed a cooperative venture.

While FIGHT's motivation for such a project is evident, it is less obvious why Xerox would invest such time and money. A combination of factors is likely responsible. First, many in FIGHT and in Rochester credit Joe Wilson's interest and integrity. Both Florence and Becker, who worked countless hours together, noted his determination to see FIGHTON through. It seems, however, that Wilson was not being entirely magnanimous. The unusual partnership Wilson forged with FIGHTON brought substantial national acclaim to Xerox for its role in reforming corporate social responsibility (CSR). The term, which came into popular parlance in the 1970s, took on new meaning in the context of Black Power.[55] Though originally a way to avoid governmental regulation, voluntary CSR came to be seen as a way to improve industry's bottom line. Companies that had once enjoyed reputations for generous giving were called to task for ignoring Black communities. As a result, Black neighborhoods and organizations became a popular target for corporate giving. This shift in CSR made great fodder for news outlets trying to interpret Black Power to the masses. Various media regularly featured stories on FIGHTON, and Xerox provided much to report. In a *New York Times* piece, a Xerox executive offered in the racially coded language so popular in the Jim Crow North, "Before we were made aware of the deprivation of the Negroes, we asked Negroes to take the same test as whites . . . but that was not a fair measure of their ability because of the lack of opportunities, family background, [and] cultural deprivation."[56] The *Rochester Democrat and Chronicle* took up the mantle, reporting, "The program of help for the disadvantaged is part of '[Xerox's] broader commitment' to seek actively solutions to social programs. 'We cannot grant equality or dignity,' the [Xerox] officials said, 'but we can provide opportunity for equality and be understanding of the different means through which men seek dignity.'"[57] This was indeed the language of Black Power.

Smooth Honky Talk

Not to be outdone by Xerox and FIGHT, Kodak searched for ways to capitalize on local calls for Black economic development. If the FIGHT-Xerox program was a new venture in communal Black capitalism, then Kodak provided, in many ways, its antithesis. Kodak's version encouraged private enterprise and entrepreneurship; it rewarded African Americans who adopted a capitalist ethos rather than a cooperative spirit. The company's various attempts to foster Black capitalism then prompted a showdown to determine who would articulate its meaning and what that meaning might be. Kodak attempted to co-opt FIGHT on multiple occasions. When that proved unsuccessful, the company excluded the Black Power organization from its plans, opting instead to work with the Urban League.

In the midst of the 1966–1967 FIGHT-Kodak controversy, both entities had been persuaded to participate in Rochester Jobs Incorporated (RJI), which kept alive some hopes that Kodak and FIGHT might successfully work together. When Kodak set out to conquer Black capitalism, it hoped to bring FIGHT into its fold. After bowing to FIGHT's demands for increased jobs and training, Kodak met with the organization to discuss the potential for a joint business venture, possibly Fightronics, FIGHT's ill-fated proposal. When Kodak quickly rejected the plan because it called for immediate Black ownership, discussions ceased. Yet when officials announced "the Kodak plan" to the national chamber of commerce, they disingenuously touted their several meetings with "Negro leaders" as evidence of Black collaboration.[58] In rejecting FIGHT's input and creating a blueprint without its counsel, Kodak officials consciously sought to define Black capitalism in a way that precluded Black Power.

Nonetheless, Kodak continued with a plan to develop four potential Black businesses; the most developed of these—described sarcastically by Xerox's Horace Becker—drew the ire of FIGHT leaders:

> It was a complete factory to make wooden pallets—"high technology." They had where you buy the wood, how you cut it, how many nails you drive in each piece, how long it will take to build the pallet and the number of people who need pallets, a list of all the customers, and its high technology. You see, you have to hit the nail on the end with the big head on it, and when you're going through the nails, you find some have the head on the wrong side and so you have to turn those over— but this was a complete book. . . . Franklin [Florence], the first time he sees it, it's all complete. Well, he went through the roof. And the next couple of meetings I had with him, all he did was carry on about those bastards.[59]

Florence's anger would have been recognizable throughout Black Power circles nationally; he understood that programs developed without community input failed precisely because "they do not mobilize the pride and yearning for self-determination which is the only thing that will really energize the ghettoes."[60] Black capitalism—FIGHT style—required Black investment at the ground level. That Kodak wished to provide—in typical paternal fashion— an unskilled, nontechnical industry to the Black community without input from that community was beyond the pale. Florence condemned it in the gendered language so typical of the era: "You are emasculating the Black community."[61] While "the Kodak plan" made waves in Congress, it went nowhere in Rochester. Without FIGHT's support and interest, Kodak's so-called community development corporation went by the wayside.

Not to be deterred, Kodak did not completely abandon Black capitalism. In the fall of 1967, Kodak executives approached the local chamber of commerce to form the Rochester Business Opportunities Corporation (RBOC) "to help inner city residents start, manage and own their own businesses."[62] Like RJI before it, RBOC was designed as a community project. It would eventually include twenty-two trustees hailing from myriad industries headquartered in Rochester: Kodak, Xerox, Bausch and Lomb, to name but a few. The elite group also included managing partners of major investment and accounting firms: Price Waterhouse, Arthur Andersen, and Pete Merritt. But in forming RBOC, "a decision was made to exclude representatives of the FIGHT organization on the ground that the new corporation should be 'business based.'"[63] While it aided select members of the Black community, RBOC was not conceptualized to provide the kind of community uplift or self-determination that FIGHT envisioned. A case study of RBOC later reported that its members felt "the project would not have got going so fast had it been forced to negotiate complex problems of community representation and ownership."[64] Understandably, FIGHT's response to RBOC was mixed. Though it would not directly attack RBOC as a tool of the establishment, FIGHT rejected this limited, corporate version of Black capitalism.[65]

RBOC was not without purpose, however. The program's first goal was to prevent future uprisings by offering a handful of African Americans a visible and economic stake in the community, while preserving Kodak's dominance in Rochester. In maintaining the status quo, RBOC would serve as an appropriate model for Richard Nixon's Office of Minority Business Enterprise down the line. To accomplish the first goal, RBOC took would-be entrepreneurs with technical skills and provided them with business training. Clarence Ingram, RBOC's general manager for nearly twenty years, explained one set of limitations a new businessman might face: "They can fix your car. Sure they'll tune it up real good, give you a nice job, but he'd never owned that place before. He didn't realize that there's overhead."[66] RBOC, then, provided new (or expanding) Black businesses—typically involving no more than a dozen employees—grants and loans as well as instruction in bidding for jobs, creating budgets, maintaining payroll, purchasing, and marketing. As interest in RBOC grew, its instructors included volunteers from local universities and businesses, many who believed in "riot prevention." Ingram theorized that a number of RBOC beneficiaries would be unable to repay their loans: "But at that time, I guess, the community, the larger community—now, I'm thinking, they looked at which is cheaper—let them tear up the city or we let them waste this little money. That's a small price to pay."[67]

Through RBOC, Kodak attempted to launch a second venture, its own Black company, in conjunction with the Urban League. Camura, as it was to be called, was presented to the Urban League as a ready-made Black business to repair Kodak cameras. While Kodak would oversee the processing, diagnoses, and return of the equipment, Camura employees would make the repairs. As with Kodak's wooden pallet proposal to FIGHT, Camura was delivered to the Urban League as a fait accompli. Unlike FIGHT however, the Urban League was prepared to enter into a predetermined business venture with Kodak. Its associate director announced, "The league has been looking for ways to help inner city people develop businesses and this looks like a good possibility."[68] Having been pegged by many in the Black community as a conservative middle-class organization, the Urban League was interested in divorcing itself from that stigma. Camura seemed an ideal and simple solution. The Urban League signed onto Kodak's program as one of many it hoped would repair its reputation in the Black community. With funding from the national On-the-Job Training program, the League set out to mirror FIGHT's efforts to train and employ the hard-core unemployed. Though not a mom-and-pop shop, Camura underwhelmed observers by employing just ten people in its first year of operation. Aware of the small impact the company was making, the Urban League defended "its economic and social significance," which "far outweigh[ed] the actual employment."[69]

The Urban League attempted optimism, citing Kodak's promise that eventual ownership of the company would be turned over to "the president and/or workers so that they will own it outright," but these promises failed to materialize.[70] By 1970, the Urban League stopped approving On-the-Job Training contracts for Camura and withdrew its support for the company, given a host of problems. A string of Camura trainees quit the program amid charges of exploitation. When the Urban League confronted Camura's manager, he "stated that his preference was for white employees because they understood that 'a business had to grow.' He further stated that . . . Black employees had given him the most trouble as far as absenteeism and production and persistently asking for raises." Despite Camura's social mission, the manager felt he could not take chances with "mediocre employees" lest his business fail. When reminded that he was reimbursed for training and providing jobs to this population, he replied, "It wasn't worth it."[71] To its credit, the Urban League withdrew support from Camura permanently. As Minister Florence anticipated, Black capitalism controlled by white capital could never benefit the Black community.

Camura, however, was just one business developed with funding from RBOC, and Kodak just one contributor. Despite its reliance on Kodak money, there were several people deeply and personally invested in RBOC's success. Ingram recalled how difficult it was to convince people of RBOC's sincerity and purpose. "The men in the streets—now I'm talkin' 'bout the brothers," he began, "they would say 'Ah, that's not going to do anything, that's another game they're gonna run on you.' So to prove that they were wrong, everybody that came into the [RBOC] office and wanted some help, they got it. But it was only—we called 'em apartheid businesses: grocery stores, dry cleaners, gas stations, garages,—you know, that kind of thing."[72] In time, RBOC came to support larger businesses: a heating and cooling company, a local radio station, and a florist, all of which, much to Ingram's joy, continued to exist into the new century.

For Kodak's purposes, RBOC and business ventures such as Camura affirmed the company as a trendsetter in the business world. Whether these programs were successfully implemented and served the populations they intended was secondary to the business of business. Kodak continued to funnel money to RBOC without concern for whether the programs could or would be successful. It simply mattered that Kodak would have ultimate say and top billing in RBOC's publicity and programming.[73] Kodak could claim that its project prevented further rioting and aided in job creation, all while maintaining its hegemony in the community. Black capitalism Kodak style, its executives claimed, was successful.

As the 1960s came to an end and Rochester faced the new decade, both the Urban League and FIGHT struggled to advance their ideological and economic agendas while simultaneously negotiating daily organizational operations. They had provided the nation with influential models of, and a voice for, Black capitalism. FIGHTON symbolized a local approach to communal Black economic development, rejecting versions of Black capitalism championed by Kodak and the Nixon administration. The ongoing struggle between community, capital, and the state to define the purpose and path of Black capitalism, however, proved consequential to both Black self-determination and community development. Writing in 1971, Geoffrey Faux noted, "Since 1967, very little money has been made available for new urban programs, particularly for those in conflict with deliberate policy decisions made by both the Johnson and Nixon administrations to discourage neighborhood-controlled urban projects."[74] This contest to define Black capitalism continued to be fought at the federal level for years with the introduction of the Community Self-Determination Act of 1968 and its revision, the Community Corporation Act of 1970.[75] In an effort to reign in criticisms like Faux's and reestablish the perception that Washington supported Black business, these two pieces of legislation wound their way through the system. Though ultimately unsuccessful, they demonstrated the ongoing contest for the soul of Black capitalism.

Minister Florence characteristically refused to remain silent about something so near and dear to the Black community. He did not favor the federal Community Self-Determination Act of 1968, precisely because he valued *community* determination, which could not be legislated by the government. For Florence, it was a right to be asserted, demanded even, by the community itself. Invited to speak at a symposium on community self-determination on "A New Role for Private Enterprise," Minister Florence used the platform to rail against the "smooth honky talk" and co-optation implicit in the legislation.[76] He declared the act a "'hypocritical piece of legislation,' and suggested that it be 'torn up, because you can't start wrong and end right.' He held that the legislation would set up 'Mickey Mouse' types of organizations, instead of giving control to the local leaders responsive to ghetto needs." Scratching notes on a pad from his hotel room, Florence prepared to prevent the legislation from going forward; he imparted what he had learned in Rochester: "The problem of the ghetto is powerlessness; if the people there don't have the power to negotiate for themselves, there will be no economic development."[77] Back in Rochester, Florence triumphantly reported to his steering committee, "National organizations are floundering, as opposed to [the] community organization which is growing stronger and has more influence today on State and National Politics than all the National Organizations with all their white money put together."[78] Both bills, the Self-Determination Act and the Community Corporation Act, were defeated.

In Rochester, however, the multiple versions of Black capitalism coexisted for some time. RBOC funded minority entrepreneurship for more than twenty years, while ownership of FIGHTON was eventually sold to an African American, Matthew Augustine. Under his directorship, FIGHTON continues to exist under the name Eltrex, providing stock options, training, and employment to Rochester's hard-core unemployed. In 2009, Robert Weems asked, "What can (and should) be done to substantively improve the plight of Black business in America?"[79] The answer may well lie in Rochester's history.

Conclusion

Paths to Freedom in Rochester

> If there is no struggle, there is no progress.
> —Frederick Douglass, 1857

The story of Rochester, New York, makes clear that even among a relatively small Black population in a medium-sized city, there was no single Black movement nor one distinct path to freedom. Black activists carved out a series of simultaneous movements, which were complicated and continuously contested. From goals to methodology, activists and organizations competed to define and stretch the boundaries of their lived experiences. And in the 1950s and 1960s, the space for such multifaceted efforts had expanded. What made this moment possible was not just a renewed effort by Black activists; Black activists had continuously fought for equality, for their freedom rights throughout the history of the United States. Rather, in the postwar world, economies were booming, opportunities were abundant, and in the face of Black insurgency, white liberals ceded some room to Black advancement.

Black folk in Rochester seized this moment, striking the hammer while the iron was hot. At the beginning of the 1960s, they used the burgeoning civil rights movement and its new strategies of direct action protest to overturn the complacent relationship between the Black leadership and the white leaders in the city. Once that was accomplished, these new Black leaders made inroads across their community, which allowed for a certain unity of action, if not of ideology. After the 1964 uprising, these leaders took advantage of the fear the disturbances caused, in Rochester and elsewhere, to enact a full-court press on the city government, the churches, and the corporations to support economic, social, and political parity for Black folk. Some scholars have argued that the most powerful legacies of this decade of urban rebellion are the modern-day campaign for law and order and the War on Drugs. They have rightly noted that the rise of a white backlash in the form of Barry Goldwater, Richard Nixon, and others was a cumulative outcome of these events.[1] But in 1964, this was only one possibility, and certainly not the most pressing prospect for Black activists in Rochester. Nor did the Rochester civil rights community condemn those insurgents engaged in the uprising, as happened in places like Harlem and elsewhere. Instead, Rochester's Black leaders used the revolt as a springboard for more oppositional organizing than occurred in other cities and certainly more than occurred within national civil rights organizations. In 1964, Black activists in Rochester saw opportunity.

By 1970, they had pressed their advantage socially, politically, and economically using multiple vehicles. Some of the more conservative activists had joined or formed new branches of traditional national organizations, such as the NAACP and the Urban League, and local organizations, such as Action for a Better Community; while others, primarily activist ministers and radical women, had launched the more militant FIGHT, which spoke directly to their immediate needs. Many in the community joined several of the organizations and worked across them to increase opportunity for Black Rochester. These organizations and the movement as a whole were about more than just strong leadership, though that mattered as well. The ordinary citizens of Rochester evinced a broad conception of the movement, one that was not limited to singular strategies for racial advancement but rather necessitated attacking the system in diverse ways. These activists partnered with politicians, with schools, with settlement houses, and with locally headquartered national businesses. And importantly, they warned of impending revolt if their demands were not considered, negotiated, or met.

At any other time, the 1964 Rochester uprising may not have yielded such results. The sheer exasperation of Black folk combined with their willingness to engage in "riots" signaled to everyone that postwar prosperity could not exclude African Americans with their silence or consent. The sharp contrast between the ghetto-like conditions in Rochester's two Black wards and the widespread wealth at the outer reaches of the city and in its suburbs created a crisis of conscience for many white residents, especially among some church leaders and their parishioners. Activists and emergent leaders understood that a moment had presented itself and that they must direct its course. The moment, however, was just that—a moment. It could not last.

By the close of the 1960s, the space that had opened was contracting once again, in Rochester and nationally. Locally, the moment passed at the confluence of several events, some of which also had national significance. FIGHT had begun as an issues-oriented organization in 1964, and in 1971 it confronted one of the deadliest issues to date. Nearby Attica state prison, the early recruiting ground for so many Muslims and the place where the Nation of Islam had gained constitutionally protected legitimacy, erupted. Inmates took several guards hostage as they seized control, and the state struggled with how to retake the prison.[2] Elliott "L. D." Barkley, a Rochester native, quickly became a spokesman for the incarcerated men. In his now famous oration, widely televised at the time, Barkley made a plea to observers of the Attica events: "We are men! We are not beasts and we do not intend to be beaten or driven as such. . . . What has happened here is but the sound before the fury of those who are oppressed. . . . We've called upon all the conscientious citizens of America to assist us in putting an end to this situation that threatens the lives of not only us, but of each and every one of you, as well."[3] Barkley's appearance sent shockwaves throughout Black Rochester, which had not yet heard there was trouble at Attica. Unable to get official information from the prison system, women such as Barkley's mother, Laverne, descended on FIGHT headquarters, pleading for assistance. Several FIGHT ministers, past and present, traveled to Attica to obtain information on their behalf. Instead of merely gathering information, the Black ministers who appeared on the scene in those early hours of the standoff were drafted to serve on the negotiating team between inmates and the state.

As the standoff concluded in tragedy, six of the thirty-two inmates murdered in the retaking of the prison had been residents of Buffalo or Rochester and thus were known to the ministers. Assuaging in part their own pain, the ministers began to organize, helping local families to bury the victims, which included L. D. Barkley. Of primary importance, they raised funds to help assist the families. Lavern Barkley had amassed a hefty telephone bill during the uprising, calling legislators, entertainers, organizers, anyone she believed might have some influence. She remembered, "I would call and ask them to go to Attica, call there, do whatever they could, because I believed that a lot of people were going to lose their lives. I did this because I was fearful." The FIGHT ministers paid the phone bill afterward.[4] They also vowed to never forget and, thus, set about aiding the Rochester survivors in their resultant legal battles. In many ways the Attica events consumed the organization, appropriating much of its available resources—financial, intellectual, and especially emotional—for several years to come.

FIGHT suffered other losses at the onset of the 1970s. Since its inception, Minister Franklin Florence had been FIGHT's most visible public face. Whether formally or informally, in his own right as president or through a figurehead,

Florence remained the dominant figure in Rochester's movements. Charismatic and flamboyant, his confrontational and bracing tactics had served FIGHT well, most notably in the struggle against Kodak. Yet within the organization, those same tactics were often less effective, and they ended up alienating many. After five years with Florence at the helm, the organization's 1970 convention doubled as a referendum on Florence's leadership. After an abortive attempt the previous year, Florence's detractors put up a credible candidate, the mild-mannered Bernie Gifford, to run against him in 1970. It was not a close contest. Despite various maneuvers by the minister and a rump of diehard supporters, not all of them consistent with FIGHT's constitution or the decorum expected of a man of the cloth, Florence lost in a landslide. Many viewed Gifford as a more measured voice for the organization. One FIGHT member described Gifford this way: "Bernie had a different style. He wasn't as—nowhere near as articulate as Franklin [Florence]. He was smart, very smart intellectually, well read, but nowhere near the charisma that Franklin had."[5] Though divisive, Florence had been a compelling, and militant, spokesman for FIGHT. Without his promotion of an oppositional identity, some of the fight left FIGHT. The bitterly fought election confirmed FIGHT's decline, both as a political force in the city and as a source of moral authority in the Black community. The organization continued to exist, but Raymond Scott, who would later take the helm, theorized with the benefit of hindsight that the Florence-Gifford election "was the demise of the organization, there. That was really the demise of it, because it was divided at that point. It had been a unified group—people maybe favored this or that—but it was a unified group. That was really the crystal clear division. . . . The spirit just wasn't there. And it never returned. It never returned; that was the demise."[6]

But internal dissension alone could not have caused the decline of the movement in Rochester. Many of the organizations that formed in the wake of the uprising were in flux; the FIGHT organization was transitioning from an issues-oriented group to an economic development corporation. It was inopportune that this conversion occurred at this moment. The nation was on the verge of deindustrialization and economic recession.[7] FIGHT continued to serve as the voice of the community in its struggles with various power holders, particularly on issues of police brutality, employment, and housing conditions. But to effect real change, they believed their strategy must progress. Thus, as the Attica events culminated in heartache and as Florence's influence waned, the organization entered a new phase of community development.

FIGHT began to operate community development corporations (CDCs), operating three substantial business ventures into the 1970s. The first of these, FIGHTON, emerged from the partnership with Xerox in the late 1960s. The company made electrical products and sold them to Kodak, Xerox, and other local businesses. Importantly, FIGHTON employed nearly two hundred people at its height. Second, FIGHT Square, a 3.6-million-dollar housing complex built on nine acres, was completed in 1972 under the auspices of FIGHT. This facility boasted 148 low-to-moderate-income residential units in ten buildings, each with a private entry and access to a yard, garden, or recreational area. The Black-owned facility also included a community space complete with an auditorium, a health center, a pharmacy, a barbershop, a beauty salon, and a laundromat. At the time, FIGHT hoped to secure additional space for an on-site childcare center.[8] FIGHT Square was conceived as part of a total community, in which residents could find work with Black-owned CDCs, such as FIGHTON, and with the businesses built into the housing community, and then invest their incomes with Black organizations and businesses. A third venture, a second housing project known as FIGHT Village, came to fruition in 1974. This facility, comprised of 246 units of low-income public housing, has been managed by Franklin Florence under various auspices into the present moment but funded through the federal Department of Housing and Urban Development (HUD). At one point, FIGHT leaders hoped it would include a shopping center as well.[9]

But the latter half of the 1970s were not kind to FIGHT, which continued to exist in a reduced fashion until 1978, when it fizzled without fanfare. The *Rochester Democrat and Chronicle* acknowledged FIGHT's passing with a post-mortem describing its slow unraveling. After a poor financial year in 1976, FIGHTON changed its name to Eltrex and sold the business to an African American, Matt Augustine, who had recently been hired to manage the company. Augustine continues to run the company with the same mission, employee base, and community spirit in which it began. In 1974, for the last time, FIGHT registered with the New York State Department of State as a charity, and by 1976, FIGHT was no longer registered. The registration was not the only cancellation in 1976. In that year, FIGHT closed its community office in the face of foreclosure for nonpayment of taxes. It appears that its last two years were spent trying to stave off repossession of its business ventures. FIGHT was unsuccessful in saving FIGHT Square, which was repossessed and sold. Though it has faced constant financial difficulties, FIGHT Village has survived.[10]

That FIGHT's CDCs met with mixed results is representative of the era. One of Black Power's greatest legacies is its insistent call for Black-controlled institutions. This included Black-owned businesses in Black neighborhoods and housing developments that flourished under the auspices of CDCs. While FIGHT was in the forefront of this movement in the late 1960s, many of these came of age in the 1970s and 1980s. As Black Power practitioners sought to "do for self," they built and maintained cooperative housing ventures, which were often supported with a mixture of public and private funds and which relied on community management and continuous financial support.

As FIGHT and many of the civil rights organizations in Rochester made the transition from an issues orientation to an economy-building emphasis, the country entered one of the greatest economic recessions of the century. The postwar boom had inflated the collective national sense of prosperity and had exaggerated what was possible financially within a capitalist system. Locally, technologically driven companies, primarily Eastman Kodak, Xerox, and Bausch and Lomb, preserved Rochester as one of the most financially comfortable cities in the country much longer than many others. It was in that flush moment, of course, that Rochester's civil rights and Black Power movements flourished and began to make economic demands of both the city government and these businesses.

This period of boom, however, was sure to bust. As Alejandro Reuss has stated, economists understand that "capitalist economies always go through boom-and-bust cycles, with recessions interrupting the process of capital accumulation and economic growth. Most of the time, these crises are shallow enough that 'normal' economic growth resumes without major changes in framework institutions," but in a moment of contraction, fear and blame typically follow.[11] By 1973, the economy was in free fall, and the nation's urban centers faced the brunt of it. This particular recession was caused by a combination of deindustrialization (a decline in manufacturing) and suburbanization. Deindustrialization caused a spike in unemployment, but it also significantly reduced tax revenues, which cities had come to rely on for their social welfare programs. Simultaneously, increasing numbers of taxpayers moved to suburbs and took their tax bases with them. Both factors had a deleterious effect on the nation's cities. That these occurrences followed on the heels of nearly a decade of racial unrest and urban revolts allowed many to lay the blame for the demise of the cities at the feet of the Black Freedom Struggle and the white liberals who had supported it. As a result, the country was "divided by two different visions for its future . . . [and] the contraction of the state also meant the shrinking of the social imagination."[12] As such, financial and moral support for Black economic development, community development corporations, and experimental training programs waned rapidly.

In Rochester, as nationally, the economic contraction created a mixed legacy for the movement. Xerox CEO Joe Wilson died in 1971, just after the company opened a new research center not in Rochester, but in Silicon Valley. This move away from Wilson's beloved Rochester reflected the larger global historical capitalist forces that were underway. Black capitalism, once a locally conceived and implemented practice, was adopted at the national level by the likes of Richard Nixon. As historian Robert Weems and others have noted, Nixon implemented Black capitalism at the national level in large part to blunt, or defang, its radical potential.[13] Thus we see in this economic contraction a contested and unresolved legacy for Black capitalism.

Furthermore, the narrative of the 1964 Rochester uprising would begin to take its modern form in this moment. Local commentator Bob Lonsberry recalled fifty years after the 1964 uprising, "The physical, economic and social damage lingers to this day. The riot destroyed the neighborhood and it remains in large part destroyed to this day. And that is nothing to celebrate."[14] One-time Rochester police officer Joseph Cimino recollected, "We [the police] thought we were on pretty good footing. . . . We were totally caught off guard [by the riot], and I still think to this day it was some overt actions at the dance that just started the whole thing."[15] In such recollections the uprising and the entire ten-year organizing effort that it birthed could be reduced in the popular imagination to a mistake on the part of the police and the destruction of a neighborhood that never recovered. Black folks were already responding to the decline of their neighborhoods during the 1964 revolt, and the subsequent rally to protect them was swept away by narratives that ignore the economic decline and hail law and order policing.

This book provides a more complete recounting of the long Black Freedom Struggle, a set of multifaceted social, political, cultural, and *economic* movements by examining the possibilities presented by the 1964 uprising in Rochester, New York. Understanding this struggle as a series of successes and failures or a wave that rises and falls ignores the incredibly repressive environment in which Black men and women have always had to live in the United States. At the very moment that the possibility of self-sufficiency and true Black Power might have been realized, the movement was forced to assume a defensive posture again. In Rochester, the Black community had raised the possibility by creating a path to bring social and economic change to fruition. The violence and repression of Attica forced the Rochester movement back into a defensive posture. The subsequent national cries for increased law-and-order policing only solidified this defensive stance, locally and nationally. And the economic recession made it possible to defund the very efforts for which they had so long fought, to abandon the moral imperative, and to simultaneously blame Black activists for the failure of the movement.

Slowly but surely the movement's most talented and dedicated supporters abandoned vehicles such as FIGHT. Remaining true to the cause, many activists turned their efforts to the individual neighborhood and block associations in this new climate. Consider, for example, Mildred Johnson, whose fiery speech at the 1963 Baden Street rally attended by Malcolm X, among others, summarized so well the collective feelings of Black Rochester, which was then under siege from police brutality. "We are Black folks first," Johnson insisted on that occasion. Johnson, who came from a family with deep activist roots in Black Rochester, later emerged as a key supporter of FIGHT. With the decline of FIGHT, Johnson transferred her considerable talents and unbounded energies to other projects, chief among them the Virginia Wilson Helping Hands Association, an organization named for her mother that provides housing assistance, legal counsel, and referrals to social service agencies and employment centers.

Mildred Johnson was hardly alone in continuing the good fight once this moment passed. After unsuccessfully contesting his ignominious loss for the FIGHT presidency in the election of 1970, including a legal challenge, Franklin Florence rejoined the fray. Almost fifty years later, he remained the senior pastor at Rochester's Central Church of Christ and served as president of the Rochester Faith Community Alliance. Florence continued to be engaged with FIGHT Village, the low-income housing project that came into being in 1969 and for which he was instrumental in securing federal funding. Still a model housing project, FIGHT Village accepts Section 8 subsidies and boasts units with up to four bedrooms, expansive and professionally cared-for lawns, and off-street playgrounds. Residents use the housing office for assistance with translation, employment issues, and legal concerns.

Then there is Walter Cooper, one of the leaders of the "Young Turks" who, on arriving in Rochester as a young professional in the 1950s, promptly took on the established Black leadership for what he viewed as its complacency and neglect of the Black community. A tireless worker and investigator, Cooper was associated with any number of organizations over the years, among them the NAACP, the Urban League, and Action for a Better Community. Cerebral and scientific in his approach to social problems, Cooper kept his distance from FIGHT and especially Florence, whose style he considered incendiary and counterproductive. Cooper would not have been fazed by FIGHT's departure from the political scene, preoccupied as he has always been with other concerns.

In 2009, the city of Rochester lauded Cooper for fifty years of community service. His other honors include appointment to the New York State Board of Regents as a regent emeritus. More recently, the city of Rochester opened the Dr. Walter Cooper Academy, an experimental school for children in kindergarten through second grade. Students make a pledge to uphold the "Cooper code." The school's motto, "Never give up," summarizes well Cooper's lifelong work. Over the past several decades, Cooper, now in his early nineties, has spent a good deal of his time prowling the hallways of the institution named after him. He has attended curriculum meetings and contacted parents to discuss their involvement in their children's education. For Cooper, these efforts have been but the latest attempt to improve the education of Black children.[16]

In Rochester, as everywhere else across the United States, the Black Freedom Struggle remains an unfinished undertaking. In the wake of one of the first urban uprisings of that era, efforts to create the FIGHT organization spawned a set of movements that not only helped to transform Rochester but also had a national impact. During its brief and sometimes glorious moment in the political ascendancy, some in Rochester's Black community enthusiastically embraced FIGHT, while others chose to work independently of it. Mildred Johnson fell into the former category, and Walter Cooper into the latter. Both stood on strong and sturdy shoulders. Whatever their ideological disposition or organizational preferences, Rochester activists were guided by the dictum of another Black Rochesterian, Frederick Douglass, who asserted that without struggle, there is no progress. Today in Rochester, as elsewhere, that struggle for progress and dignity continues.

ACKNOWLEDGMENTS

This book would not have been possible without substantial financial and institutional support from numerous sources, including the History Department at Binghamton University, the Charlotte W. Newcombe Foundation, the Partnership Trust and the New York State Archives, Bloomfield College, and a two-week National Endowment for the Humanities (NEH) workshop on the Jim Crow North created by Jeanne Theoharis and Komozi Woodard. Ireton Consulting improved the revision and editing of this work in every possible way. Michael McGandy at Cornell University Press showed an interest in this work before the research had really begun. For his willingness to stick with the project through its completion, I am so very grateful.

Archival staff from the University of Illinois Chicago Special Collections, Rochester Public Library, Rochester Museum and Science Center, King Center for Research, Sanford Historical Society, Rochester Municipal Archives and Record Center, the New York State Archives, the Ryerson Image Centre, and the University Archives of the State University of New York at Buffalo assisted with locating materials and making the most productive use of them. Chris Christopher generously shared her research and connections from the film *July '64* with me, while city historian Christine Ridarsky connected me to several archives and collections. Portions of this work appeared earlier as "FIGHTing for the Soul of Black Capitalism: Struggles for Black Economic Development in Postrebellion Rochester," in *The Business of Black Power: Community Development, Capitalism, and Corporate Responsibility in Postwar America*, 45–67, edited by Laura Warren Hill and Julia Rabig (Rochester, NY: University of Rochester Press, 2012, reprinted with permission; and "'We Are Black Folks First': The Black Freedom Struggle in Rochester, NY and the Making of Malcolm X," *The Sixties: A Journal of History, Politics, and Culture* 3, no. 2 (December 2010): 163–185, reprinted with permission of Taylor and Francis (http://www.informaworld.com). Kevin Heard, the associate director of Binghamton University's GIS Campus Core Facility, created the demographic map in chapter 1, which is printed with permission. Many thanks to the Eastman

Kodak Company, the *Rochester Democrat and Chronicle* (the *USA Today* Network), the Werner Wolff family, and the Xerox Corporation, Xerox Historical Archives, for permission to print images in the text.

This research was made infinitely more fruitful by the staff of University of Rochester's Rare Books, Special Collections, and Preservation, River Campus Libraries. Richard Peek, Nancy Martin, Melissa Mead, Melinda Wallington, and, most especially, Phyllis Andrews supported me throughout this project. With institutional support from the UR, Phyllis and I collaborated on the Rochester Black Freedom Struggle Oral History Project, which underscores every portion of this book. Phyllis's capable student assistants further transcribed hundreds of hours of interviews. I am forever indebted to the participants of that interview project, most especially Dr. Walter Cooper, Minister Franklin Florence, Clarence Ingram, Horace Becker, Connie and John Mitchell, Charlie Price, the Reverend Marvin Chandler, Minister Raymond Scott, Herb White, and Daryl Porter, many of whom offered their personal archive collections for my use. All of these interviewees imbued this book with honesty, humility, joy, heartache, and faith that in telling their stories, their contributions to the struggle would continue. I deeply regret that so many of them transitioned before its publication.

I have been blessed with exceptional mentors, teachers, and advisers who have shaped my intellectual and personal development, including Emilye Crosby, Joe McCartin, Anne MacPherson, Jamie Spiller, the late Akbar Muhammad, Diane Sommerville, John Stoner, Mark Reisenger, Jeanne Theoharis, Komozi Woodard, Brian Purnell, Sandy VanDyk, and Paul Genega, among others. My companions in the 2015 NEH workshop and the subsequent North East Freedom North Studies Writing Collective—Kristopher Bryan Burrell, Crystal Moten, Say Burgin, and Peter Levy—inspired and guided the final revisions to this work. More importantly, their generous spirit and collaboration make scholarship production so much more fulfilling and enjoyable.

In many ways, my grandparents Irene and Bernie taught me my first history lessons, sharing with me stories, photos, and even their early marital correspondence from the farm in upstate New York. My parents, Don Warren and Susan Ahouse, provided me a firm intellectual foundation upon which to build. My sisters and lifelong companions, Lisa Aulgur and Emily Gilbert, have always been my home. I am blessed with cousins who often feel more like siblings: Brandy, Stephen, Joe, Jill, Kari, and Alana, thank you for the laughter— always the laughter.

The most incredible group of comrades has sustained me in every way. For their lifetime of love, kindness, support, intellectual engagement, childcare, laughter, tears, and most importantly, their companionship, I thank Holen

Robie, Melody Ross Wilson, Mark Schmidt, Sarah Hillman, Erica Ellison Ko-nopski, Emily Hill Mehlenbacher, Geoff Schutte, Andrew Dudley, Sandra Sanchez-Lopez, Carlos Cortissoz Mora, Jodie Broecker Taylor, Janelle Edwards, the late Karen Clark, Kikuyu Mau Calhoun, Julia Rabig, Nishani Frazier, Shan-non King, Brandon Fralix, Freddie Harris Ramsby, Jonterri Gadson, Nixon Cleophat, Nora McCook, and Michelle Chase. Two individuals have carried so much of this load, and they deserve more credit than this humble offering can provide. Denise Ireton demonstrated numerous acts of friendship and kindness both to me and to my son Liam on a daily basis. Additionally, this experience has been improved in every way by the love, support, and intel-lectual engagement of Michael O. West. My constant companion, Liam, had just learned to walk when I started down this path. Now a junior in high school, he is still quick to remind me, and anyone who will listen, that his mother is "not like a *real* doctor or anything."

NOTES

Introduction

1. "No. HS-7. Population of the Largest 75 Cities: 1900–2000," US Census Bureau, Statistical Abstract of the United States: April 1, 2003, https://www.census.gov/statab/hist/HS-07.pdf, accessed October 30, 2014, Wayback Machine.

2. Though present early on in Rochester, the most spectacular display of Black theology and Black economic development might very well have occurred some years later, with the creation of the Black Manifesto produced at the 1969 Black Economic Development Conference in Detroit, an event arranged by Black clergy.

3. Rochester was no stranger to social protest movements. In fact, the abolition and women's rights movements of the nineteenth century garnered several interesting case studies. Indeed, much has been written about this city's earlier movements. Of the bulk of Rochester's twentieth century, however, historians have had little to say, despite its continued tradition of dissent and a demand for social and economic justice, which most glaringly coalesced in this new struggle for Black rights. For examples, see Paul Johnson, *A Shopkeeper's Millennium: Society and Revivals in Rochester, NY, 1815–1837* (New York: Hill and Wang, 1978); Nancy Hewitt, *Women's Activism and Social Change: Rochester, NY, 1822–1872* (Ithaca, NY: Cornell University Press, 1984); and Milton Sernett, *North Star Country: Upstate New York and the Crusade for African American Freedom* (Syracuse, NY: Syracuse University Press, 2002).

4. The "Freedom North" studies began in earnest with the publication of Jeanne Theoharis and Komozi Woodard, eds., *Freedom North: Black Freedom Struggles outside the North, 1940–1980* (New York: Palgrave Macmillan, 2003); and Theoharis and Woodard, eds., *Groundwork: Local Black Freedom Movements in America* (New York: New York University Press, 2005). Other studies that are central to this literature include Martha Biondi, *To Stand and Fight: The Struggle for Civil Rights in Postwar New York City* (Cambridge, MA: Harvard University Press, 2003); Matthew Countryman, *Up South: Civil Rights and Black Power in Philadelphia* (Philadelphia: University of Pennsylvania Press, 2006); Patrick D. Jones, *The Selma of the North: Civil Rights Insurgency in Milwaukee* (Cambridge, MA: Harvard University Press, 2010); Clarence Lang, *Grassroots at the Gateway: Class Politics and Black Freedom Struggle in St. Louis, 1936–75* (Ann Arbor: University of Michigan Press, 2009); Donna Jean Murch, *Living for the City: Migration, Education, and the Rise of the Black Panther Party in Oakland, California* (Chapel Hill: University of North Carolina Press, 2010); Robert O. Self, *American Babylon: Race and the Struggle for Postwar Oakland* (Princeton, NJ: Princeton University Press, 2003); Thomas J. Sugrue, *The Origins of the Urban Crisis: Race and Inequality in Postwar Detroit*

(Princeton, NJ: Princeton University Press, 2005); Komozi Woodard, *A Nation within a Nation: Amiri Baraka (LeRoi Jones) and Black Power Politics* (Chapel Hill: University of North Carolina Press, 1999); and Brian Purnell and Jeanne Theoharis with Komozi Woodard, *The Strange Careers of the Jim Crow North: Segregation and Struggle outside of the South* (New York: New York University Press, 2019).

5. See Christopher Strain, *Pure Fire: Self-Defense as Activism in the Civil Rights Era* (Athens: University of Georgia Press, 2005); Charles E. Cobb Jr., *This Nonviolent Stuff'll Get You Killed: How Guns Made the Civil Rights Movement Possible* (New York: Basic Books, 2014); and Akinyele Dmowale Umoja, *We Will Shoot Back: Armed Resistance in the Mississippi Freedom Movement* (New York: New York University Press, 2014).

6. See Michael Flamm, *In the Heat of Summer: The New York Riots of 1964 and the War on Crime* (Philadelphia: University of Pennsylvania Press, 2016).

7. At the 2009 Association for the Study of African-American Life and History (ASALH) conference in Cincinnati, Ohio, young Black Power scholars in several sessions struggled to place their current work in the Black Freedom Struggle historiography, which privileges the social, cultural, and political expressions of Black Power at the expense of economic expressions. Likewise, these same scholars felt frustrated by the literature in business history, which has traditionally ignored the Black Power movement altogether. Their various efforts, however, will likely bring about a significant change in the historiography, bringing together Black Power studies and business history. See Laura Warren Hill and Julia Rabig, eds., *The Business of Black Power: Community Development, Capitalism, and Corporate Responsibility in Postwar America* (Rochester, NY: University of Rochester Press, 2012); Brian Purnell, *Fighting Jim Crow in the County of Kings: The Congress of Racial Equality in Brooklyn* (Lexington: University Press of Kentucky, 2013). See also Julia Rabig, *The Fixers: Devolution, Development, and Civil Society in Newark, 1960–1990* (Chicago: University of Chicago Press, 2016); Nishani Frazier, *Harambee City: The Congress of Racial Equality in Cleveland and the Rise of Black Power Populism* (Fayetteville: University of Arkansas Press, 2017); Joshua Davis, *From Head Shops to Whole Foods: The Rise and Fall of Activist Entrepreneurs* (New York: Columbia University Press, 2017).

8. Early examples of this work include Robert E. Weems Jr., *Desegregating the Dollar: African-American Consumerism in the Twentieth Century* (New York: New York University Press, 1998); Emilye Crosby, *A Little Taste of Freedom: The Black Freedom Struggle in Claiborne County, Mississippi* (Chapel Hill: University of North Carolina Press, 2005); Self, *American Babylon*; and Countryman, *Up South*. For more recent and intentional examinations of the economic threads of Black Power, see Hill and Rabig, eds., *Business of Black Power*; Michael Ezra, ed., *The Economic Civil Rights Movement: African Americans and the Struggle for Economic Power* (New York: Routledge, 2013); and Jessica Gordon Nembhard, *Collective Courage: A History of African American Cooperative Economic Thought and Practice* (University Park, PA: Penn State University Press, 2014).

9. See Victoria Wolcott, "Recreation and Race in the Postwar City: Buffalo's 1956 Crystal Beach Riot," *Journal of American History* 93, no. 1 (June 2006): 63–90; Weems, *Desegregating the Dollar*; and Crosby, *Little Taste of Freedom*. There are, however, a few exceptions here. Both Matthew Countryman and Thomas Sugrue note the tension between traditional civil rights strategies and those engaged in the economic development more often associated with Black Power. See Countryman, *Up South*; and

Sugrue, *Sweet Land of Liberty: The Forgotten Struggle for Civil Rights in the North* (New York: Random House, 2008).

10. Robert E. Weems Jr. and Lewis A. Randolph, "The Ideological Origins of Richard Nixon's 'Black Capitalism' Initiative," *Review of Black Political Economy* 29, no. 1 (Summer 2001): 49–61; Weems and Randolph, "The National Response to Richard M. Nixon's Black Capitalism Initiative: The Success of Domestic Détente," *Journal of Black Studies* 32, no. 1 (September 2001): 66–83; and Dean Kotlowski, *Nixon's Civil Rights: Politics, Principle, and Policy* (Cambridge, MA: Harvard University Press, 2002).

11. This work responds to and builds on three important recent trends in the historiography of civil rights and Black Power. First, it draws on the temporal extension of both movements called for by Jacquelyn Dowd Hall. See Hall, "The Long Civil Rights Movement and the Political Uses of the Past," *Journal of American History* 91, no. 4 (March 2005): 1233–1263. For examples of this literature, see Timothy B. Tyson, *Radio Free Dixie: Robert F. Williams and the Roots of Black Power* (Chapel Hill: University of North Carolina Press, 1999); Woodard, *A Nation within a Nation*; Theoharis and Woodard, eds., *Freedom North*; Angela Dillard, *Faith in the City: Preaching Radical Social Change in Detroit* (Ann Arbor: University of Michigan Press, 2007); Hasan Jeffries, *Bloody Lowndes: Civil Rights and Black Power in Alabama's Black Belt* (New York: New York University Press, 2009); Martha Biondi, *To Stand and Fight: The Struggle for Civil Rights in Postwar New York City* (Cambridge, MA: Harvard University Press, 2003). To be sure, not all scholars of the Black Freedom Struggle support these historiographic shifts. Sundiata Keita Cha-Jua and Clarence Lang have argued that by stretching the parameters of the traditional civil rights movement, scholars have obscured rather than clarified the issue by placing the Black Freedom Struggle "outside of time and history, beyond the processes of life and death, and change and development." See Cha-Jua and Lang, "The 'Long Movement' as Vampire: Temporal and Spatial Fallacies in Recent Black Freedom Studies," *Journal of African-American History* 92, no. 2 (Spring 2007): 265–288. These same scholars reject the lionization of the Black Power movement in favor of the civil rights movement. For a fuller description of this literature and the subsequent shift in the literature, see Peniel Joseph, "The Black Power Movement: A State of the Field," *Journal of American History* 96, no. 3 (December 2009): 752. Second, the Black Freedom Struggle has been reenvisioned spatially. Studies of the movement in the North and West radically depart from the previous literature, which located a singular type of movement that privileged the South. See Countryman, *Up South*; Self, *American Babylon*; Matthew Lassiter and Joseph Crespino, eds., *The Myth of Southern Exceptionalism* (New York: Oxford University Press, 2009). See also Kimberley L. Phillips, *AlabamaNorth: African-American Migrants, Community, and Working-Class Activism in Cleveland, 1915–45* (Urbana: University of Illinois Press, 1999), which argues that both the civil rights and Black Power movements often drew from common sources, ideologically and organizationally. See Jeffries, *Bloody Lowndes*. Finally, this literature privileges the community as a central point of organization. In these local studies, federal policies, national organizations, and leading figures do not become peripheral; rather, their historical positions are clarified and illuminated further by local contextualization. Neither movement was monolithic, nor were national events and organizations received identically around the nation. See, for example, Theoharis and Woodard, eds., *Groundwork*; Emilye Crosby, ed., *Civil Rights History from the Ground Up:*

Local Struggles, a National Movement (Athens: University of Georgia Press, 2011); Crosby, *Little Taste of Freedom*; and Patrick D. Jones, *The Selma of the North: Civil Rights Insurgency in Milwaukee* (Cambridge, MA: Harvard University Press, 2009).

12. See, for example, Allen J. Matusow, *The Unraveling of America: A History of Liberalism in the 1960s* (New York: Harper and Row, 1984); and Todd Gitlin, *The Sixties: Years of Hope, Days of Rage* (New York: Bantam Books, 1987).

13. Ruth Forsyth, *The Rochester Area Selected Demographic and Social Characteristics* (Rochester, NY: Monroe Community College, 1984).

14. Dillard, *Faith in the City*, 89.

15. The term "hard-core unemployed" was widely used in this period to denote a person who was not easily employed because he or she had insufficient education or training, a criminal record, had suffered long periods of unemployment, or had never been gainfully employed.

16. Sugrue, *Sweet Land of Liberty*, 429.

1. Black Rochester at Midcentury

1. "Baden Street Settlement, Fiftieth Anniversary, 1901–1951," Rochester, 1951, Baden St. Settlement Files, Social Welfare History Archives, University of Minnesota Library, Minneapolis, digitized March 12, 2018; Social Welfare History Project, Virginia Commonwealth University Libraries, Richmond, http://socialwelfare.library.vcu.edu/organizations/baden-street-settlement-1901-1951/.

2. Timothy B. Tyson, *Radio Free Dixie: Robert F. Williams and the Roots of Black Power* (Chapel Hill: University of North Carolina Press, 1999), 71.

3. See, for example, Joe William Trotter, *Black Milwaukee: The Making of an Industrial Proletariat, 1915–45* (Urbana: University of Illinois Press, 1985); James R. Grossman, *Land of Hope: Chicago, Black Southerners, and the Great Migration* (Chicago: University of Chicago Press, 1989); James N. Gregory, *The Southern Diaspora: How the Great Migrations of Black and White Southerners Transformed America* (Chapel Hill: University of North Carolina Press, 2005); Elizabeth Clark-Lewis, *Living In, Living Out: African-American Domestics and the Great Migration* (Washington, DC: Smithsonian Institution Press, 1994); Greta de Jong, "Staying in Place: Black Migration, the Civil Rights Movement, and the War on Poverty in the Rural South," *Journal of African-American History* 90, no. 4 (Autumn 2005): 387–409; Carole Marks, "Black Workers and the Great Migration North," *Phylon* 46, no. 2 (1985): 148–161; Carole Marks, *Farewell—We're Good and Gone: The Great Black Migration* (Bloomington: Indiana University Press, 1989); Allan Spear, *Black Chicago: The Making of a Negro Ghetto, 1890–1920* (Chicago: University of Chicago Press, 1967); Gilbert Osofsky, *Harlem, The Making of a Ghetto: Negro New York, 1890–1930* (Chicago: Ivan R. Dee, 1996); and Kenneth Kusmer, *A Ghetto Takes Shape: Black Cleveland, 1870–1930* (Urbana: University of Illinois Press, 1976).

4. Trotter, *Black Milwaukee*, 39.

5. Gregory, *Southern Diaspora*, 18.

6. Gregory, 15–17.

7. Father Quintin Primo recalled, for example, that one day he received a call from the head custodian at Kodak. Kodak was looking to hire "janitors of color" for good pay and benefits. The company required only that a potential candidate for the custodial

position have a minimum of two years in college. See the Right Reverend Quintin E. Primo Jr., *The Making of a Black Bishop* (Wilmington, DE: Cedar Tree Books, 1998), 80.

8. William Ringle, "A Tale of Two Cities: From Sanford, Fla., to Rochester, N.Y.," *Rochester Times-Union*, March 10, 1969, 1A.

9. Victoria Sandwick Schmitt, "Goin' North," *Rochester History* 54, no. 1 (1992): 6. See also Neil Foley, *The White Scourge: Mexicans, Blacks, and Poor Whites in Texas Cotton Culture* (Berkeley: University of California Press, 1997), 165; Eugene Barrington, "New Beginnings: The Story of Five Black Entrepreneurs Who Migrated from Sanford, Florida to Rochester, New York" (PhD diss., Syracuse University, 1976), 24; and Dorothy Nelkin, *On the Season: Aspects of the Migrant Labor System* (Ithaca, NY: State School of Industrial and Labor Relations, Cornell University, 1970), 11.

10. Patricia DuPont, Carl H. Feuer, and Jean Kost, "Black Migrant Farmworkers in New York State: Exploitable Labor," *Afro-Americans in New York Life and History* 12, no. 1 (January 1988): 9.

11. DuPont, Feuer, and Kost, "Black Migrant Farmworkers," 78.

12. Joyce Woelfle Lehmann, *Migrant Farmworkers of Wayne County, New York: A Collection of Oral Histories from the Back Roads* (Lyons, NY: Wayne County Historical Society Bicentennial Project, 1990), 26.

13. Lehmann, *Migrant Farmworkers*, 36–37.

14. Lehmann, 5.

15. "About Mott's: Company History," 2019, http://www.motts.com/about. See also chris1967-ga, "Q: Corporate Historical," Google Answers, October 25, 2002, http://answers.google.com/answers/threadview?id=68866.

16. Nelkin, *On the Season*, 21.

17. Lehmann, *Migrant Farmworkers*, 8.

18. Nelkin, *On the Season*, 26.

19. Nelkin, 26.

20. Lehmann, *Migrant Farmworkers*, 78.

21. Schmitt, "Goin' North," 22.

22. Ira Katznelson, *When Affirmative Action Was White: An Untold History of Racial Inequality in Twentieth-Century America* (New York: W. W. Norton, 2005), 27–29.

23. Nelkin, *On the Season*, 64.

24. Gregory, *Southern Diaspora*, 11; DuPont, Feuer, and Kost, "Black Migrant Farmworkers," 11.

25. Schmitt, "Goin' North," 4.

26. Ringle, "Tale of Two Cities," 1A.

27. Barrington, "New Beginnings," 12.

28. Barrington, 54.

29. Barrington, 229.

30. John and Constance Mitchell, interview by Laura Warren Hill, July 12, 2008, transcript, Rochester Black Freedom Struggle Project, Rare Books, Special Collections, and Preservation, River Campus Libraries, University of Rochester; herein referred to as Mitchell interview.

31. Charles Buddy Granston, interview by Laura Warren Hill, July 6, 2009, transcript, Rochester Black Freedom Struggle Project, Rare Books, Special Collections, and Preservation, River Campus Libraries, University of Rochester.

32. Darryl Porter, Walter Cooper, and Laura Warren Hill, interview by Norma Holland, *Many Voices, Many Visions*, WHAM-TV, May 24, 2009.

33. Trent Jackson, interview by Chris Christopher, *July '64*, directed by Carvin Eison, DVD (Brockport, NY: ImageWordSound, 2006).

34. Walter Cooper, interview by Laura Warren Hill, May 21, 2008, transcript, Rochester Black Freedom Struggle Project, Rare Books, Special Collections, and Preservation, River Campus Libraries, University of Rochester; herein referred to as Cooper interview.

35. Earl Caldwell, "Chapter 7: Boll Weevil," *Caldwell Journals*, Maynard IJE History Project, Oakland, CA: Robert C. Maynard Institute for Journalism Education, 1999, http://www.localcommunities.org/servlet/lc_procserv/dbpage=page&gid=000 910000009674825948437 65.

36. Caldwell, "Boll Weevil."

37. Frederick Douglass quoted in Eugene E. DuBois, *The City of Frederick Douglass: Rochester's African-American People and Places* (Rochester: Landmark Society of Western New York, 1994).

38. Adolph Dupree, "Rochester Roots/Routes, Part III," *About . . . Time*, September 1984, 17.

39. I employ the use of courtesy titles, drawing on the practice of scholar Charles M. Payne, who argues, "Southern Blacks had to struggle for the use of 'courtesy titles' and thus often had a different appreciation for them. More particularly, the use of titles was self-consciously a token of respect and affection that [people] commanded even from young men and women who [sic] were frequently contemptuous of social convention." See Payne, *I've Got the Light of Freedom: The Organizing Tradition and the Mississippi Freedom Struggle* (Berkeley: University of California Press, 1995), 6.

40. Over the course of his lifetime, George Eastman bestowed $51,000,000 on the University of Rochester. He was integral in the creation of the medical school. A plaque affixed to the medical school reads, "The School of Medicine and Dentistry was established in the University of Rochester in 1920 by the gifts of George Eastman and the General Education Board founded by John D. Rockefeller and is dedicated to the advancement of knowledge and to instruction in medicine and dentistry for the promotion of the health and happiness of mankind." See Arthur J. May, "George Eastman and the University of Rochester: His Role, His Influence," *University of Rochester Library Bulletin* 26, no. 3 (Spring 1971).

41. Adolph Dupree, "Rochester Roots/Routes, Part II," *About . . . Time*, August 1984, 12.

42. Dupree, "Rochester Roots/Routes, Part II," 21.

43. Rochester legend suggests the pair was responsible for acceptance of the first Black blood donors to the American Red Cross as well.

44. Dupree, "Rochester Roots/Routes, Part II," 12.

45. Bennett Parmington, "Dr. Charles Terrell Lunsford," Field Reports from Mt. Hope Cemetery, Rochester, NY (December 22, 2008), http://hdl.handle.net/1802/6338; see also "A Shocking Inner City Crime" clipping, box 5A, folder 8, Franklin Florence Papers, Rare Books, Special Collections, and Preservation, River Campus Libraries, University of Rochester.

46. Mitchell interview; Dupree, "Rochester Roots/Routes, Part V," *About . . . Time*, November 1984, 32.

47. Primo, *Making of a Black Bishop*, 64.

48. Glenn Claytor, interview by Laura Warren Hill, August 21, 2008, transcript, Rochester Black Freedom Struggle Project, Rare Books, Special Collections, and Preservation, River Campus Libraries, University of Rochester; herein referred to as Claytor interview.

49. Claytor interview.

50. Claytor interview.

51. Primo, *Making of a Black Bishop*, 68–73.

52. Interestingly, Cooper was a beneficiary of Lunsford's agitation some decades earlier. Cooper was hired by Eastman Kodak only after the company reluctantly began to hire some African Americans with PhDs in chemistry and biology.

53. "Education: Should All Northern Schools Be Integrated?" *Time*, September 7, 1962.

54. Cooper interview.

55. Claytor interview.

56. Jack Germound, interview by Chris Christopher, *July '64*, directed by Carvin Eison, DVD (Brockport, NY: ImageWordSound, 2006).

57. Dupree, "Rochester Roots/Routes, Part III," 33.

58. Dupree, "Rochester Roots/Routes, Part V," 34.

59. Reuben Davis, interview by Laura Warren Hill, July 9, 2009, transcript, Rochester Black Freedom Struggle Project, Rare Books, Special Collections, and Preservation, River Campus Libraries, University of Rochester.

60. Dupree, "Rochester Roots/Routes, Part V," 32.

61. Dupree, 32; Cooper interview; Mitchell interview.

62. Mitchell interview.

63. 1985 Presentation of the Annual Rotary Award to Constance M. Mitchell, May 21, 1985; Clarissa St. Reunion 10th Anniversary publication, 2005. Constance and John Mitchell provided these materials for use by the author.

64. Mitchell interview.

65. Claytor interview.

66. Mitchell interview.

67. Mitchell interview.

68. Mitchell interview.

69. Mitchell interview.

70. Cooper interview; Claytor interview; Mitchell interview.

71. Claytor interview.

72. Darryl Porter, interview by Laura Warren Hill, June 10, 2008, transcript, Rochester Black Freedom Struggle Project, Rare Books, Special Collections, and Preservation, River Campus Libraries, University of Rochester.

73. Claytor interview.

74. 1985 Presentation and Clarissa St. Reunion.

2. Uniting for Survival

1. Chapter 2 was originally published as "'We Are Black Folks First': The Black Freedom Struggle in Rochester, NY and the Making of Malcolm X," *The Sixties: A Journal of History, Politics and Culture* 3, no. 2 (December 2010): 163–185. Some changes have been

made to this version. Used with permission from *The Sixties*, Taylor & Francis Ltd., http://www.informaworld.com. For the anecdote, see Gloster Current to Messrs. Wilkins, Morsell, Moon, and Odom, memorandum, February 19, 1963; Gloster Current to Rev. J. Oscar Lee, February 21, 1963; Gloster Current to NAACP branches, Re: NAACP and the Muslims, undated; all three in Papers of the NAACP, Part 29: Branch Department Files, Series B: Branch Newsletters, Annual Branch Activities Reports, and Selected Branch Department Subject Files, 1966–1972, Folder "009059-010-0492: Black Muslims, Nation of Islam, and police brutality, 1962–1963 and undated," Pro-Quest History Vault; herein referred to as Folder 009059-010-0492, NAACP papers.

2. "Negroes Call for Unity to Protest 'Abuses,'" *Rochester Democrat and Chronicle*, February 18, 1963, 15; "The Rochester Image Two-Faced? Angry Voices Raised by Opposing Groups," *Rochester Democrat and Chronicle*, March 13, 1963, 6. Both articles are in box 58, folder 766, Industrial Areas Foundation Records, Special Collections and University Archives, University of Illinois at Chicago.

3. Scholars have built upon the popular perceptions created by contemporary newspaper accounts that drew sweeping distinctions between the separatist platform of the NOI and the integrationist agenda of the NAACP and the nonviolent strategies of the early CORE movement. For examples of this scholarship, see C. Eric Lincoln, *The Black Muslims in America* (Boston: Beacon Press, 1961), 141–145; Kevin Mumford, *Newark: A History of Race, Rights, and Riots in America* (New York: New York University Press, 2007), 81; Angela Dillard, *Faith in the City: Preaching Radical Social Change in Detroit* (Ann Arbor: University of Michigan Press, 2007), 232–233; Komozi Woodard, *A Nation within a Nation: Amiri Baraka (LeRoi Jones) and Black Power Politics* (Chapel Hill: University of North Carolina Press, 1999), 62; James H. Cone, *Martin and Malcolm and America: A Dream or a Nightmare* (Maryknoll, NY: Orbis Books, 1991; reprint 2007), 200; and Judson Jeffries, ed., *Black Power in the Belly of the Beast* (Urbana: University of Illinois Press, 2006), 3.

For examples of popular reporting, see Michael Clark, "Rise in Racial Extremism Worries Harlem Leaders," *New York Times*, January 25, 1960, 1, 18. Here, NAACP president Roy Wilkins told reporters, "The Temple of Islam was no better in its racial creed than the Ku Klux Klan. We also feel . . . that any cult that seeks to make a minority believe that it can solve its problems through racial hatred is misleading the people and spreading destruction." The same article quoted C. Sumner Stone of the *New York Age*, "The NAACP and the Urban League are doing a good job, but are not emotionally satisfying. . . . When you're angry, you want to hear angry words." The article opined, "The purveyors of angry words in Harlem are to be found mainly among followers of Elijah Muhammad and Malcolm X."

4. Adolph Dupree, "Rochester Roots/Routes, Part V," *About . . . Time*, November 1984, 23.

5. Hasan Kwame Jeffries identifies freedom rights as "the assortment of civil and human rights that emancipated African Americans identified as the crux of freedom. Framing the civil rights movement as a fight for freedom rights acknowledges the centrality of slavery and emancipation to conceptualizations of freedom; incorporates the long history of black protest dating back to the daybreak of freedom and extending beyond the Black Power era; recognizes African Americans' civil and human rights objectives; and captures the universality of these goals. Moreover, it al-

lows for regional and temporal differentiation, moments of ideological radicalization, and periods of social movement formation." In Jeffries, *Bloody Lowndes: Civil Rights and Black Power in Alabama's Black Belt* (New York: New York University Press, 2009), 4.

6. Blake McKelvey, "Housing and Urban Renewal: The Rochester Experience," *Rochester History* 17, no. 4 (October 1965): 19.

7. McKelvey, "Housing and Urban Renewal," 19.

8. Olive Le Boo to Mayor Frank Lamb, July 27, 1964, BIN 1274, folder "Riots of 1964, Letters from Olive Le Boo"; and A citizen residing at 230 Trafalgar St. to Mayor Frank Lamb, July 29, 1964, Frank Lamb Collection, Mayoral Papers, BIN 1274, folder "Riots of 1964; Correspondence from Individuals," both in Frank Lamb Collection, Mayoral Papers, Rochester Municipal Archives and Record Center.

9. "As We See It: Community Leadership Needed to Stop Attacks on Police," *Rochester Times-Union*, August 22, 1961; "A Start toward Better Relations," *Rochester Times-Union*, August 25, 1961; and "A Way to Improve Racial Problems," *Rochester Democrat and Chronicle*, August 26, 1961.

10. Desmond Stone, "The Tense, Sensitive No Man's Land of Race Relations," *Rochester Times-Union*, February 19, 1963, "S.C.A.C" folder, Walter Cooper papers. This set of papers was generously offered to the author for use. With Dr. Cooper's permission, they have since been deposited with the Rare Books, Special Collections, and Preservation, River Campus Libraries, University of Rochester. All references refer to their original organization in folders by Dr. Cooper and will not necessarily correspond with the archival system employed by the University of Rochester; herein referred to as Cooper papers.

11. Walter Cooper, interview by Laura Warren Hill, May 21, 2008, transcript, Rochester Black Freedom Struggle Project, Rare Books, Special Collections, and Preservation, River Campus Libraries, University of Rochester; herein referred to as Cooper interview.

12. Some residents cited at least thirteen cases they viewed as truly egregious. Cooper interview; Franklin Florence, interview by Laura Warren Hill, September 19, 2008, transcript in author's personal collection; herein referred to as Florence interview; and Glenn Claytor, interview by Laura Warren Hill, August 21, 2008, transcript, Rochester Black Freedom Struggle Project, Rare Books, Special Collections, and Preservation, River Campus Libraries, University of Rochester.

13. Cooper interview; Florence interview; "Two Cops Hurt Subduing Man," *Rochester Democrat and Chronicle*, August 23, 1962, "RVF Police Cases and Incidents 1959–1969" clipping file, Rochester Public Library; herein referred to as RPL. See also *The People of the State of New York v. Rufus Fairwell Preliminary Hearing* transcript, box 18, folder 15, Howard Coles Papers, Rochester Museum and Science Center; herein referred to as Coles papers.

14. "Detective Testifies on Fairwell," *Rochester Times-Union*, May 19, 1964, "RVF Police Cases and Incidents 1959–1969" clipping file, RPL; "U.S. Probing Fairwell Case, Rally Told," *Rochester Democrat and Chronicle*, November 5, 1962, "RVF Police Cases and Incidents 1959–1969" clipping file, RPL.

15. The "man with a gun" story was repeated so many times that it became rather cliché throughout the city. See "Muslim Case Goes to Jury," *Rochester Democrat and Chronicle*, March 25, 1964; "Muslim Trial Set Monday," *Rochester Democrat and Chronicle*,

February 27, 1964; "Officers' Injuries Told to Muslim Case Jury," *Rochester Democrat and Chronicle*, March 14, 1964; and "Police Deny Watch on Muslim Hall," *Rochester Times-Union*, May 17, 1963. All articles are in the "Black Muslims" clipping file, RPL.

15. For descriptions of the arrest, see "Rochester: Cops' Newest Target in Harassment Plot," *Muhammad Speaks*, February 4, 1963, 5.

16. For more on the Wilmington Ten, see Larry Reni Thomas, *The True Story behind the Wilmington Ten* (Hampton, VA: U. B. & U. S. Communications Systems, 1982).

17. Statement of A. C. White, February 5, 1963, NAACP and Police Brutality folder, Cooper papers. This statement indicates that it "was not signed by Mr. White, because of the extent of injuries of his arm and hands!!!" which included "a broken left arm, a shattered bone in the left wrist, a broken bone in the right hand, a broken finger on the right hand, . . . a dislocated finger on the right hand, ribs and side . . . bruised from the kicking, and sore until [he] could hardly breathe."

18. Florence interview.

19. Florence interview.

20. Florence interview.

21. For this list, Blake McKelvey included the Federation of Churches, which seemed to have changed around 1961 from the Federation of Churches of Rochester and Vicinity to the Rochester Area Council of Churches. McKelvey, "A History of the Police of Rochester, New York," *Rochester History* 25, no. 4 (October 1963): 25.

22. The investigation by the Justice Department would eventually be dropped without a conviction of the officers. In exchange, the city of Rochester paid a very handsome settlement to Rufus Fairwell for his injuries. See "Police, Firefighters Back Homer on Fairwell Case," *Rochester Democrat and Chronicle*, November 23, 1962; "Indictments Hit by Police Group," *Rochester Democrat and Chronicle*, n.d; "City Agrees to Provide Results of Police-Abuse Probe to Group," *Rochester Democrat and Chronicle*, February 21, 1963. All of these articles are in the NAACP and Police Brutality folder, Cooper papers. See also "The United Appeal of the United Action Committee for Rufus Fairwell," box 18, folder 15, Coles papers; "U.S. Probing Fairwell Case Rally Told," *Rochester Democrat and Chronicle*, November 5, 1962, "RVF Police Cases and Incidents, 1959–1969" clipping folder, RPL.

23. For more on the Nation of Islam, see Michael A. Gomez, *Black Crescent: The Experience and Legacy of African Muslims in the Americas* (Cambridge: Cambridge University Press, 2005).

24. Charles and Pauline Price, interview by Laura Warren Hill, August 6, 2008, transcript, Rochester Black Freedom Struggle Project, Rare Books, Special Collections, and Preservation, River Campus Libraries, University of Rochester; herein referred to as Price interview.

25. Minister Franklin Florence indicated that he accompanied Malcolm X and Freddie Thomas to a meeting with the city fathers prior to the invasion of the mosque wherein Malcolm X provided them with information regarding the NOI in an effort to preempt any run-ins with the police. See Florence interview.

26. For more on the 1971 Attica riot, see Heather Thompson, *Blood in the Water: The Attica Prison Uprising of 1971 and Its Legacy* (New York: Pantheon, 2016).

27. For a more complete examination of the NOI's formation and practices, see Garrett Felber, *Those Who Know Don't Say: The Nation of Islam, the Black Freedom Move-*

ment, and the Carceral State (Chapel Hill: University of North Carolina Press, 2020); Ula Yvette Taylor, *The Promise of Patriarchy: Women and the Nation of Islam* (Chapel Hill: University of North Carolina Press, 2017); Lincoln, *Black Muslims in America*; E. U. Essien-Udom, *Black Nationalism: A Search for an Identity in America* (Chicago: University of Chicago Press, 1962); Clifton Marsh, *The Lost-Found Nation of Islam in America* (Lanham, MD: Scarecrow Press, 2000); Dennis Walker, *Islam and the Search for African-American Nationhood: Elijah Muhammad, Louis Farrakhan, and the Nation of Islam* (Atlanta: Clarity Press, 2005); Jeffrey Ogbar, *Black Power Radicals and African-American Identity* (Baltimore: Johns Hopkins University Press, 2004); Michael Gomez, *Black Crescent: The Experience and Legacy of African Muslims in the Americas* (Cambridge, MA: Cambridge University Press, 2005); Richard Brent Turner, *Islam in the African-American Experience* (Bloomington: Indiana University Press, 1997); and Claude Andrew Clegge, *An Original Man: The Life and Times of Elijah Muhammad* (New York: St. Martin's Press, 1997).

28. These cases ultimately determined that the NOI would be a constitutionally protected religion.

29. *WE: Rochester's Only Newsmagazine* 19, no. 12 (January 7, 1963), clipping, Folder 009059-010-0492, NAACP papers.

30. Malcolm's talk that evening was a variation of the commonly known "House Slave, Field Slave" speech. See Charles Holcomb, "Muslim Tells of All-Negro Nation Goal," *Rochester Times-Union*, January 29, 1963, 22; and "Muslim Urges Nation in U.S for Negroes," *Rochester Democrat and Chronicle*, January 23, 1963; both in Folder 009059-010–0492, NAACP papers.

31. Wendell Phillips, "About the Wendells," *Wendells Write* (blog), 2009, http://wendellswrite.com/about/.

32. Holcomb, "Muslim Tells of All-Negro Nation Goal."

33. Rodney Brown, *Silent Leader: The Biography of Dr. Freddie L. Thomas* (Rochester, NY: Brown Publishing, 2015).

34. Chad Oliveiri, "Remembering Brother Malcolm: Thoughts on the Prophet, Forty Years after His Death," interview with Constance Mitchell, *Rochester City Newspaper*, February 16, 2005, *City Newspaper* digital archives. See also John and Constance Mitchell, interview by Laura Warren Hill, July 12, 2008, transcript, Rochester Black Freedom Struggle Project, Rare Books, Special Collections, and Preservation, River Campus Libraries, University of Rochester; herein referred to as Mitchell interview.

35. Mitchell interview; see also Holcomb, "Muslim Tells of All-Negro Nation Goal," 22.

36. After one of the era's first race riots occurred in Rochester on July 24–27, 1964, the local police reported in an internal memorandum that much of the responsibility for this event lay with Malcolm X and the Black Muslims: "The incident of January 6, 1963 involving a response by police officers to an emergency call at a location on North Street where there was found to be a meeting of Muslims and every indication that the call was a set-up on the part of some persons who desired to incite an incident and ferment [*sic*] unrest among the Negroes is another classic example. Following this, Malcolm X appeared in our community and preaching hate against the whites and supremacy for the Negros [*sic*], literally frightened a large number of our residents. Threats were made of blood in our streets and rioting at that time which prompted many of our clergy into becoming more aggressive locally in the

civil rights movement. The action of those clergymen involved in all faiths resulted in much unfavorable publicity against the police." See Inter-Departmental Correspondence from W. M. Lombard, Chief of Police to Donald J. Corbett, Commissioner of Public Safety, Attention: Porter W. Homer, City Manager, September 29, 1964, BIN 301, boxes 4 and 5 combined, Summer 1964-General, City Manager Subject Files C, Public Emergency Riot, Rochester Municipal Archives and Record Center.

37. "'Human Rights' Violated, Muslims Say," *Rochester Democrat and Chronicle*, January 8, 1963, 19. Interestingly, just weeks after Malcolm made this charge publicly, Rochester city police interrupted a Protestant church in full garb with K9 units in tow. See Florence interview. See also "Supervisors Get Report: Democrats Laud Anti-Bias Unit," *Rochester Democrat and Chronicle*, October 12, 1962; and "Supervisor Cites 1961 Record: City Cops Charged in 16 Complaints," undated; both articles are in the NAACP and Police Brutality folder, Cooper papers.

38. Interestingly, Monroe County, with the city of Rochester at its heart, had both a county Human Rights Commission and an office of the State Human Rights Commission. In the first nine months of 1962 alone, the county commission investigated more than 750 cases, approximately 725 of them initiated by nonwhite persons. Of the sixteen police brutality cases referred to this commission, all sixteen were against the Rochester City Police Department.

39. At this time, James Meredith had gained considerable national and international attention in his fight to desegregate the University of Mississippi through a federal lawsuit. See "Rochester, New York, Incident," in FBI Papers, NY 105-8999, Miscellaneous NOI Activity, 17–20, http://wonderwheel.net/work/foia/1963/040263-050263/misc-noi.pdf, April 14, 2010, Wayback Machine; and "Jailed Muslims Fasting, or Dieting?" *Rochester Times-Union*, February 15, 1963, 15.

40. "Muslim Assails Police 'Hostility,'" *Rochester Democrat and Chronicle*, February 15, 1963, Folder 009059-010-0492, NAACP papers.

41. For examples, see RVF Black Muslims clipping folder, RPL.

42. "Muslims Bar Firemen from Hall," *Rochester Democrat and Chronicle*, January 14, 1963, "RVF Black Muslims" clipping folder, RPL; and "Rochester Negroes Unite for Freedom: Hit Muslims' Persecution, Protest Police Brutality," *Muhammad Speaks*, March 18, 1963, 11.

43. Bruce Perry, ed., *Malcolm X: The Last Speeches* (New York: Pathfinder Press, 1989), 151–181.

44. A hand-drawn flyer that circulated throughout the Black community in Rochester after the 1964 uprising listed Loftus Carson as a "Tom," and therefore someone to be wary of (unfiled, Cooper papers).

45. "Muslim Assails Police 'Hostility,'" *Rochester Democrat and Chronicle*, February 15, 1963, Folder 009059-010-0492, NAACP papers; "Muslim Head Pleased by Conference," *Rochester Times-Union*, January 18, 1963, Black Muslims folder, RPL; and "Muslim Leader, Police Confer," *Rochester Democrat and Chronicle*, January 18, 1963, Black Muslims folder, RPL.

46. Louis DeCaro, *On the Side of My People: A Religious Life of Malcolm X* (New York: New York University Press, 1996), 185.

47. "Muslim March in N.Y. Protests Arrests Here," *Rochester Democrat and Chronicle*, February 14, 1963, RVF Black Muslims clipping folder, RPL.

48. "Rochester Negroes Unite for Freedom," *Muhammad Speaks*, March 18, 1963, 11.

49. "Black Muslims Released on $500 Bail Each," *Rochester Democrat and Chronicle*, undated, Folder 009059-010-0492, NAACP papers.

50. "Meeting Set at Settlement," *Rochester Times-Union*, February 16, 1963, Folder 009059-010-0492, NAACP papers.

51. "Negroes Call for Unity to Protest 'Abuses,'" *Rochester Democrat and Chronicle*, February 18, 1963, Folder 009059-010-0492, NAACP papers; author's personal correspondence with Walter Cooper, July 21, 2008.

52. "Rochester Negroes Unite for Freedom: Hit Muslims' Persecution, Protest Police Brutality," *Muhammad Speaks*, March 18, 1963, 11.

53. Current to Wilkins et al., February 19, 1963, NAACP papers.

54. Current to NAACP branches, NAACP papers (emphasis in original).

55. "NAACP Hits Separatists," *Rochester Times-Union*, January 17, 1963, Folder 009059-010-0492, NAACP papers.

56. "Rise of Muslims Laid to Bias," *Rochester Democrat and Chronicle*, January 31, 1963, Folder 009059-010-0492, NAACP papers; Florence interview.

57. Walter Cooper, "7.24.64: Reflections on the Rochester Riots," *Rochester City Newspaper*, July 21, 2004, *City Newspaper* digital archives.

58. Full-page advertisement in local newspaper, February 22, 1963, NAACP and Police Brutality folder, Cooper papers.

59. "City Agrees to Provide Results of Police-Abuse Probe to Group," *Rochester Democrat and Chronicle*, February 21, 1963, NAACP and Police Brutality folder, Cooper papers.

60. "Talks Continue into Late Hour on Police Acts," *Rochester Democrat and Chronicle*, February 25, 1963; "Review Board Progress Cited," *Rochester Times-Union*, February 27, 1963; "Board May Be Month Away," *Rochester Democrat and Chronicle*, February 28, 1963. All of these articles are in the NAACP and Police Brutality folder, Cooper papers.

3. A Quiet Rage Explodes

1. Temperatures had exceeded ninety degrees for several days leading up to the dance and then remained abnormally high well into the evening of July 24, 1964. See "Weather Reports throughout the Nation," *New York Times*, July 24, 1964, 52.

2. Contemporary accounts by public officials disputed stories that a dog bite occurred. However, footage of the riot does in fact show a young person bandaged after a canine bite. See Carvin Eison, dir., *July '64*, DVD (Brockport, NY: ImageWordSound, 2006).

3. Thomas Sugrue, *The Origins of the Urban Crisis: Race and Inequality in Postwar Detroit* (Princeton, NJ: Princeton University Press, 1996); Sidney Fine, *Violence in the Model City: The Cavanagh Administration, Race Relations, and the Detroit Riot of 1967* (Ann Arbor: University of Michigan Press, 1989); Leonard Gordon, *A City in Racial Crisis: The Case of Detroit Pre- and Post-1967 Riot* (Dubuque, IA: W. C. Brown, 1971); Hubert G. Locke, *The Detroit Riot of 1967* (Detroit: Wayne State University Press, 1969); Gerald Horne, *Fire This Time: The Watts Uprising and the 1960s* (Charlottesville: University Press of Virginia, 1995); Robert M. Fogelson, *The Los Angeles Riots* (Salem, NH: Ayer, 1988); Peter Rossi, ed., *Ghetto Revolts* (New Brunswick, NJ: Transaction Books, 1973); David Sears and John McConahay, *The Politics of Violence: The New Urban Blacks and the Watts Riot* (Boston: Houghton Mifflin, 1973).

4. "Hot Summer: Race Riots in North," *New York Times*, July 26, 1964, E1. The article's author claimed that "the contagion of racial violence last week began in Harlem, swept across the East River to the Bedford-Stuyvesant section of Brooklyn, flared back briefly to lower Manhattan, and then late in the week leaped 300 miles to Rochester." This type of reductionist reporting has encouraged scholars to focus on large urban centers as representative of the era, rather than to understand the context and particularities of location. I argue that Rochester is worthy of study in its own right for what it can tell us about the relationship between rioting and Black organizing in this era. A local article reaffirmed the belief in small, white cities that rioting would not break out; see "The Negro Influx: Problems Remain But Much Has Been Done," *Rochester Times-Union*, August 20, 1964; Rochester Riots and Profile, Walter Cooper papers. This set of papers, herein referred to as Cooper papers, was generously offered to the author for use. With Dr. Cooper's permission, they have since been deposited with the Rare Books, Special Collections, and Preservation, River Campus Libraries, University of Rochester. All references refer to their original organization in folders by Dr. Cooper and will not necessarily correspond with the archival system employed by the University of Rochester.

5. Whitney M. Young, "Middle Cities in Peril," June 6, 1964, BIN 1274, folder "Riots of 1964; Correspondence from Individuals," Frank Lamb Collection, Mayoral Papers, Rochester Municipal Archives and Record Center; herein referred to as Lamb Collection.

6. The term "second-tier city" describes a city that falls into one of two categories. The first refers to population. During the twentieth century, Rochester, for example, did not crack the top twenty list of most-populated cities. At its apex in 1930, Rochester ranked twenty-two, with a population of 328,132. The second category describes cities that experienced the largest African American in-migration rates during the Second Great Migration, specifically during the years 1955–1959. These second-tier cities did not expand considerably during the First Great Migration, but instead became popular destinations for African Americans later in the century. While they could not compete with larger cities in terms of population, their rates were impressive. Many such migrants first traveled to large cities such as Detroit, Chicago, and New York, then moved to smaller cities such as Rochester, Auburn, and Elmira in New York; Racine and Milwaukee in Wisconsin; Spokane, WA; and Sacramento, CA. See Townsand Price-Spratlen, "Urban Destination Selection among African Americans during the 1950s Great Migration," *Social Science History* 32, no. 3 (Fall 2008): 446.

7. Eison, *July '64*.

8. Trent Jackson, interview by Chris Christopher, in Eison, *July '64*.

9. Franklin Florence, interview by Chris Christopher, in Eison, *July '64*.

10. Thomas Allen, Report on Rochester, N.Y. Incident, July 1964, p. 2, Papers of the NAACP, Part 27: Selected Branch Files, 1956–1965, Series B: The Northeast, Folder "001504-006-0001, Rochester, New York branch operations, 1964–1965," ProQuest History Vault.

11. Allen, Report on Rochester.

12. "'Hoodlums on the Unfiled': Interview with Rochester's Congressman, Frank J. Horton," *U.S. News and World Report*, August 10, 1964, 40.

13. "We Demand," undated, BIN 1274, folder "Riots of 1964, Letters about the Riots; City Ordinances ordering curfew, list of demands from Mr. Nathaniel Wise," Lamb Collection.

14. Rochester mayor Frank Lamb, quoted in Eison, *July '64*.

15. Porter Homer to the Council, Re: Riots of July 1964, April 27, 1965, BIN 1274, folder "Riots of 1964, Letters from Businesses and other Groups," Lamb Collection.

16. "Rochester Police Battle Race Riot: Arrest of Negro Sets Off Melee by 1,000 in 50-Block Area of Upstate City," *New York Times*, July 25, 1964, 1.

17. John and Constance Mitchell, interview by Laura Warren Hill, July 12, 2008, transcript, Rochester Black Freedom Struggle Project, Rare Books, Special Collections, and Preservation, River Campus Libraries, University of Rochester; herein referred to as Mitchell interview.

18. Mitchell interview.

19. For a full description of Peck's relationship to the community, see chapter 1. See also Walter Cooper, interview by Laura Warren Hill, May 21, 2008, transcript, Rochester Black Freedom Struggle Project, Rare Books, Special Collections, and Preservation, River Campus Libraries, University of Rochester; herein referred to as Cooper interview; Glenn Claytor, interview by Laura Warren Hill, August 21, 2008, transcript, Rochester Black Freedom Struggle Project, Rare Books, Special Collections, and Preservation, River Campus Libraries, University of Rochester; Mitchell interview; and Eison, *July '64*.

20. Charles "Buddy" Granston, interview by Laura Warren Hill, July 6, 2009, transcript, Rochester Black Freedom Struggle Project, Rare Books, Special Collections, and Preservation, River Campus Libraries, University of Rochester.

21. James Malone to Seymour Scher, "Arrest Statistics, Preliminary Report," August 5, 1964, BIN 301, boxes 4 and 5 combined, Summer 1964-General, City Manager Subject Files C, Public Emergency Riot, Rochester Municipal Archives and Record Center, Rochester, NY; herein referred to as Public Emergency Riot files.

22. Daryl Porter, interview by Chris Christopher, in Eison, *July '64*.

23. Arthur Whitaker, interview by Chris Christopher, in Eison, *July '64*.

24. Eison, *July '64*.

25. Thomas Bell Jr., VP and GM of ITC, to Mayor Lamb and Public Advisory Board, August 8, 1964, bin 1274, folder "Riots of 1964," Lamb Collection.

26. Loma Allen, interview by Laura Warren Hill, August 7, 2008, transcript, Rochester Black Freedom Struggle Project, Rare Books, Special Collections, and Preservation, River Campus Libraries, University of Rochester; herein referred to as Allen interview.

27. Herb White, interview by Laura Warren Hill, August 2008, transcript, Rochester Black Freedom Struggle Project, Rare Books, Special Collections, and Preservation, River Campus Libraries, University of Rochester; herein referred to as White interview.

28. Marvin Chandler, interview by Laura Warren Hill, May 13, 2009, transcript, Rochester Black Freedom Struggle Project, Rare Books, Special Collections, and Preservation, River Campus Libraries, University of Rochester; White interview.

29. During the three days of rioting, three people were killed in a helicopter crash as a public official sought to get a closer look at events on the ground. A fourth man staggered into the road at another point and was hit by a car. He later died as a result of his injuries.

30. Constance Mitchell, interview by Chris Christopher, in Eison, *July '64*.

31. Charles and Pauline Price, interview by Laura Warren Hill, August 6, 2008, transcript, Rochester Black Freedom Struggle Project, Rare Books, Special Collections, and Preservation, River Campus Libraries, University of Rochester; herein referred to as Price interview.

32. Price interview.

33. Many major cities that experienced riots formed commissions to study the causes of the rebellion. In 1968, the federal government published the results of a national commission based on investigations in several cities; it is commonly referred to as the Kerner Report. See United States, *The Kerner Report: The 1968 Report of the National Advisory Commission on Civil Disorders* (New York: Pantheon Books, 1998).

34. United States Department of Justice, Federal Bureau of Investigation Report, 1964, bin 1274, folder "Riots of 1964, Letters about the Riots; City Ordinances ordering curfew, list of demands from Mr. Nathaniel Wise," Lamb Collection.

35. "Crisis in Race Relations: Rochester: Where a Race Riot Hit a 'Model' City," *U.S. News and World Report*, August 10, 1964, 37, BIN 1274, folder "Riots of 1964, Magazine Articles about the Riots, Other Related Material from Watts to Civil Rights," Lamb Collection.

36. For example, Darryl B. Harris, "The Logic of Black Urban Rebellions," *Journal of Black Studies* 28, no. 3 (January 1998): 368–385; Susan Olzak and Suzanne Shanahan, "Deprivation and Race Riots: An Extension of Spilerman's Analysis," *Social Forces* 74, no. 3 (March 1996): 931–961; Susan Olzak, Suzanne Shanahan and Elizabeth H. McEnearey, "Poverty, Segregation, and Race Riots: 1960 to 1993," *American Sociological Review* 61, no. 4 (August 1996): 590–613; and Mary C. King, "'Race Riots' and Black Economic Progress," *Review of Black Political Economy* 30, no. 4 (Spring 2003): 51–66.

37. More recently, scholars have begun to examine the ways that self-defense facilitated the movement, making nonviolence safe. See Christopher Strain, *Pure Fire: Self-Defense as Activism in the Civil Rights Era* (Athens: University of Georgia Press, 2005); Akinyele Umoja, *We Will Shoot Back: Armed Resistance in the Mississippi Freedom Movement* (New York: New York University Press, 2014); and Charles Cobb, *This Nonviolent Stuff Will Get You Killed: How Guns Made the Civil Rights Movement Possible* (New York: Basic Books, 2014).

38. Allen interview.

39. "We Demand," undated, BIN 1274, folder "Riots of 1964, City Ordinances Ordering Curfew, list of demands from Mr. Nathaniel Wise," Lamb Collection.

40. "Black Nationalist Movement Leaders Gaining Strength in Rochester," *Rochester Democrat and Chronicle*, July 27, 1964, BIN 1274, folder "Riots of 1964, Letters about the Riots; City Ordinances Ordering Curfew, List of Demands from Mr. Nathaniel Wise," Lamb Collection.

41. "Black Nationalist Movement Leaders," Lamb Collection.

42. Eison, *July '64*.

43. Allen, Report on Rochester, p. 1, NAACP papers.

44. Notes Relating to Attempt to Obtain New York National Guard Assistance in Rochester, undated, BIN 301, boxes 4 and 5 combined, Public Emergency Riot files.

45. John D. Madl, "Experiences—Techniques Used in Riots and Riot Control: A Study Based on Disorders in New York City, NY, Rochester, NY, and Philadelphia, PA, Summer-1964," BIN 1274, folder "Riots of 1964, Letters from Businesses and other Groups," Lamb Collection.

46. Madl, "Experiences," Lamb Collection.

47. "Riot Organized or Spontaneous?" *Rochester Democrat and Chronicle*, July 26, 1964, 1; "8 p.m. Curfew Ordered in City after Night-Long Negro Rioting, *Rochester Times-Union*, July 25, 1964, 1.

48. Chuck Mangione, interview by Chris Christopher, in Eison, *July '64*.

49. Jackson interview, in Eison, *July '64*.

50. "Friends of Negroes but Druggist Isn't Spared," *Rochester Times-Union*, July 27, 1964, Clipping File, Rochester Race Riot Papers, D.185, Rare Books, Special Collections, and Preservation, River Campus Libraries, University of Rochester.

51. Pictures located in the Rochester Race Riot Papers attest to this. See box 4, Photo Album, Rochester Race Riot Papers, D.185, Rare Books, Special Collections, and Preservation, River Campus Libraries, University of Rochester.

52. Mitchell interview.

53. Thomas Sugrue, *Sweet Land of Liberty: The Forgotten Struggle for Civil Rights in the North* (New York: Random House, 2008), 225, 332.

54. Matthew Countryman, *Up South: Civil Rights and Black Power in Philadelphia* (Philadelphia: University of Pennsylvania Press, 2006), 172.

55. Komozi Woodard, *A Nation within a Nation: Amiri Baraka (LeRoi Jones) and Black Power Politics* (Chapel Hill: University of North Carolina Press, 1999), 80.

56. See, for example, Horne, *Fire This Time*.

57. Clarence G. DePrez, Deputy Chief of Police, to W. M. Lombard, Chief of Police, August 3, 1964, Preliminary Report of Riot Investigation, BIN 301, boxes 4 and 5 combined, Public Emergency Riot files (emphasis in original).

58. Peter Hickey, "He's Aching but Alive Thanks to Army Truck," *Rochester Times-Union*, July 25, 1964, 1.

59. Data compiled from arrest records in box 4, 1964–1966, Rochester Race Riot Papers, D.185, Rare Books, Special Collections, and Preservation, River Campus Libraries, University of Rochester.

60. DePrez to Lombard, August 3, 1964, Public Emergency Riot files.

61. Mitchell interview, in Eison, *July '64*.

62. "Dr. Clark Warns That Riots Could Break Out Elsewhere," *New York Times*, July 22, 1964, 18.

63. Mitchell interview, in Eison, *July '64*.

64. "8 p.m. Curfew Ordered in City," 1.

65. Joseph E. Middlebrooks, Colonel, GS, NYARNG to Mayor, June 7, 1967, BIN 301, boxes 4 and 5 combined, Public Emergency Riot files.

66. Madl, "Experiences," Lamb Collection.

67. Lt. Col. Rex Applegate, "New Riot Control Weapons," *Ordnance* (July–August 1964): 67–70, BIN 1274, folder "Riots of 1964," Lamb Collection.

68. Applegate, "New Riot Control Weapons," Lamb Collection.

69. Jerry E. Bishop, "Police vs. Riots: How Forceful Should They Be in Putting Down Disorders?" undated article, BIN 1274, folder "Correspondence, Riots of 1964," Lamb Collection.

70. Colonel William F. Sheehan, "Command Report: Aid to Civil Authority, Rochester, NY 26 Jul–4 Aug 1964," received by Rochester City Manager's office on November 23, 1964, BIN 301, boxes 4 and 5 combined, Public Emergency Riot files.

71. Northern California Chapter of Radio and Television News Directors Association, "Broadcast Guidelines for Coverage of Civil Disorders," February 23, 1967, BIN 301, boxes 4 and 5 combined, Public Emergency Riot files (emphasis in original).

72. Six-City Study—A Survey of Racial Attitudes in Six Northern Cities: Preliminary Findings, June 1967, BIN 301, boxes 4 and 5 combined, Public Emergency Riot files.

4. Build the Army

1. In this chapter title, "Build the Army" was a term used at the first organizational meeting of FIGHT, a new community organization formed in Rochester after the uprising. The temporary committee determined its initial call would "build the army." See "Agenda of Rochester's Temporary Committee," March 30, 1965, FIGHT Steering, B, box 3B, Franklin Florence Papers, Rare Books, Special Collections, and Preservation, River Campus Libraries, University of Rochester; herein referred to as Florence papers.

2. Peter Levy, *The Great Uprising: The Urban Race Revolts of the 1960s* (New York: Cambridge University Press, 2018).

3. Adam Fairclough, *To Redeem the Soul of America* (Athens: University of Georgia Press, 1987), 197.

4. Kristopher Burrell, "Outsmarting Racism: New York's Black Intellectuals and Theorizing Northern Racism, 1945–1968" (PhD diss., CUNY Graduate Center, 2011).

5. "Who Speaks for the Negro?" *New York Times*, July 30, 1964, 26.

6. "Who Speaks," *New York Times*, 26.

7. For further discussion of the national NAACP's relationship with the Rochester branch, see chapter 2. For more on the divisive split between Black activists and the NAACP in Rochester, see chapter 1. Certain Black members of the local NAACP attempted to picket the homes of particular slumlords with poor reputations. One such slumlord contributed funds to the NAACP, so the picketing was called off at the behest of the National NAACP offices; see Franklin Florence, interview by Laura Warren Hill, September 19, 2008, transcript in author's personal collection; herein referred to as Florence interview.

8. In fact, the president of the Black Power organization that formed in 1965 refused to meet with CORE because he claimed it was an all-white organization. See Ed Chambers to Saul Alinsky, April 21, 1965, box 40, folder 619, Industrial Areas Foundation Records, Special Collections and University Archives, University of Illinois at Chicago; herein referred to as IAF records.

9. For further discussion of Rochester's Nation of Islam branch, see chapter 2.

10. Kristopher Burrell, "Where from Here? Ideological Perspectives on the Future of the Civil Rights Movement, 1964–1966," *Western Journal of Black Studies* 36, no. 2 (Spring 2012): 137–148.

11. For more on Herb White and the Board for Urban Ministry, see Herb White, interview by Laura Warren Hill, August 2008, transcript, Rochester Black Freedom Struggle Project, Rare Books, Special Collections, and Preservation, River Campus Libraries, University of Rochester; herein referred to as White interview. See also P. David Finks, "Crisis in Smugtown: A Study of Conflict, Churches, and Citizen Organizations in Rochester, NY, 1964–1969" (PhD diss., Union Graduate School, 1975).

12. Marvin Chandler, interview by Laura Warren Hill, May 13, 2009, transcript, Rochester Black Freedom Struggle Project, Rare Books, Special Collections, and Preservation, River Campus Libraries, University of Rochester.

13. Florence interview.

14. White interview; Michael Harrington, *The Other America: Poverty in the United States* (New York: Macmillan, 1962); Harvey Cox, *The Secular City: Secularization and Urbanization in Theological Perspective* (New York: Macmillan, 1966).

15. White interview.

16. Charles Silberman, *Crisis in Black and White* (New York: Vintage Books, 1964), 213.

17. Silberman, *Crisis in Black and White*, 213.

18. Finks, "Crisis in Smugtown," 9.

19. Girls Scouts of Western New York, "Georgiana Farr Sibley, 1887–1980," *Stories in Stone: Biographies*, Friends of Mount Hope Cemetery, 2009, http://www.fomh.org/Data/Documents/GeorgianaFarrSibley.pdf.

20. For a discussion of King and the SCLC's work in the North, see Adam Fairclough, *To Redeem the Soul of America* (Athens: University of Georgia Press, 1987), and David Garrow, *Bearing the Cross: Martin Luther King, Jr., and the Southern Christian Leadership Conference* (New York: William Morrow, 1986).

21. Phillip Benjamin, "Dr. King Confers with Mayor on City and U.S. Rights Issues," *New York Times*, July 28, 1964, 15.

22. "Statement by Martin Luther King, Jr., on New York Riots," July 27, 1964, King Papers, Speeches, Sermons, Etc., Series III, box 6, May 30, 1964–Oct 30, 1964, King Center for Research, King Library and Archives, Atlanta.

23. Martin Luther King Jr., to Dr. David Eisenberg, June 2, 1964, King Papers, box 51, folder 22 "Roch, NY, B'Nai B'rith, 1964–1967," King Center for Research, King Library and Archives, Atlanta.

24. Fairclough, *To Redeem the Soul of America*, 197.

25. Finks, "Crisis in Smugtown."

26. Andrew J. Young, "SCLC Dispatches Anti-Riot Team North: Finds Teen-Agers Hostile to Everyone," *Southern Christian Leadership Conference Newsletter* 2, no. 8 (July-August), King Papers, Speeches, Sermons, Etc., Series III, box 6, May 30, 1964–Oct 30, 1964, King Center for Research, King Library and Archives, Atlanta.

27. Desmond Stone, "What Price Violence? A Tense Struggle Goes on to Change Views of Negro," *Rochester Riots: A Scar or a Spur* (Rochester, NY: *Rochester Times-Union*, August 1964), box 11, folder 17, Howard Coles Papers, Rochester Museum and Science Center; herein referred to as Coles papers.

28. Finks, "Crisis in Smugtown"; see also Stephen Rose, "Rochester's Racial Rubicon," *Christianity and Crisis*, March 22, 1965, 55–59; and James Ridgeway, "Saul Alinsky in 'Smugtown,'" *New Republic*, June 26, 1965, 15–17, Alinsky folder, Walter Cooper Papers. This set of papers was generously offered to the author for use. With Dr. Cooper's permission, they have since been deposited with the Rare Books, Special Collections, and Preservation, River Campus Libraries, University of Rochester. All references refer to their original organization in folders by Dr. Cooper and will not necessarily correspond with the archival system employed by the University of Rochester; herein referred to as Cooper papers.

29. Stone, "What Price Violence?" On the young men's hostility to the strategy of nonviolence, see also Fairclough, *To Redeem the Soul of America*, 196–197.

30. Reuben Davis, interview by Laura Warren Hill, July 9, 2009, transcript, Rochester Black Freedom Struggle Project, Rare Books, Special Collections, and Preservation, River Campus Libraries, University of Rochester; herein referred to as Davis interview.

31. John and Constance Mitchell, interview by Laura Warren Hill, July 12, 2008, transcript, Rochester Black Freedom Struggle Project, Rare Books, Special Collections,

and Preservation, River Campus Libraries, University of Rochester; herein referred to as Mitchell interview.

32. Young, "SCLC Dispatches Anti-Riot Team North."

33. R. D. G. Wadhwani, "Kodak, FIGHT, and the Definition of Civil Rights in Rochester, NY: 1966–1967," *Historian* 60, no. 1 (Fall 1997): 60. There are several other possible explanations; however, on the surface, it appears that Rochester may have been tainted by the riot. Perhaps SCLC felt the ministers had already invested in a more radical form of organizing than they were prepared to support. However, local historians have suggested that the SCLC's recommendation that the council of churches work with Alinsky and the IAF suggest that the SCLC felt Rochester's problems were economic in nature and required an economically based form of organizing. While SCLC declined to organize in Rochester, James Bevel had private conversations with Franklin Florence and Constance Mitchell, two of Rochester's young Black leaders, regarding Bevel's desire to quite the SCLC. He discussed with both leaders "some cooperative ventures in Rochester." See Finks, "Crisis in Smugtown."

34. Fairclough, *To Redeem the Soul of America*, 197.

35. Finks, "Crisis in Smugtown."

36. Young, "SCLC Dispatches Anti-Riot Team North."

37. For more information on the Industrial Areas Foundation and Saul Alinsky, see Robert Bailey Jr., *Radicals in Urban Politics: The Alinsky Approach* (Chicago: University of Chicago Press, 1974); Saul Alinsky, *Rules for Radicals: A Practical Primer for Realistic Radicals* (New York: Vintage Books, 1989); and Sanford D. Horwitt, *Let Them Call Me Rebel: Saul Alinsky, His Life and Legacy* (New York: Knopf, 1989).

38. Harold S. Hacker, "Who Is Saul Alinsky" (February 1965; revised March 1965), unpublished paper, Cooper papers.

39. Finks, "Crisis in Smugtown," 35; see also Mitchell interview.

40. For a thorough discussion of these approaches, see Finks, "Crisis in Smugtown," 35; and Nicholas von Hoffman, "Reorganization in the Casbah," unpublished paper, Alinsky folder, Cooper papers.

41. Hacker, "Who Is Saul Alinsky," Cooper papers.

42. Saul Alinsky, "The Professional Radical: Conversations with Saul Alinsky," *Harper's*, June 1965, 37–47, Alinsky folder, Cooper papers.

43. Mitchell interview; White interview.

44. Mitchell interview.

45. Ed Chambers, interview by Laura Warren Hill, August 9, 2008, transcript, Rochester Black Freedom Struggle Project, Rare Books, Special Collections, and Preservation, River Campus Libraries, University of Rochester; herein referred to as Chambers interview.

46. Sanford D. Horwitt, "Citizenship through Acting Collectively," *Los Angeles Times*, July 20, 1997; also published under the title "Alinsky: More Important Now Than Ever."

47. Finks also argued that this use of language was important because "the class unrest orientation brought in some support which would have been absent were it merely racial trouble." Finks, "Crisis in Smugtown," 39.

48. James F. Findlay Jr., *Church People in the Struggle: The National Council of Churches and the Black Freedom Movement, 1950–1970* (New York: Oxford University Press, 1993), 172.

49. "*Playboy* Interview: Saul Alinsky," *Playboy*, March 1972.

50. White interview.

51. White interview.

52. Florence interview.

53. Florence interview.

54. Florence interview.

55. The Board for Urban Ministry's Herb White recalled, "I don't think I ever met Malcolm, but he was very much an absent presence in Rochester, because Minister Florence and one or two of the other Black clergy knew him personally and struggled with their own theological opinions to remain Christian and Black and nationalistic." See White interview.

56. Agenda of Rochester's Temporary Committee, March 30, 1965, FIGHT Steering, box 3B, folder 23, Florence papers (emphasis in original).

57. "Negroes Say Unit Sets Own Policy," *Rochester Democrat and Chronicle*, undated article, box 58, folder 766, IAF records.

58. Summary notes, Steering Committee, March 29, 1965, FIGHT Steering, box 3B, folder 23, Florence papers.

59. Summary notes, Florence papers.

60. Florence interview.

61. Marvin Chandler, "Remembering FIGHT" (speech, Colgate Rochester Crozier Divinity School, Rochester, October 3, 2005), in author's possession.

62. Florence interview.

63. Florence interview.

64. Florence interview.

65. Florence interview.

66. See box 3B, folder 25, Florence papers.

67. FIGHT Steering Committee Meeting, April 5, 1965; FIGHT Steering Committee Meeting, April 7, 1965; FIGHT Steering Committee Meeting, April 5, 1966; all minutes found in box 3B; folder 23–24, Florence papers.

68. Mitchell interview.

69. Frank Riessman, "A Comparison of Two Social Action Approaches: Saul Alinsky and the New Left," September 1965, unpublished paper, unfiled, Cooper papers.

70. Nicholas von Hoffman, "Reorganization in the Casbah," undated, Alinsky folder, Cooper papers.

71. Official FIGHT Groups, undated, box 3B, folder 14, Florence papers.

72. "How It's Being Waged, The Do-It-Yourself War on Poverty—an article reprinted from the *Detroit Free Press*," August 22, 1965, box 58, folder 765, IAF records.

73. James Ridgeway, "Saul Alinsky in 'Smugtown,'" *New Republic*, June 26, 1965, 15–17, Alinsky folder, Cooper papers.

74. Florence interview; White interview.

75. Mitchell interview.

76. Davis interview.

77. Porter interview.

78. Gus Newport, interview by Laura Warren Hill, March 27, 2009, transcript, Rochester Black Freedom Struggle Project, Rare Books, Special Collections, and Preservation, River Campus Libraries, University of Rochester; herein referred to as Newport interview.

79. Franklin Florence, "Speech FF Buffalo," undated, box 62, folder 791, IAF records.

80. Angela Dillard, *Faith in the City: Preaching Radical Social Change in Detroit* (Ann Arbor: University of Michigan Press, 2007), 89.

81. Steering Committee Minutes, April 14, 1965, box 3B, folder 23, Florence papers.

82. Steering Committee Minutes, April 24, 1965; Housing Committee Minutes, July 8, 1965; and Steering Committee Minutes, July 13, 1965. All three sources are from box 3B, folder 23, Florence papers.

83. Steering Committee Minutes, November 16, 1965, box 3B, folder 23, Florence papers.

84. Lillian B. Rubin, "Maximum Feasible Participation: The Origins, Implications, and Present Status," *Annals of the American Academy of Political and Social Science* 385, no. 1 (September 1969): 14–29. See also Daniel Patrick Moynihan, *Maximum Feasible Misunderstanding: Community Action in the War on Poverty* (New York: Free Press, 1969); Edward Schmitt, *President of the Other America: Robert Kennedy and the Politics of Poverty* (Amherst: University of Massachusetts, 2010); Susan Youngblood Ashmore, *Carry It On: The War on Poverty and the Civil Rights Movement in Alabama, 1964–1972* (Athens: University of Georgia Press, 2008); and Robert Bauman, *Race and the War on Poverty: From Watts to East L.A.* (Norman: University of Oklahoma Press, 2008).

85. Desmond Stone, "Poverty War a Challenge," *Rochester Times-Union*, January 15, 1965, Cooper papers.

86. Cooper interview.

87. Proceedings and Debates of the 89th Congress, 1st sess., *Congressional Record* (July 21, 1965): 16982–16983, Cooper papers.

88. Report from Sidney Lindenberg et al. to J. M Friedman et al., February 21, 1967, box 59, folder 772, IAF records.

89. Ed Chambers to Saul Alinsky, memo, November 22, 1965, box 40, folder 619, IAF records.

90. Chambers to Alinsky, IAF records.

91. Joseph C. Brownell to Dear Sirs, December 22, 1965, Personal folder, Cooper papers.

92. Earl Caldwell, "Poverty War: Advancing or Retreating?" *Rochester Democrat and Chronicle*, November 28, 1965, Cooper papers.

93. Desmond Stone, "Antipoverty Debate Held," *Rochester Times-Union*, January 11, 1966, Nominating Committee of ABC, Inc. folder, Cooper papers.

94. Quoted in Stone, "Antipoverty Debate."

95. Quoted in Stone, "Antipoverty Debate."

96. Quoted in Stone, "Antipoverty Debate."

97. *FIGHTER (Rochester)* 1, no. 3 (January 1966): 4, unfiled, Cooper papers.

98. Stone, "Antipoverty Debate," Cooper papers.

99. Walter Cooper to Minister Franklin Florence, January 7, 1966, Nominating Committee of ABC, Inc. folder, Cooper papers.

100. Brian Donovan, "Three in FIGHT Asked to Join Agency," *Rochester Times-Union*, undated, Nominating Committee of ABC, Inc. folder, Cooper papers.

101. Ed Chambers to Saul Alinsky, memo, January 27, 1966, box 40, folder 619, IAF records.

102. ABC Fact Sheet, distributed at Friends of FIGHT meeting, January 1966; "Friends of FIGHT Raps 'Imbalance,'" *Rochester Times-Union*, January 12, 1966. Both documents are in Cooper papers.

103. Loren Crabtree, "Finding Guide, Baden Street Settlement House Records," July 1967 (digitized 2007), Social Welfare History Archives, Department of Archives and Special Collections, University of Minnesota, Minneapolis, https://archives.lib.umn.edu/.

104. Lindenberg to Friedman, IAF records.

105. "Convention of Poor Approved by ABC," *Rochester Democrat and Chronicle*, February 23, 1967, 5B, box 56, folder 754, IAF records.

106. "ABC Directors Shirk Real Job," *Rochester Times-Union*, September 15, 1967, 10A, box 61, folder 782, IAF records.

107. Franklin Florence, interview by Laura Warren Hill, Summer 2008, transcript in author's personal collection.

108. The issue of the Urban League's arrival in Rochester has been debated for decades. In our 2008 interview, Walter Cooper insisted that the corporate community, including his employer, Eastman Kodak, had played no role in excluding the Urban League from Rochester. However, several contemporary sources have contradicted this assertion. David Finks argued that "faced with . . . growing militancy and the immanent [*sic*] arrival of the Alinsky organizers, the white leadership . . . invited the National Urban League to set up a chapter in Rochester . . . although the Urban League had been denied entrance to Rochester by these same groups several times before the '64 riots." James Ridgeway, a reporter for the *New Republic*, expanded upon Fink's assertion, suggesting the incredible sway of the Community Chest in Rochester: "For a number of years the city toyed with the wild possibility of bringing in the Urban League. When Alinsky's people arrived the businessmen got together $40,000 and suddenly the League opened an office." See Finks, "Crisis in Smugtown," 49; and Ridgeway, "Saul Alinsky in 'Smugtown.'"

109. Ridgeway, "Saul Alinsky in 'Smugtown.'"

110. Cooper interview.

111. Marcus Alexis, interview by Laura Warren Hill, March 27, 2009, transcript, Rochester Black Freedom Struggle Project, Rare Books, Special Collections, and Preservation, River Campus Libraries, University of Rochester.

5. Confrontation with Kodak

1. Prakash Sethi, *Business Corporations and the Black Man: An Analysis of Social Conflict: The Kodak-FIGHT Controversy* (Scranton, PA: Chandler Publications, 1970), 16. See also Raymond A. Schroth, "Self-Doubt and Black Pride," *America*, April 1, 1967, 502–505, box 56, folder 754, Industrial Areas Foundation Records, Special Collections and University Archives, University of Illinois at Chicago; herein referred to as IAF records.

2. As a point of reference, Xerox, Rochester's second-largest corporation, ranked 171. For a complete listing of Fortune 500 companies in 1966, see "1966 Full List," *Fortune 500: A Database of 50 Years of Fortune's List of America's Largest Corporations*, CNNMoney, 2018, http://money.cnn.com/magazines/fortune/fortune500_archive/full/1966/.

3. Jules Loh, "'Rochester's Agony' . . . As an Outsider Sees It," *Rochester Democrat and Chronicle*, April 23, 1967, 4M.

4. "The Fight That Swirls around Eastman Kodak," *Business Weekly*, April 29, 1967, 38–41, box 57, folder 759, IAF records.

5. "Fight That Swirls."

6. James Farmer, foreword to Sethi, *Business Corporations*.

7. Schroth, "Self-Doubt and Black Pride."

8. Sethi, *Business Corporations*, 21.

9. This phrase was suggested in FIGHT's working papers for posters for a rally to be held February 14, 1967 (box 58, folder 763, IAF records). The claim, of course, was a play on John L. Lewis's statement that "a man's right to a job transcends the right of private property." See "The Professional Radical: Conversations with Saul Alinsky," *Harper's Magazine*, June 1965, 37–47, Alinsky folder, Walter Cooper papers. This set of papers was generously offered to the author for use. With Dr. Cooper's permission, they have since been deposited with the Rare Books, Special Collections, and Preservation, River Campus Libraries, University of Rochester. All references refer to their original organization in folders by Dr. Cooper and will not necessarily correspond with the archival system employed by the University of Rochester; herein referred to as Cooper papers.

10. "$20,353,788 Earned by Eastman Kodak," *New York Times*, April 8, 1931, 36.

11. Beginning in 1912, Kodak paid a yearly wage dividend to its workers; in 1930, that wage dividend amounted to an average of $135 per employee. This is the equivalent of $1,650 in 2009. By 1956, the dividend had increased to $687 per employee. This is the equivalent of $6,589 in 2020. See "Eastman Employees to Share $2,378,647: Annual Wage Dividend Will Be Divided Today among 17,601 Workers," *New York Times*, July 1, 1930, 41.

12. It is also interesting to note that George Eastman, founder of Eastman Kodak, sent large sums of money to Black colleges and universities, including Tuskegee, Meharry, and Hampton. The company refused, however, to hire their graduates. See Laura Warren Hill, "Strike the Hammer While the Iron Is Hot: The Black Freedom Struggle in Rochester, NY, 1940–1970" (PhD diss., Binghamton University, 2010).

13. Sethi, *Business Corporations*, 23.

14. "Jackson Condemns 'Parasite' Finance," *New York Times*, January 16, 1938, 4.

15. The company's expansion resulted in part from military war orders for sensitive aerial photography equipment, portable darkrooms, and a special V-mail program that delivered mail to and from touring soldiers at a rate of thirty-five million letters per month. See "Eastman Prepares for Post-War Output," *New York Times*, March 24, 1944, 24; and "$219,759,664 Sales by Eastman Kodak," *New York Times*, April 3, 1943, 22.

16. After serving a "key role in the development of the Social Security Program" and having served on multiple federal committees, Eastman Kodak treasurer and director Marion B. Folsom was named under secretary of the treasury in the Eisenhower administration. See John D. Morris, "Official of Kodak and Chairman of C.E.D May Supervise Internal Revenue Bureau," *New York Times*, December 12, 1952, 47.

17. "Kodak to Sponsor Sullivan TV Show," *New York Times*, June 24, 1957, 35.

18. Juliet E. K. Walker, *The History of Black Business in America: Capitalism, Race, and Entrepreneurship*, 2nd ed. (Chapel Hill: University of North Carolina Press, 2009); Adolph Dupree, "Rochester Roots/Routes, Part II," *About . . . Time*, August 1984, 14.

19. Walker, *History of Black Business*; Dupree, "Roots/Routes, Part II," 14.

20. On Caledonia Street alone, without ever entering a white-owned establishment, African Americans could rent a room, get a haircut or hair styling, visit a Black doctor or dentist, and buy groceries, a newspaper, artwork, and furniture. In the surrounding neighborhood, they could plan a homegoing service, play billiards, drink a whiskey while listening to a Black musician, and get their car serviced, all in Black-owned businesses. For a more complete record of Black Rochester's business activity, see Dupree, "Roots/Routes, Part II," 22.

21. Dupree, "Roots/Routes, Part II," 22. The Jentonses' grocery stored boasted a "full line of fancy and staple groceries, southern produce" and undoubtedly to the delight of local residents, a confectionary.

22. Dupree, "Roots/Routes, Part II," 20.

23. See, for example, selected coverage in the *New York Times*: "Strike-Free Kodak Credits 'Dividends,'" December 12, 1948; "Rail Wage Demands Opposed: Profit Sharing Proposed at Method of Avoiding Further Bankruptcies," November 4, 1941; "Eastman Charted Path for Industry," March 15, 1932; "A Way to Save Children," September 1, 1940; "Wider Programs of Health Urged," September 12, 1944; and "Kodak Says Rochester Offers Few Skilled Negroes," July 29, 1964. See also letter from FIGHT to Kodak, September 14, 1966, unfiled, Cooper papers.

24. Quoted in Schroth, "Self-Doubt and Black Pride," IAF records.

25. Dupree, "Roots/Routes, Part II," 12.

26. "Kodak Says Rochester Offers Few Skilled Negroes," *New York Times*, July 29, 1964.

27. Marvin Chandler, interview by Laura Warren Hill, May 13, 2009, transcript, Rochester Black Freedom Struggle Project, Rare Books, Special Collections, and Preservation, River Campus Libraries, University of Rochester; herein referred to as Chandler interview.

28. Clarence Ingram, interview by Laura Warren Hill, July 12, 2008, transcript, Rochester Black Freedom Struggle Project, Rare Books, Special Collections, and Preservation, River Campus Libraries, University of Rochester.

29. Charles and Pauline Price, interview by Laura Warren Hill, August 6, 2008, transcript, Rochester Black Freedom Struggle Project, Rare Books, Special Collections, and Preservation, River Campus Libraries, University of Rochester; herein referred to as Price interview.

30. Price interview.

31. Loh, "Rochester's Agony."

32. "Fight That Swirls."

33. Germaine Knapp and Rhona Genzel, interview by Laura Warren Hill, August 20, 2008, transcript, Rochester Black Freedom Struggle Project, Rare Books, Special Collections, and Preservation, River Campus Libraries, University of Rochester.

34. Loh, "Rochester's Agony."

35. Lewis G. Robinson, Director, Jomo Freedom Kenyatta House, to Franklin Florence, December 6, 1966, box 3C, folder 29, Franklin Florence Papers, Rare Books, Special Collections, and Preservation, River Campus Libraries, University of Rochester; herein referred to as Florence papers.

36. Transcription of remarks given by Saul Alinsky and Franklin Florence on WORK-TV, October 26, 1966, box 61, folder 782, IAF records.

37. "Fight That Swirls."

38. "Fight That Swirls." Florence frequently made this argument in public interviews.

39. Loh, "Rochester's Agony"; James Ridgeway "Attack on Kodak," *New Republic*, January 21, 1967, 11–13, box 56, folder 754, IAF records; Chandler interview.

40. "Kodak, FIGHT at Impasse on Job Talks," *Rochester Democrat and Chronicle*, January 12, 1967, 3B, box 56, folder 754, IAF records.

41. Chandler interview.

42. December 20th Agreement, box 3C, folder 29, Florence papers.

43. December 20th Agreement.

44. "Kodak, FIGHT Remain Firm in Their Positions in Job Dispute," *Rochester Times-Union*, April 26, 1967, box 61, folder 784, IAF records.

45. "Mulder Loses Post at Kodak," *Rochester Democrat and Chronicle*, May 19, 1967, 1; "Kodak Directors Drop Executive," *New York Times*, May 19, 1967. Both articles are in box 56, folder 754, IAF records.

46. Loh, "Rochester's Agony."

47. Nicholas van Hoffman, "Picture's Fuzzy as Kodak Fights FIGHT," *Washington Post*, January 9, 1967, box 56, folder 754, IAF records.

48. Desmond Stone, "The Kodak-FIGHT Dispute: How It Began, Why It Continues," *Rochester Times-Union*, April 21, 1967.

49. Loh, "Rochester's Agony"; "New Threat for Employers? What a Negro Group Seeks from Kodak," *U.S. News and World Report*, May 8, 1967, box 61, folder 784, IAF records.

50. "Militant Rights Group Expected to Attend Kodak Annual Meeting," *Wall Street Journal*, April 24, 1967, box 56, folder 753, IAF records.

51. Ridgeway, "Attack on Kodak."

52. "Kodak Charges FIGHT with Power Drive," *Rochester Times-Union*, January 6, 1967.

53. "Fight That Swirls."

54. Loh, "Rochester's Agony."

55. Loh, "Rochester's Agony."

56. Brian Donovan, "Carmichael Pledges Boycott," *Rochester FIGHTER*, February 1967, Florence papers.

57. Schroth, "Self-Doubt and Black Pride."

58. Donovan, "Carmichael Pledges Boycott."

59. Transcript of WNYR broadcast, January 20, 1967, box 61, folder 784, IAF records.

60. "Churchmen Back FIGHT on Jobs," *Rochester Democrat and Chronicle*, January 4, 1967, box 56, folder 753, IAF records. See also "1967 General Resolution, Eastman Kodak Dispute with FIGHT I," Social Justice Statements, Unitarian Universalist Association, 2019, http://www.uua.org/statements/eastman-kodak-dispute-fight-i.

61. Henry B. Clark to All Members of the Commission on Urban Life, January 5, 1967, box 58, folder 765, IAF records.

62. For examples of this church support, see "High Noon at Flemington," *Christianity and Crisis*, May 29, 1967, box 56, folder 753, IAF records; and "Church Groups to Question Kodak at Annual Meeting," *Presbyterian Life*, May 1, 1967, box 56, folder 754, IAF records.

63. The rallying cry differed between Florence, who wanted other men of God to put their stocks where their sermons were, and Alinsky, who asked those same men to keep their sermons but provide their stock. See Franklin Florence to Dear Friends, May 2, 1967, box 57, folder 759, IAF records; Franklin Florence to Dear Friends, May 24, 1967, box 61, folder 784, IAF records; and ". . . And Kodak Will Ask, 'How High?'" *Fortune*, June 1, 1967, box 57, folder 759, IAF records.

64. For a select example, see Robert E. Weems, *Desegregating the Dollar: African-American Consumerism in the Twentieth Century* (New York: New York University Press, 1998); Emilye Crosby, *A Little Taste of Freedom: The Black Freedom Struggle in Claiborne County, Mississippi* (Chapel Hill: University of North Carolina Press, 2005); Robert O. Self, *American Babylon: Race and the Struggle for Postwar Oakland* (Princeton, NJ: Princeton University Press, 2003); and Matthew Countryman, *Up South: Civil Rights and Black Power in Philadelphia* (Philadelphia: University of Pennsylvania Press, 2006).

65. "Church Groups to Question Kodak at Annual Meeting," *Presbyterian Life*, May 1, 1967, box 56, folder 754, IAF records.

66. "Focus on Flemington" was the title for FIGHT's new stockholder strategy.

67. Kodak's annual meetings were held in Flemington, New Jersey, for tax purposes. Despite its Rochester headquarters, Kodak incorporated in New Jersey rather than New York because the neighboring state claimed more liberal corporate tax laws. The legal firm responsible for Kodak's incorporation and documentation boasted more than sixty Fortune 500 clients including United Fruit, American Tobacco, Republic Steel, and Standard Oil. See "Kodak Holds Its Meeting amid Racial Protests," *New York Times*, April 26, 1967, box 61, folder 784, IAF records.

68. Loh, "Rochester's Agony."

69. "Kodak Will Ask."

70. Edwin Kruse to Minister Florence, April 9, 1967, box 58, folder 764, IAF records.

71. Rolf Meyersohn to Minister Florence, April 11, 1967, box 58, folder 764, IAF records.

72. M. J. Rossant, "All You Need Is One Share," *New York Times*, May 7, 1967, box 56, folder 754, IAF records.

73. Rossant, "All You Need."

74. Barbara Carter, "The FIGHT against Kodak," *Reporter*, April 20, 1967, 28–31, box 57, folder 759, IAF records.

75. "FIGHT Gets Support in Kodak Feud," *Rochester Times-Union*, April 11, 1967, 6B, box 56, folder 753, IAF records.

76. "FIGHT Gets Support."

77. "Kodak, FIGHT Remain Firm in Their Positions in Job Dispute," *Rochester Times-Union*, April 26, 1967, box 61, folder 784, IAF records.

78. Earl C. Gottschalk Jr., "Militant Rights Group Expected to Attend Kodak Annual Meeting," *New York Times*, April 24, 1967, box 56, folder 753, IAF records.

79. "Vaughn Defends Kodak Role in Dispute," *Rochester Times-Union*, April 25, 1967, box 56, folder 754, IAF records.

80. Carter, "FIGHT against Kodak."

81. "Mediation Sought by Javits," *Rochester Democrat and Chronicle*, April 15, 1967, box 56, folder 754, IAF records.

82. Ed Chambers to Saul Alinsky, internal memo, April 18, 1967, box 39, folder 613, IAF records.

83. Potential signs considered by FIGHT, box 58, folder 764, IAF records. See also images of the Flemington picket, which shows these slogans used on signs, box 119, folder 1, Kodak Historical Collection #003, D.319, Rare Books, Special Collections, and Preservation, River Campus Libraries, University of Rochester.

84. "Kodak Picketed on Negro Hiring," *World Journal Tribune*, April 25, 1967, box 57, folder 762, IAF records.

85. Bus Captains Instructions, box 3C, folder 31, Florence papers.

86. Betty Flynn, "Negro Protest Stirs Kodak Uproar," *Chicago Daily News*, April 25, 1967, box 56, folder 754, IAF records.

87. "Kodak Picketed on Negro Hiring," *World Journal Tribune*, April 25, 1967, box 57, folder 762, IAF records.

88. Flynn, "Negro Protest"; "FIGHT Chairman Bolts Meeting in Dispute with Kodak," *Buffalo Evening News*, April 25, 1967, box 61, folder 784; "Plan Protest at Kodak Meeting," *Kansas City (MO) Times*, April 25, 1967, box 57, folder 759; "Kodak Picketed on Negro Hiring," *New York World Journal Tribune*, April 25, 1967, box 57, folder 762; "Rights Debate Disrupts Kodak Meeting," *Chicago Sun-Times*, April 26, 1967, box 61, folder 784; "Civil Rights Group Turns Kodak Parley into Shouting Match," *Pittsburgh Press*, April 26, 1967, box 57, folder 762; "Action Group Declares War on Kodak at Tumultuous Stockholders' Session," *Washington Post*, April 26, 1967, box 57, folder 762; "Negroes Protest Kodak Policies, Disrupt Meeting," *Cleveland Press*, April 26, 1967, box 57, folder 762; "Kodak Holds Its Meeting amid Racial Protests," *New York Times*, April 26, 1967, box 61, folder 784; "Kodak Refuses to Restore Negro Job Pact"; "Rights Group Vows 'War' against Concern," *Wall Street Journal*, April 26, 1967, box 57, folder 762. All of the preceding articles are in the IAF records.

89. "Kodak Gives $15,000 to Flemington School," *Rochester Democrat and Chronicle*, May 5, 1967, box 61, folder 784; John Kifner, "Negro Ad Agency Hired by Kodak," *New York Times*, April 28, 1967, box 56, folder 753. Both articles are in the IAF records.

90. The 1965 Moynihan report, titled "The Negro Family: A Case for National Action," stirred a great debate in the nation for its portrayal of the African American family as pathological and Black woman as promiscuous. The US Department of Labor has the full text available on its website (https://www.dol.gov/). For discussions of the text, see Deborah Gray White, *Too Heavy a Load* (New York: Norton, 1999), 198–203; Michele Wallace, *Black Macho and the Myth of the Superwoman* (New York: Verso, 1990), 30–31, 109–116; and Annelise Orleck, *Storming Caesars Palace: How Black Mothers Fought Their Own War on Poverty* (Boston: Beacon Press, 2005), 81.

91. Timothy Crouse, "Moynihan Helped Smooth Way for Kodak-FIGHT Reconciliation," *Crimson*, July 3, 1967.

92. Louis K. Eilers telegram, box 3C, folder 31, Florence papers.

93. John and Constance Mitchell, interview by Laura Warren Hill, July 12, 2008, transcript, Rochester Black Freedom Struggle Project, Rare Books, Special Collections, and Preservation, River Campus Libraries, University of Rochester.

94. "Fight That Swirls."

95. For example, shortly after the Flemington meeting, "Mrs. Porter Brown, general executive of the board of missions of the Methodist church [attended] the May 19 annual meeting of General Motors Corp. to question GM about its 'deep involvement' in South Africa." See "In the Kodak Dispute, Churches Take a New Civil-Rights Tack," *National Observer*, May 3, 1967, box 57, folder 762, IAF records.

96. Edward B. Fiske, "Churches Flex Their Economic Muscle," *New York Times*, April 16, 1967, E11, box 56, folder 54, IAF records.

6. FIGHTing for the Soul of Black Capitalism

1. Chapter 6 was originally published as "FIGHTing for the Soul of Black Capitalism: Struggles for Black Economic Development in Postrebellion Rochester" in *The Business of Black Power: Community Development, Capitalism, and Corporate Responsibility in Postwar America*, edited by Laura Warren Hill and Julia Rabig, 45–67 (Rochester, NY: University of Rochester Press, 2012). Used with permission from University of Rochester Press in partnership with Boydell & Brewer. The chapter title is obviously a play on W. E. B. Dubois, *The Souls of Black Folk* (Chicago: A. C. McClurg and Co., 1903).

2. Malcolm X, "The Ballot or the Bullet," speech, Cleveland, April 1964.

3. Juliet E. K. Walker, *The History of Black Business in America: Capitalism, Race, Entrepreneurship* (New York: Twayne Publishers, 1998). See also Abram L. Harris, *The Negro as Capitalist: A Study of Banking and Business among American Negroes* (New York: Negro University Press, 1936).

4. Here Walker engages E. Franklin Frazier, *Black Bourgeoisie* (Glencoe, IL: Free Press, 1957); and Nathan Glazer and Daniel Patrick Moynihan, *Beyond the Melting Pot: The Negroes, Puerto Ricans, Jews, Italians, and Irish of New York City* (Cambridge: MIT Press, 1963).

5. See Booker T. Washington, *Up from Slavery* (New York: Dover Publications, 1995 [1901]); Daniel R. Fusfield and Timothy Bates, *The Political Economy of the Urban Ghetto* (Carbondale: Southern Illinois University Press, 1984); Essien Udosen Essien-Udom, *Black Nationalism: A Search for an Identity in America* (Chicago: University of Chicago Press, 1962); C. Eric Lincoln, *The Black Muslims in America* (Boston: Beacon Press, 1961); and Wilson J. Moses, *Classical Black Nationalism: From the American Revolution to Marcus Garvey* (New York: New York University Press, 1996).

6. See, for example, Robert Allen, *Black Awakening in Capitalist America* (Garden City, NY: Doubleday, 1969); and Earl [Hutchinson] Ofari, *The Myth of Black Capitalism* (New York: Monthly Review Press, 1970).

7. Frazier, *Black Bourgeoisie*; Ofari, *Myth of Black Capitalism*; Allen, *Black Awakening in Capitalist America*.

8. For a more complete account of Black business development in the twentieth century, see chapter 1.

9. Robert E. Weems Jr., *Business in Black and White: American Presidents and Black Entrepreneurs in the Twentieth Century* (New York: New York University Press, 2009), 31.

10. For example, Walker rightly privileges the experiences of Black businesspeople and practitioners in her narrative. Her discussion of Black capitalism, however, is driven by the relationship between national figures (Stokely Carmichael and Martin Luther King Jr.) and organizations (the Nation of Islam) and the federal government (the Small Business Association) in the promotion of Black capitalism. Weems spends just two pages to note the relationship between corporations and black activists in the development of Black capitalism. Of importance to this piece, however, is that he highlights the relationship between Xerox and FIGHT as a model of Black economic development in this era.

11. Steven M. Gelber, *Black Men and Businessmen: The Growing Awareness of a Social Responsibility* (Port Washington, NY: Kennikat Press, 1974), 161.

12. "Rev. Gene Bartlett, 79: Led Divinity School," *New York Times*, November 11, 1989, 33.

13. Peter B. Taub, "Industries to Recruit in Inner City Here," *Rochester Times-Union*, September 14, 1967, 1.

14. Romney went on to become Nixon's first secretary of housing and urban development. See Alexander Polikoff, "Beyond Ghetto Gilding," response to Owen Fiss, "What Should Be Done for Those Who Have Been Left Behind?" in Forum: Moving Out of the Ghetto, *Boston Review* 25, no. 3 (Summer 2000), digital, *Boston Review* archive.

15. Gelber, *Black Men and Businessmen*, 181.

16. Richard Nixon, "Statement on the Merger of the National Alliance of Businessmen and Plans for Progress," June 13, 1969, The American Presidency Project, Gerhard Peters and John T. Woolley, directors, https://www.presidency.ucsb.edu/node/239441. There is further information to be found regarding the National Alliance of Businessmen in contemporary accounts of Black capitalism. See, for example, William F. Haddad and G. Douglas Pugh, eds., *Black Economic Development* (Englewood, NJ: Prentice Hall, 1969), especially Howard J. Samuels, "Compensatory Capitalism," 61–74. The papers in this volume were first used as background reading for the Thirty-fifth American Assembly which met at Arden House, Harriman, New York, April 24–27, 1969 to discuss Black Economic Development. They now appear for general readership and as background for additional Assemblies in the United States.

17. In 1969, Germaine Knapp and her husband came to Rochester when he obtained a job with Xerox through the NAB to hire and train the hard-core unemployed for the various job programs Xerox had undertaken. As a result, Knapp herself would be hired to work for Step Up, a GED and job training program sponsored by Xerox and FIGHT. See Germaine Knapp and Rhona Genzel, interview by Laura Warren Hill, August 28, 2008, transcript, Rochester Black Freedom Struggle Project, Rare Books, Special Collections, and Preservation, River Campus Libraries, University of Rochester.

18. Neil Ulman, "Negro Pioneer: Philadelphia's Rev. Sullivan Preaches Self-Help, Not Protest," *Wall Street Journal*, 15 April 1966, box 56, folder 754, Industrial Areas Foundation Records, Special Collections and University Archives, University of Illinois at Chicago; herein referred to as IAF records. See also "Symposium: 'The Lion of Zion: Leon H. Sullivan and the Pursuit of Social and Economic Justice,'" *Journal of African American History* 96 (Winter 2001), 39–95.

19. Of some import to FIGHT, Sullivan derived his brand of Black Power from the community, a strategy to which FIGHT subscribed. He organized a "10–36 plan," wherein each member of his congregation invested ten dollars for a period of thirty-six months. This initial seed money created Zion Investment Associates, which laid out the money for Sullivan's various economic development plans, including the symbolic conversion of a jail cell into a job training center, a garment manufacturing company that employed women, and a shopping plaza with sixteen Black-managed businesses. Zion turned its profits back to the community: two-fifths to the initial investors, one-fifth in profit-sharing plans for the employees, and two-fifths into a nonprofit charitable trust used for further economic development in the community.

20. Martin Skala, "Inner City Enterprises: Current Experience," in Haddad and Pugh, eds., *Black Economic Development*, 151–70; Matthew Countryman, *Up South: Civil Rights and Black Power in Philadelphia* (Philadelphia: University of Pennsylvania Press, 2006).

21. Proposal, box 61, folder 782, IAF records.

22. Skala, "Inner City Enterprises," 157.

23. Ideological opposition to capitalism was a driving force for a growing number of Black activists, including James Forman and Richard Allen, leaders of the Black Panther Party. Bobby Seale, chair of the Black Panther Party, argued, "In our view it is a class struggle between the massive proletarian working class and the small, minority ruling class. Working-class people of all colors must unite against the exploitative, oppressive ruling class." See Seale, *Seize the Time: The Story of the Black Panther Party and Huey P. Newton* (Baltimore: Black Classic Press, 1991), 72. See also Charles E. Jones, ed., *The Black Panther Party [Reconsidered]* (Baltimore: Black Classic Press, 1998), 337–358; Jama Lazerow and Yohuru Williams, eds., *In Search of the Black Panther Party: New Perspectives on a Revolutionary Movement* (Chapel Hill: Duke University Press, 2006); Allen, *Black Awakening in Capitalist America*; and Ofari, *Myth of Black Capitalism*.

24. Lincoln, *Black Muslims in America*, 88.

25. Walker, *History of Black Business in America*, 272.

26. The Nation of Islam's Honorable Elijah Muhammad organized all his economic enterprises under the motto "Do for self."

27. Weems, *Business in Black and White*, 130.

28. Robert E. Weems Jr., and Lewis A. Randolph argue that Nixon's promotion of Black capitalism created a "national discourse." While I agree with them that Nixon's plan garnered much criticism and discussion in the Black community, I suggest this debate was underway in Rochester before Nixon fancied a 1968 presidential run. The national discourse that emerged reflects the efforts of local communities to negotiate power. See Weems and Randolph, "The National Response to Richard M. Nixon's 'Black Capitalism' Initiative: The Success of Domestic Détente," *Journal of Black Studies* 32, no. 1 (September 2001): 66–83.

29. General Ideas for a Florence Talk to Rochester Business Leaders, box 62, folder 791, IAF records.

30. *FIGHTON Today: Beginning of the Beginning* (published circa 1969), box 57, folder 762, IAF records.

31. Rather than serve as competition for the film conglomerate Eastman Kodak, Haloid's presence in Rochester, like that of many small companies in the Flower City, served its wealthiest industrial neighbor. Haloid and others prevented federal antitrust lawsuits from disrupting Kodak's dominance. As one historian put it, "[Haloid's] very existence was ideal legal evidence that Eastman Kodak was not really a monopoly." See Charles D. Ellis, *Joe Wilson and the Creation of Xerox* (Hoboken, NJ: John Wiley and Sons, 2006), 21.

32. Minister Franklin Florence originally proposed the idea of FIGHTON to Xerox CEO Joe Wilson under the name "Operation Mainstream." The phrase, however, had wider national use. Minister Florence was likely familiar with the provision that "Amendments to the Economic Opportunity Act to provide for the direct employment of the adult poor in conservation and beautification efforts are officially labeled 'Operation Mainstream.'" The economist Frank Davis argued, "If we apply this definition with respect to business and employment opportunities of the Black community, we would expect the policy of Black Capitalism to place Black entrepreneurs in the principal or dominant course of American business." See Frank G. Davis, *The Economics of Black Community Development* (Chicago: Markham Publishing, 1972), 93.

33. General Ideas for a Florence Talk.

34. Stewart Perry, "National Policy and the Community Development Corporation," *Law and Contemporary Problems* 36, no. 2 (Spring 1971): 297–308.

35. "Xerox Corporation Back Black Business: Cites FIGHTON as Example of Progress," *Chicago Defender*, June 27, 1968, box 62, folder 791, IAF records.

36. Ellis, *Joe Wilson*, 3–4.

37. Ellis, *Joe Wilson*, 6–16.

38. Ellis, *Joe Wilson*, 237.

39. Ellis, *Joe Wilson*, 242.

40. Horace Becker, interview by Laura Warren Hill, August 20, 2008, transcript, Rochester Black Freedom Struggle Project, Rare Books, Special Collections, and Preservation, River Campus Libraries, University of Rochester; herein referred to as Becker interview.

41. "FIGHT," episode of *Need to Know*, originally aired February 3, 2000, WXXI (public broadcasting), Rochester, digital copy accessed May 7, 2007; the online version is no longer available.

42. Basic Goals of FIGHT's New Job Program, undated, box 3C, folder 34, Franklin Florence Papers, Rare Books, Special Collections, and Preservation, River Campus Libraries, University of Rochester; herein referred to as Florence papers.

43. "Xerox Plans to Hire 150 for 'Step Up,'" *Rochester Democrat and Chronicle*, February 28, 1967, box 61, folder 78, IAF records. Plans for Step Up were underway by the fall of 1965 between Xerox and its union affiliate, Local 14a of the Amalgamated Clothing Workers of America. See Xerox Management letter, October 26, 1965, box 58, folder 765, IAF records.

44. Joseph Schumpeter is quoted in Walker, *History of Black Business in America*, xxi.

45. US Department of Labor press release, "Negro Group to Open Rochester, NY, Plant with Aid of Xerox," June 13, 1968, box 62, folder 791, IAF records.

46. Introduction, FIGHTON Proposal "Operation Mainstream:" Joint Study, FIGHT and Xerox, box 4, folder 1, Florence papers.

47. Skala, "Inner City Enterprises," 168.

48. Skala, "Inner City Enterprises," 168.

49. FIGHT's fact sheet on enterprises, box 3, folder 43, Florence papers.

50. FIGHT's fact sheet on enterprises.

51. "FIGHT," *Need to Know*.

52. Millicent Hartzog, interview by Laura Warren Hill, November 21, 2008, transcript, Rochester Black Freedom Struggle Project, Rare Books, Special Collections, and Preservation, River Campus Libraries, University of Rochester.

53. Darryl Porter, interview by Laura Warren Hill, June 10, 2008, transcript, Rochester Black Freedom Struggle Project, Rare Books, Special Collections, and Preservation, River Campus Libraries, University of Rochester.

54. Minister Florence to DeLeon McEwen, memo, May 22, 1969, box 4a, folder 7, Florence papers.

55. In the past twenty years there has been an explosion in the literature on corporate social responsibility. See, for example, Andrew Crane, et al., *The Oxford Handbook of Corporate Responsibility* (New York: Oxford University Press, 2008); Edmundo Werna, *Corporate Social Responsibility and Urban Development: Lessons from the South*

(New York: Palgrave Macmillan, 2009); and David Crowther et al., *The Ashgate Research Companion to Corporate Social Responsibility* (Burlington, VT: Ashgate, 2008).

56. "The Slums: Business Rolls Up a Sleeve," *New York Times*, January 8, 1968, box 61, folder 782, IAF records.

57. "Xerox Plans to Hire 150."

58. Chamber of Commerce of the United States of America, "Rochester Business Opportunities Corporation Helps Ghetto Dwellers Own Businesses," in *Urban Action Clearinghouse Case Study* (Washington, DC: Chamber of Commerce of the US, 1968), appendix A.

59. Becker interview.

60. General Ideas for a Florence Talk.

61. General Ideas for a Florence Talk.

62. Chamber of Commerce, "Rochester Business Opportunities Corporation," appendix A.

63. Chamber of Commerce, "Rochester Business Opportunities Corporation," appendix A.

64. Chamber of Commerce, "Rochester Business Opportunities Corporation," appendix A.

65. See, for example, "FIGHT Industry to Open Soon," *Rochester Democrat and Chronicle*, March 6, 1968, box 57, folder 756, IAF records; note and article sent from Minister Franklin Florence to Ed Chambers, IAF organizer, box 56, folder 753, IAF records.

66. Clarence Ingram, interview by Laura Warren Hill, July 12, 2008, transcript, Rochester Black Freedom Struggle Project, Rare Books, Special Collections, and Preservation, River Campus Libraries, University of Rochester; herein referred to as Ingram interview.

67. Ingram interview.

68. "Urban League Responds to Kodak Plan," *Rochester Times-Union*, December 1, 1967, box 61, folder 782, IAF records.

69. Dr. Andrew Billingsley (Consultant), "Rochester Urban League," undated, Urban League Folder, Walter Cooper papers. This set of papers was generously offered to the author for use. With Dr. Cooper's permission, they have since been deposited with the Rare Books, Special Collections, and Preservation, River Campus Libraries, University of Rochester. All references refer to their original organization in folders by Dr. Cooper and will not necessarily correspond with the archival system employed by the University of Rochester; herein referred to as Cooper papers.

70. Billingsley, "Rochester Urban League."

71. Laplois Ashford, Executive Director, to John J. Rolle, Project Director OJT, March 10, 1970, Urban League Board, 1970 folder, Cooper papers.

72. Ingram interview.

73. "FIGHT Industry to Open Soon," *Rochester Democrat and Chronicle*, March 6, 1968, box 61, folder 782, IAF records.

74. Geoffrey P. Faux and Twentieth Century Fund, Task Force on Community Development Corporations, *CDCs: New Hope for the Inner City; Report of the Twentieth Century Fund Task Force on Community Development Corporations* (New York: Twentieth Century Fund, 1971), 30–31.

75. Faux and Twentieth Century Fund, *CDCs*, 16–17.

76. In 1970 *Time* magazine published an article titled "The Beginnings of Black Capitalism" in which the author noted sharp Black skepticism of federal programs that promised much and delivered little. The Nixon administration, in particular, was singled out as drawing the ire of African Americans who believed it to be little more than "smooth honky talk." See "The Beginnings of Black Capitalism," *Time*, April 6, 1970.

77. A. Wright Elliott, "'Black Capitalism' and the Business Community," in Haddad and Pugh, eds., *Black Economic Development*, 76.

78. Points for Steering Committee, December 17, 1968, box 3B, folder 24, Florence papers.

79. Weems, *Business in Black and White*.

Conclusion

1. Michael Flamm, *In the Heat of the Summer: The New York Riots of 1964 and the War on Crime* (Philadelphia: University of Pennsylvania Press, 2016).

2. Heather Ann Thomson, *Blood in the Water: The Attica Prison Uprising of 1971 and Its Legacy* (New York: Pantheon, 2016).

3. Attica Inmates, "Declaration to the People of America," September 9, 1971, read by L. D. Barkley, quoted in *Attica Prison Uprising 101: A Primer*, edited by Mariame Kabe, September 2011, digital version by Project NIA, "Resources," *NIA Dispatches*, https://niastories.wordpress.com/resources/.

4. Interview with Lavern Barkley, conducted by Blackside Inc., on August 22, 1989, for *Eyes on the Prize II: America at the Racial Crossroads 1965 to 1985* (PBS), Henry Hampton Collection, Film and Media Archive, Washington University Libraries, St. Louis, http://digital.wustl.edu/eyesontheprize/index.html.

5. Raymond Scott, interview by Laura Warren Hill, July 11, 2008, transcript, Rochester Black Freedom Struggle Project, Rare Books, Special Collections, and Preservation, River Campus Libraries, University of Rochester; herein referred to as Scott interview.

6. Scott interview.

7. Dan Lovely, "Leadership, Recognition the Key Gain," *Rochester Democrat and Chronicle*, July 10, 1974, sec. A.

8. Homer King, "A Profile of FIGHT Square," *Rochester Democrat and Chronicle*, August 7, 1978, sec. A.

9. Lovely, "Leadership"; Michael Wentzel, "FIGHT Village Owes Funds: HUD Says Lost Money Must Be Repaid," *Rochester Democrat and Chronicle*, November 4, 1996, sec. B.

10. Dan Olmstead, "Fight Had Gone Out of FIGHT, Inc.," *Rochester Democrat and Chronicle*, August 7, 1978, sec. A.

11. Alejandro Reuss, "That '70s Crisis: What Can the Crisis of U.S. Capitalism in the 1970s Teach Us about the Current Crisis and Its Possible Outcomes?" *Dollars and Sense: Real World Economies*, no. 285 (November/December 2009), http://www.dollarsandsense.org/archives/2009/1109reuss.html.

12. Kim Phillips-Fein, "The Legacy of the 1970s Fiscal Crisis," *Nation*, special New York issue, May 6, 2013, https://www.thenation.com/article/archive/legacy-1970s-fiscal-crisis/.

13. See Robert E. Weems Jr., *Business in Black and White: American Presidents and Black Entrepreneurs in the Twentieth Century* (New York: New York University Press, 2009); Robert E. Weems Jr., and Lewis A. Randolph, "The National Response to Richard M. Nixon's 'Black Capitalism' Initiative: The Success of Domestic Détente," *Journal of Black Studies* 32, no. 1 (September 2001), 66–83.

14. Bob Lonsberry, "Riots of 1964 Are Nothing to Celebrate," Bob Lonsberry (blog), July 14, 2014, http://www.lonsberry.com/writings.cfm?story=3734&go=4.

15. James Goodman, "1964 Riots Revisited: 3 Days That Shook Rochester," *Rochester Democrat and Chronicle*, July 20, 2014, https://www.democratandchronicle.com/story/news/2014/07/19/roberta-abbott-buckle-rochester-riots/12855941/.

16. The Cooper Academy is a public school open to all children. However, in 2020, Rochester city schools were 85.48 percent Black and Latino.

INDEX

Page numbers followed by *f* refer to figures

CPSIA information can be obtained
at www.ICGtesting.com
Printed in the USA
LVHW112250140821
695327LV00019B/1818